IMAGES of America

WESTCHESTER COUNTY

PROTECT AND SERVE

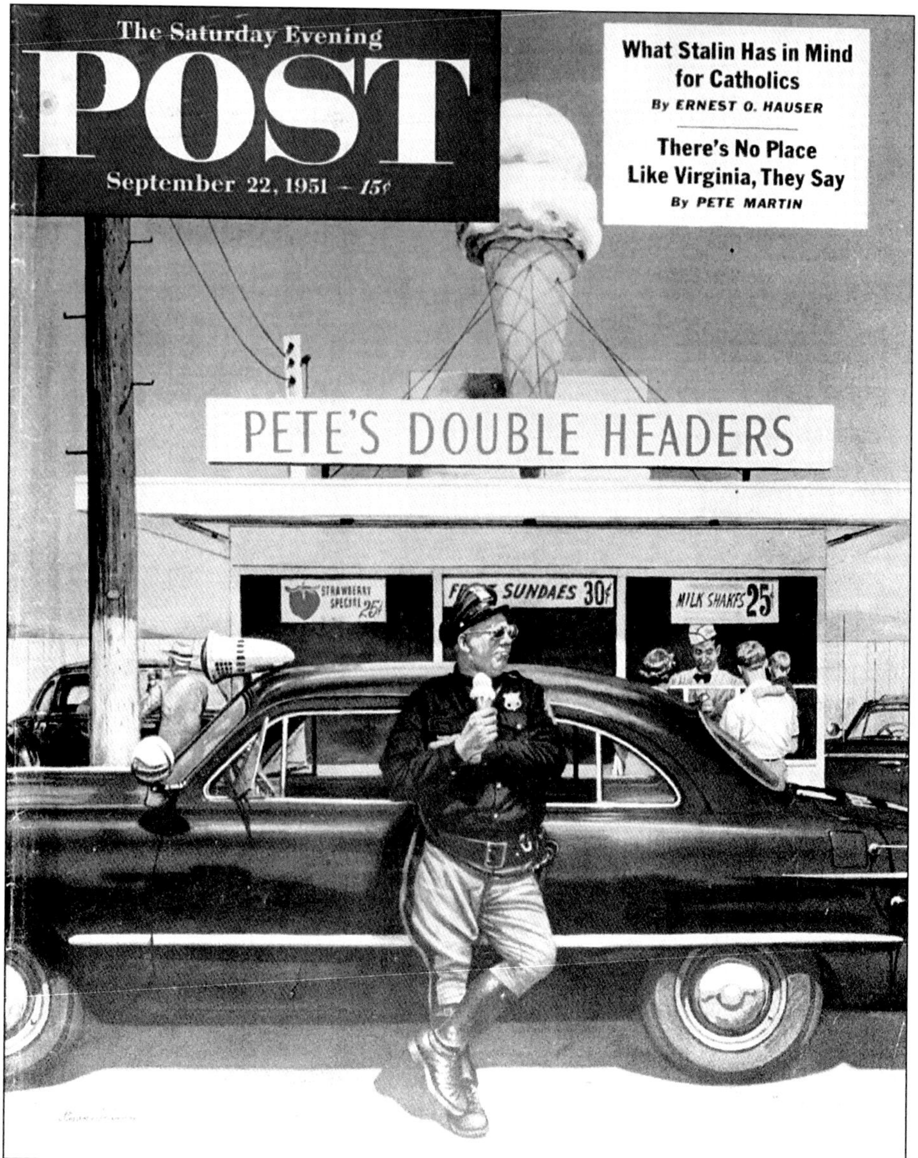

This is a *Saturday Evening Post* cover illustration from the September 22, 1951 issue. This illustration depicts police officer Fred Vosatka Sr. of the Westchester County Parkway Police in front of Pete's Double Headers ice-cream stand. It is believed that the ice-cream stand was located on Yonkers Avenue in the city of Yonkers and that Vosatka posed for the artist in Ridge Road Park in the town of Greenburgh. The notes accompanying the illustration state, "As cops are human beings, Stevan Dohanos easily found one for a model who actually was an incurable ice-cream-cone addict. He also was a candy fiend. He said that his wife often upbraided him for eating sweets, claiming that his belt was beginning to slip down under his stomach. 'It doesn't, of course,' the officer exclaimed. 'I just wear it loose to have my muscles free and unhindered. Well buy me a cone and I'll pose, but if my wife hears about this I'll get hail Columbia.' So Dohanos has painted dark glasses on the chap, hoping that the Mrs. won't recognize him, but will think of him as a typical American policeman, thus mellowing her attitude toward sugar in the diet and bringing peace into her husband's life." (CPC.)

IMAGES
of America

WESTCHESTER COUNTY
PROTECT AND SERVE

Michael J. Lavin and Frank J. Donovan

ARCADIA
PUBLISHING

Copyright © 2001 by Frank J. Donovan and Michael J. Lavin
ISBN 978-0-7385-0951-8

Published by Arcadia Publishing
Charleston, South Carolina

Printed in the United States of America

Library of Congress Catalog Card Number: 2001092558

For all general information contact Arcadia Publishing at:
Telephone 843-853-2070
Fax 843-853-0044
E-mail sales@arcadiapublishing.com
For customer service and orders:
Toll-Free 1-888-313-2665

Visit us on the Internet at www.arcadiapublishing.com

On the cover: Members of the Westchester County Parkway Police Department stop at the New Haven Railroad viaduct over the Hutchinson River Parkway in Mount Vernon c. 1930. The first two-mile section of the parkway was opened on December 24, 1927. In the background is the railroad bridge that carried the New York, Westchester & Boston Railroad through what is now Wilson Woods Park. Traces of this bridge and railroad line remain.

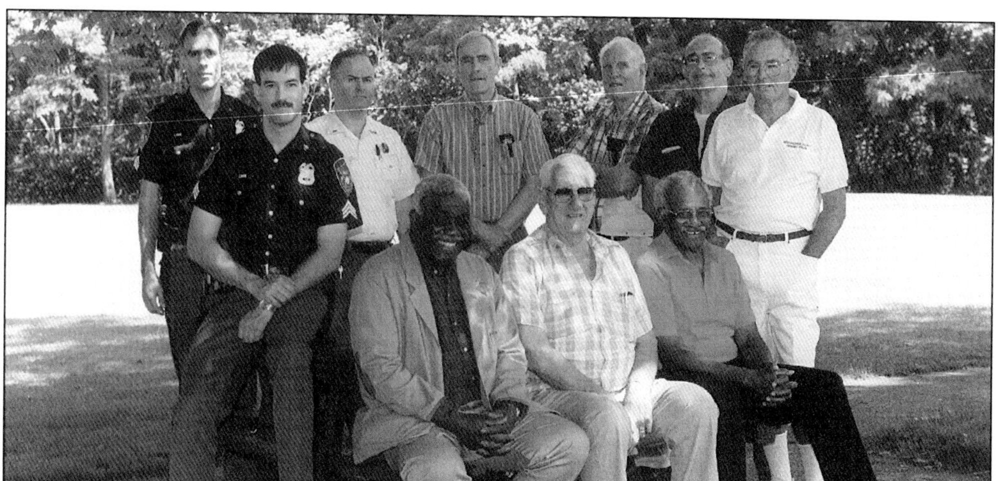

Gathered outside the Westchester County Records Center in Elmsford on June 8, 2001, with the authors are some of the present and retired members of the Westchester County Department of Public Safety who helped to make this book possible. From left to right are the following: (front row) Sgt. Michael Lavin, James Brooks, John Rosko, and Clarence Holst; (back row) Sgt. Frank Donovan, Lt. Robert O'Connor, Thomas Eaton, Richard Crawford, Frederic Arone, and Robert Trimpe.

Contents

ACKNOWLEDGMENTS

Those photographs and illustrations that have not come from the collection of the Westchester County Department of Public Safety Historical Committee have a parenthetical notation at the end of the caption. The following sources have kindly provided material for this book: the Westchester County Historical Society (WCHS), White Plains Historical Society (WPHS), Curtis Publishing Company (CPC), and Blackinton & Company (BCI).

The authors are deeply indebted to the following retired members for their generous assistance in locating and providing access to the vast majority of the material included in this book: Stephen Acunto, Frederic Arone, James Brooks, Francis Conklin, Richard Crawford, Thomas Eaton, Eric Facey, Clarence Holst, William Nelson, Walter Nugent, John Rosko, Courtland "Babe" Swift, and Robert C. Trimpe.

We would like to thank the following active members of the Westchester County Department of Public Safety as well for their assistance in preparing this book for publication: Chief Inspectors Roger R. Rokicki and Louis S. Liberatore, Lt. Robert O'Connor, Dets. James Harrison, William Mackey, and Roger Piccirilli, and Laura Galligan.

Also, we would like to thank the staff of the Westchester County Records Center, whose kind assistance was greatly appreciated, especially Patricia Dohrenwend, Sharalee Falzerano, Elaine Massena, Diana Maull, and William Prusak.

A special note of thanks to Commissioner Louis S. D'Aliso for the support and encouragement that he extended to the authors during the preparation of this book.

Finally, we wish to acknowledge the support of our families in this endeavor, especially Frank's wife, Tamra, and my wife, Maureen, and my three children, Emily, Michael, and Katie.

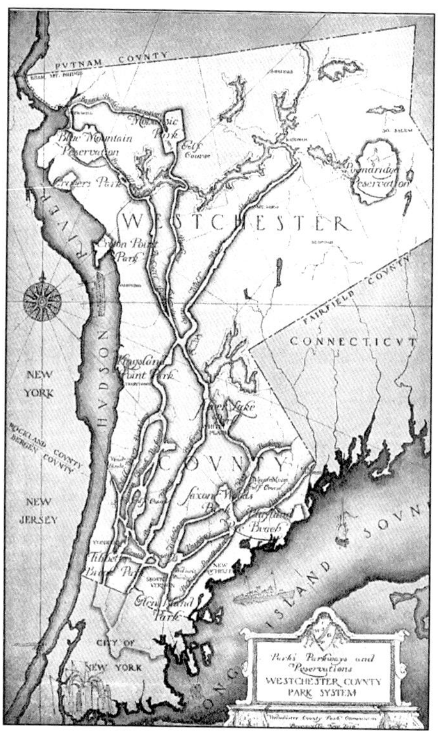

This map from the 1928 report of the Westchester County Park Commission shows the parks, parkways, and reservations of the Westchester County Park System.

INTRODUCTION

It was the desire of many members of the Westchester County Department of Public Safety to celebrate the 20-year anniversary of the department on July 1, 1999, which led to the creation of this book. The original intent of the authors was to collect and publish a brief history of the department solely for the enjoyment of the present and retired members of the department. However, during the process of collecting material for the book, it became apparent that these photographs and the stories told in their captions, although primarily focused on the history of this organization, also had a broader appeal to anyone interested in the history of law enforcement in Westchester County. Therefore, the decision was made to make this publication available to the general public. The authors hope that you will enjoy reading this book as much as they have enjoyed compiling it.

The Westchester County Department of Public Safety was created on July 1, 1979, by the merger of the Westchester County Sheriff's Department and the Westchester County Parkway Police. Since that time, the department has provided primary police coverage for county parks, parkways, and facilities. The department has also provided specialized police services to neighboring jurisdictions since its inception. Such specialized services include bomb and ballistics technicians, aviation and marine patrols, Stop DWI and DARE programs, as well as investigative support for narcotics, warrants, and major case investigations.

The history of the Westchester County Department of Public Safety can be traced back through the office of the sheriff to 1683, when the governor and council of New York appointed Benjamin Collier of Sing Sing. Sheriffs of the county continued to be appointed by the governor until 1846. After 1846, the people elected sheriffs throughout the state to a three-year term of office. The New York State Constitution, adopted in 1846, also made provisions for the office of under sheriff. The under sheriff, attorney, deputy sheriffs, jailers, and clerks were all appointed by the sheriff. The first sheriff to be elected to office was James M. Bates of Bedford. In 1898, when William Molloy of New Rochelle was sheriff, the salary was $10,000 per annum and his staff consisted of an attorney, an under sheriff, and nine deputy sheriffs, of whom one was designated as the jailer and another was designated as the clerk. The last sheriff of Westchester County prior to the merger was Thomas J. Delaney. Many of the sheriffs made notable contributions to law enforcement during their terms of office. Among those whose achievements are known to us today are Addison Johnson (1895–1897), William J. Doyle (1912–1914), Charles E. Nossetter (1918–1920), Arthur S. Maudlin, and Daniel F. McMahon (1968–1973).

Addison Johnson by his persistent efforts was responsible for the construction of a modern and well-equipped county jail. After leaving office, he went on to become warden of the Sing Sing State Prison, where he made a great number of reforms. William J. Doyle was a pioneer of criminal identification who was instrumental in the creation of the Police Society of Westchester County. He was also responsible for the creation of the Fingerprint and Bertillon Bureau of Identification within the Westchester County Office of the Sheriff. The Bertillon method of criminal identification involved the use of measurements of a person's anatomy as a positive means of identifying a person. This was an important technological improvement at a time when the transmission of photographs was only as fast as the mail and fingerprints were not as widely used as they are today. Charles E. Nossetter was responsible for expanding upon the familiar concept of the posse, wherein the sheriff summonses and deputizes a body of men for some special purpose. As a result of unrest in Westchester County during World War I, due to fear of saboteurs, spies, and enemy agents, Nossetter formed a standing posse of well-trained and well-equipped men who were ready to act upon short notice. The Sheriff's Emergency Force was formed in 1918 and consisted of 125 able-bodied men under the command of 4 lieutenants,

6 sergeants, and 10 corporals. It was formed along the lines of a regular army cavalry unit, complete with field kitchens, supply wagons, and three medical officers. In response to questions concerning the efficacy of the unit, Nossetter activated it as a test, and the entire unit was assembled and ready for duty in less than an hour. Such a feat would be difficult to duplicate today. As a result of this successful demonstration, the board of supervisors passed a resolution to officially recognize the Sheriff's Emergency Force. Arthur S. Maudlin acting in cooperation with 46 other police departments in Westchester County created a four-zone system of police response within the county. This plan required each police agency in a particular zone to notify every other police agency within that zone whenever a crime took place. The intent of the plan was to make it more difficult for the perpetrator of a crime in a particular jurisdiction to flee from that place through the neighboring jurisdictions. Maudlin was also a great proponent of the use of fingerprints in the manner of William J. Doyle. Daniel F. McMahon implemented many improvements designed to make the operations of the sheriff's department more professional. He was widely recognized for his efforts in drug enforcement, the creation of a crime lab, a ballistics unit, and a county-wide hotline to facilitate interagency police communications.

The history of the Westchester County Department of Public Safety can also be traced back through the Westchester County Parkway Police to June 1, 1926, when the first 15 members of the Westchester County Park Commission Parkway Patrol Force were sworn in. The early history of the parkway police was very eloquently set down by Robert Robischon in 1940 for publication in the program for the ninth annual entertainment and reception of the Westchester County Parkway Patrolmen's Benevolent Association. We will not attempt to retell the story ourselves; instead we have included this material in its entirety later in the book. The rest of the story, as it has been made known to us, will be told in the captions that accompany each photograph.

The history presented here is incomplete at best, but we hope that you will find something that you value in this work. We look forward to continuing this work and hearing from others who can help us to add to our understanding of the history of the department and the people and places that have been so closely associated with it. It has been our distinct pleasure to meet so many of those who preceded us in the field of law enforcement, whose paths we might not otherwise have crossed.

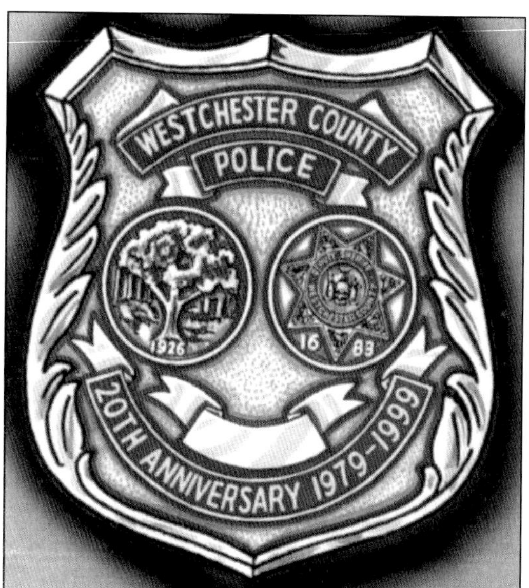

Preproduction artwork for the 20-year anniversary shield is shown in this view. (BCI.)

One

The Westchester County Sheriff's Department: 1683–1979

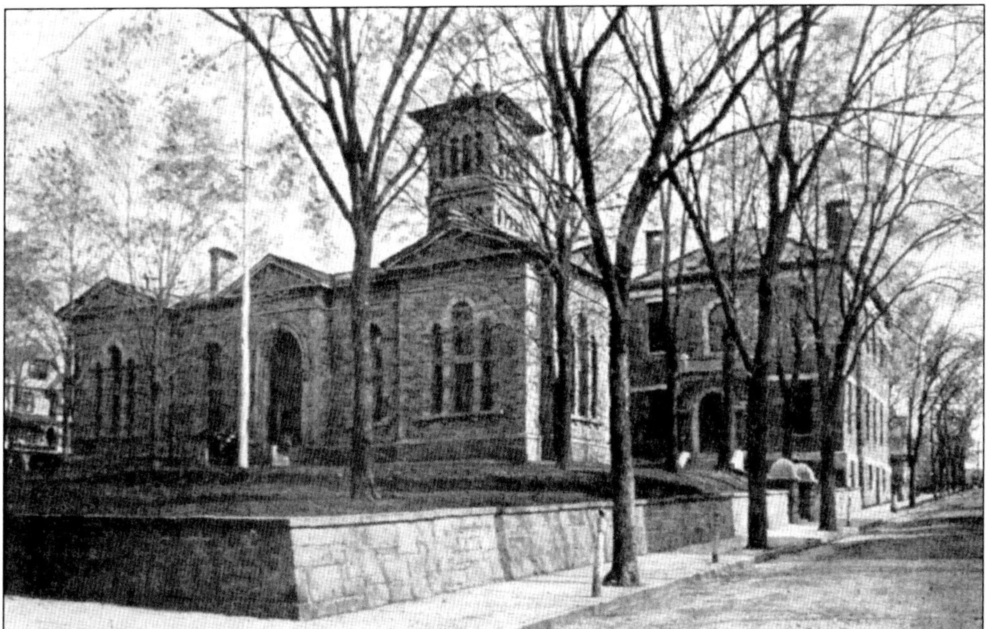

This is a view of the Westchester County Courthouse, located on Main Street in White Plains. It was built in 1855 and contained the Westchester County sheriff's office, as well as courtrooms. This courthouse was demolished in 1915 to make room for a new courthouse on the same site. (WCHS.)

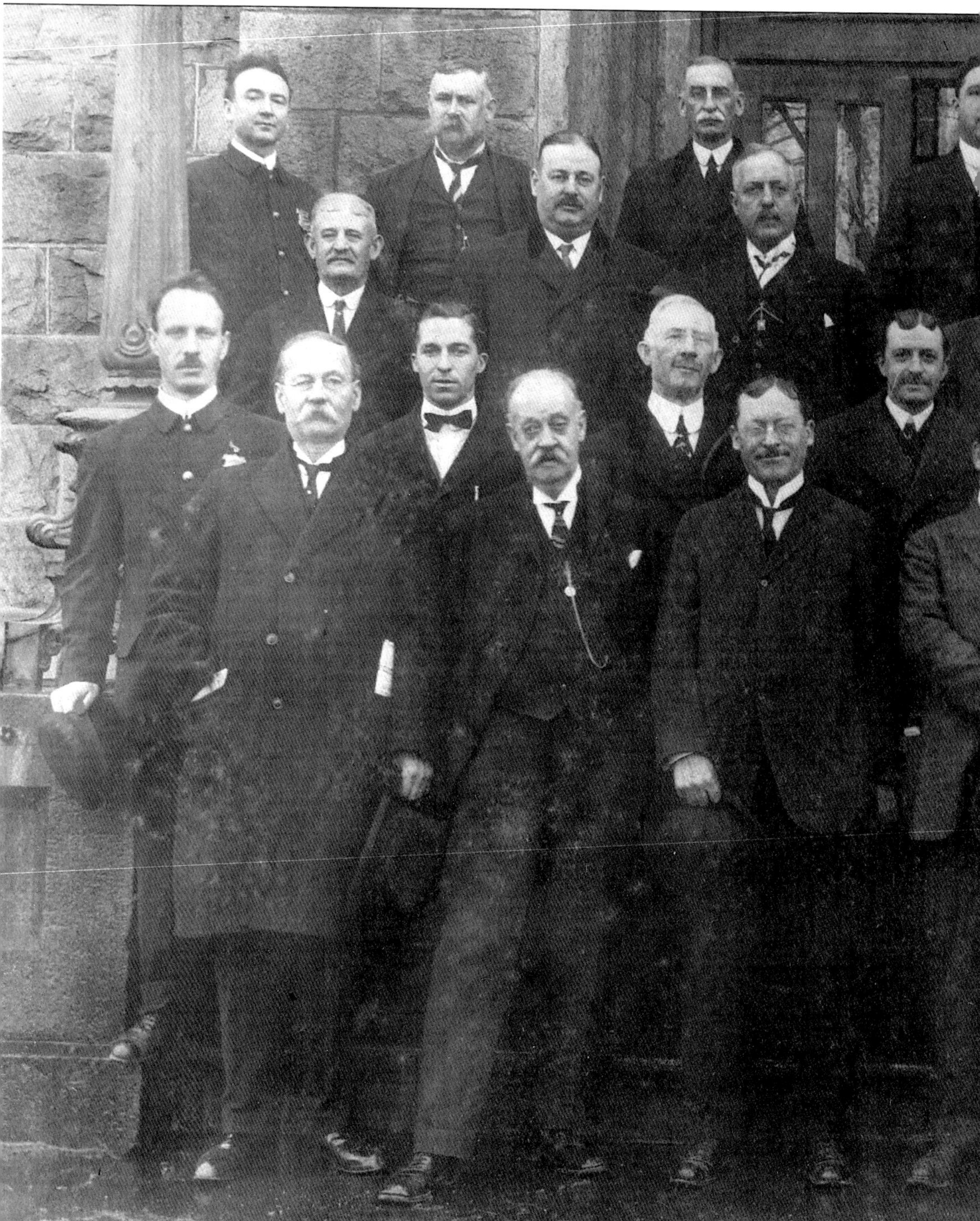

Sheriff William J. Doyle (front row, fourth from left) and his staff stand in front of the 1855 courthouse, on Main Street in White Plains. The boy (front row, third from right) is believed to be his only son, William James Doyle Jr. The Westchester County Sheriff's Department consisted of 34 full-time deputy sheriffs in 1914, along with 123 special deputy sheriffs,

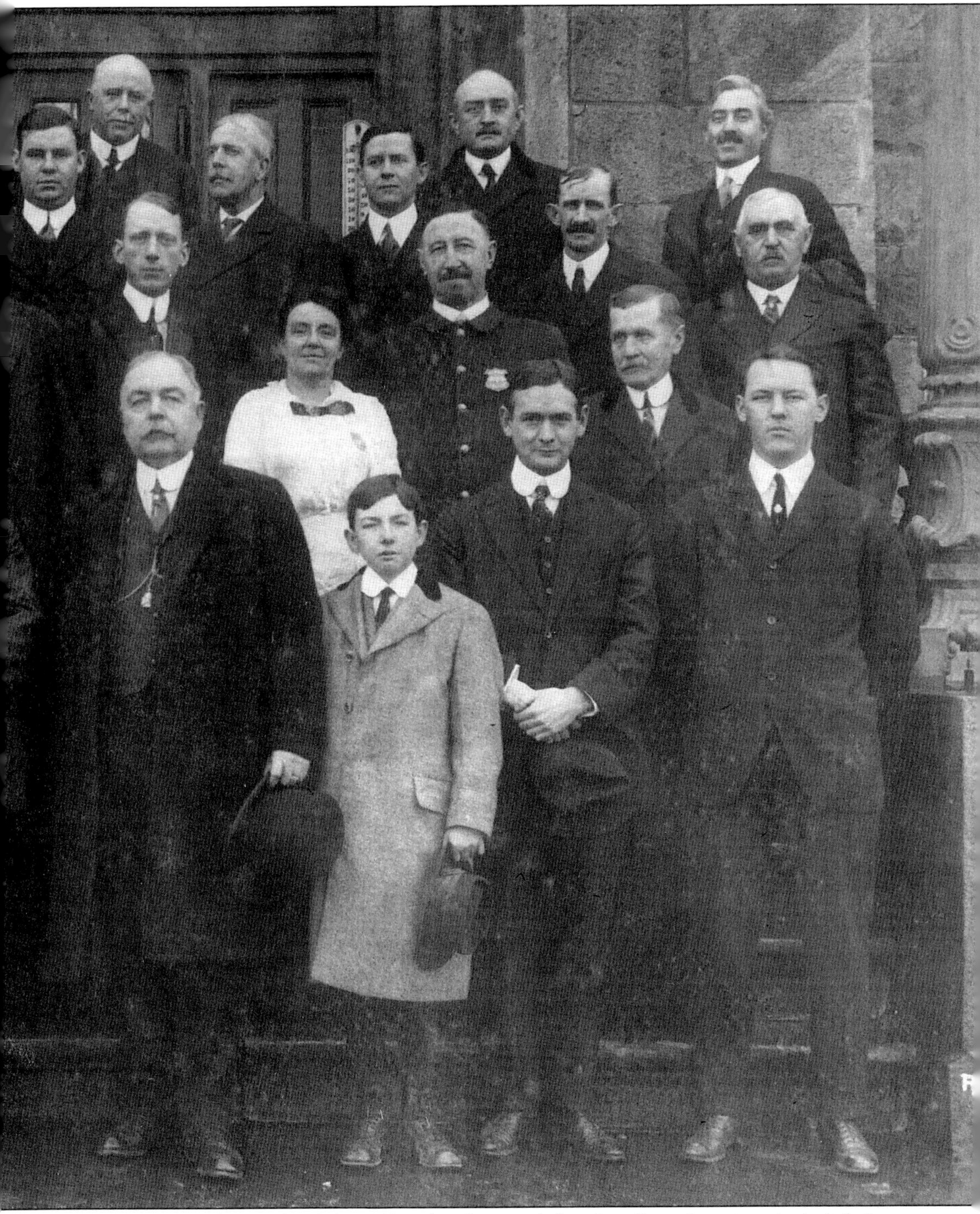

7 motorcycles, and a pack of dogs. Regular duties of the sheriff at that time included the investigation of murders and other serious crimes, the administration of the county jail and courts, and the execution of warrants.

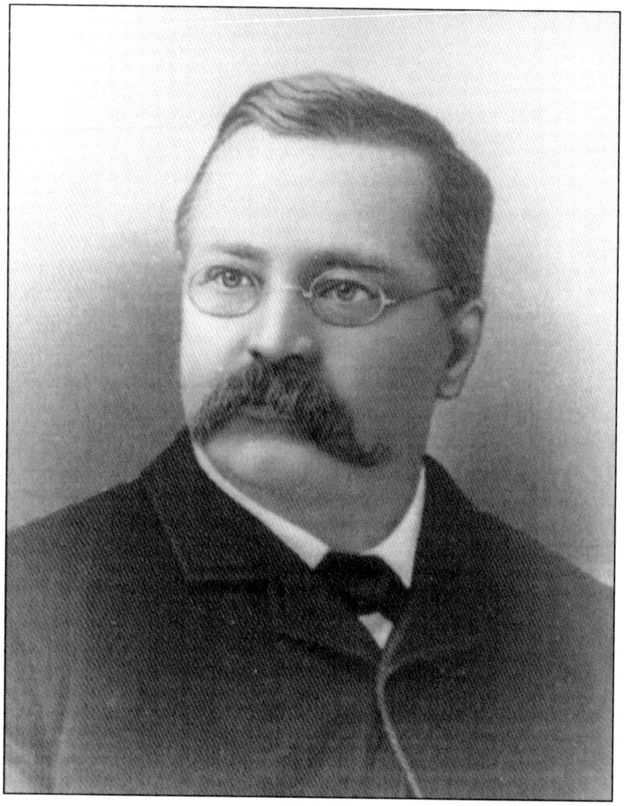

Stephen D. Horton of Cortlandt served as Westchester County sheriff from 1883 to 1885. He was born in Peekskill on February 17, 1837, and was educated at the Peekskill Academy. He had a successful business career and was the director of the Westchester County National Bank for 27 years. His son, Stephen F. Horton, was a prominent physician in city of Peekskill.

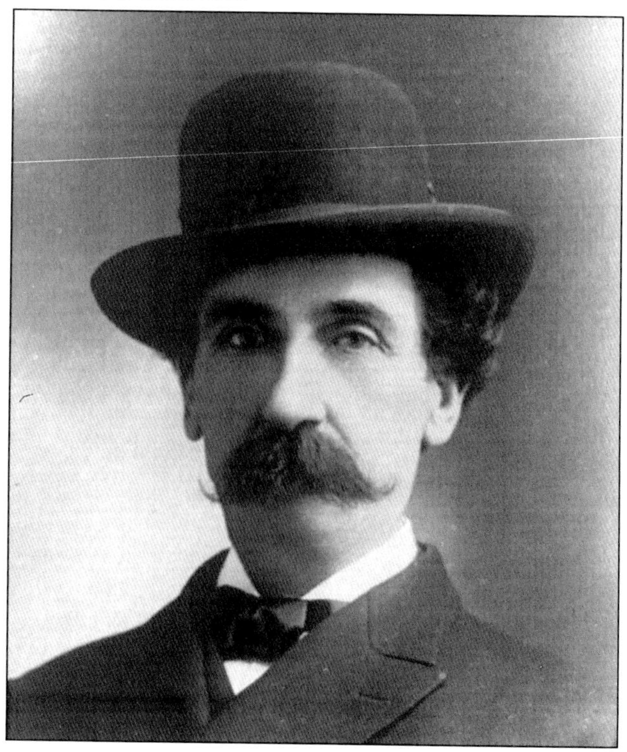

Addison Johnson of Rye was sheriff from 1895 to 1897. He was born on January 22, 1857, in Greenwich, where he lived until 10 years of age, at which time his family moved to Port Chester. His first public office was as supervisor of the town of Rye, where he served from 1892 until elected sheriff of Westchester County in 1895. As sheriff, he introduced modern business methods and lobbied for the construction of a new jail. As a result, the jail, located on Martine Avenue in White Plains, was enlarged and modernized at a cost of $65,000. In 1899, Johnson went on to become the agent and warden of Sing Sing State Prison and was highly regarded for the reforms that he put into practice.

Samuel C. Miller of White Plains was elected sheriff in 1901. He was born on August 1, 1848, in the city of Cincinnati, Ohio, and died on June 2, 1905. In 1862, his family moved to White Plains and he remained there for the rest of his life. He served as postmaster of White Plains from 1878 to 1886 and as a village trustee and then village president from 1896 to 1900, when he resigned to assume the office of Westchester County sheriff. During his term, state law allowed the sheriff to appoint a counsel at $1,500 per annum, a clerk at $1,200 per annum, a jailer at $1,200 per annum, an assistant jailer at $900 per annum, three deputy sheriffs at $1,500 each per annum, a day watchman and a night watchman at the jail for $900 each per annum, and a cook at the jail for $500 per annum.

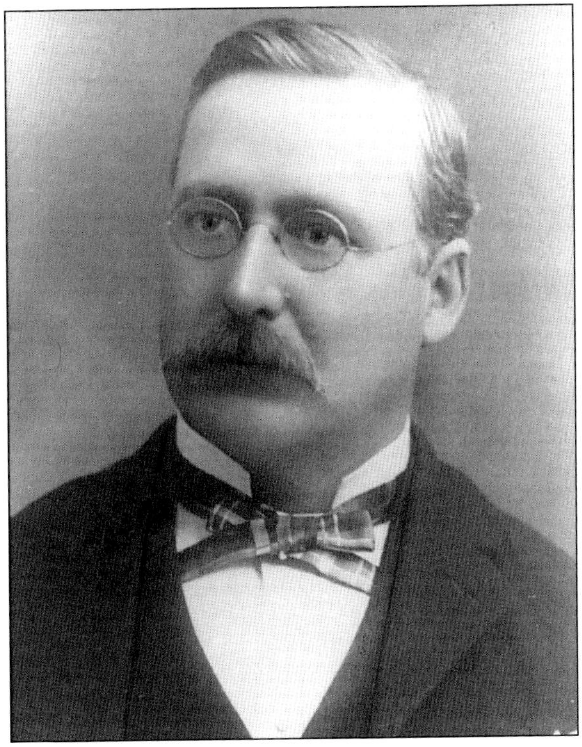

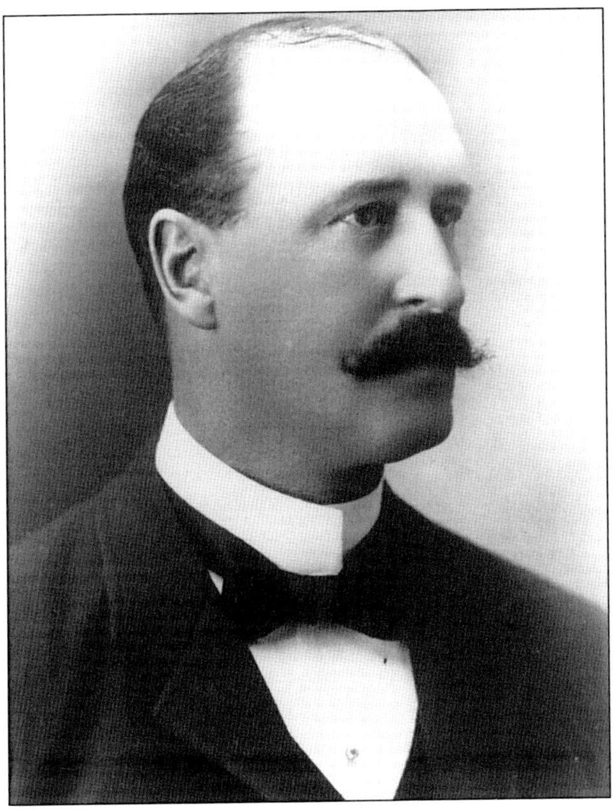

James S. Merritt was born in Port Chester on November 9, 1859. At an early age he began his business career as a peddler and, in later days, was a business partner of Addison Johnson; the firm of Johnson & Merritt was dissolved when Johnson was elected sheriff in 1895. Merritt went on to become a successful real estate broker and served as postmaster of Port Chester from 1900 to 1904. He relinquished that position to accept the office of sheriff. As a result of the just and careful manner in which he carried out his duties, he left office without being involved in any kind of lawsuit resulting from his duties—a remarkable achievement at the time.

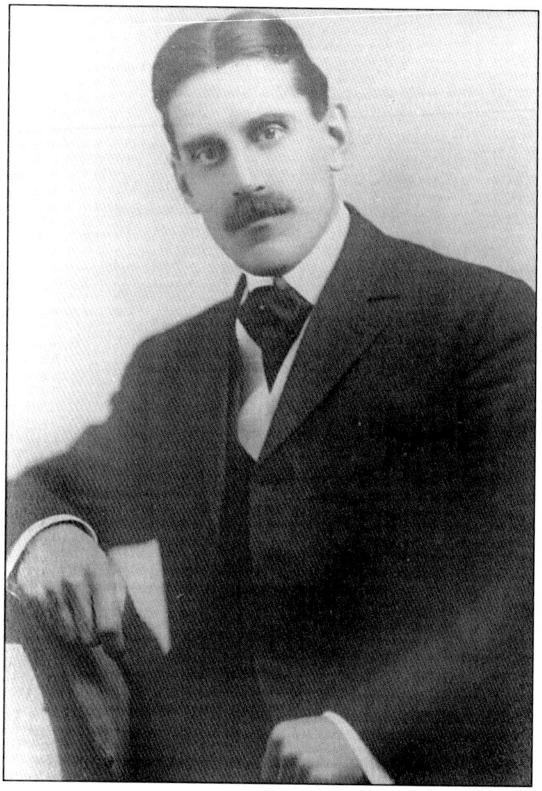

Henry Scherp, the 66th sheriff of Westchester County, served from 1910 to 1911. He was born in Yonkers on June 24, 1872. He was involved in the newspaper and printing trade early in his life and was regarded as a studious reader throughout his life. He moved to New Rochelle, where he became involved in politics and served as city commissioner of charities from 1902 to 1906. In 1906, he was elected to the Westchester County Board of Supervisors, where he served briefly before accepting the position of under sheriff to Sheriff Charles M. Lane in 1907. When Sheriff Lane died in 1909, Scherp was designated by Governor Hughes to complete his term of office as sheriff. Scherp died on October 9, 1911, as a result of injuries he received in an automobile accident on October 3, 1911. He was succeeded by his under sheriff, William J. Doyle. The salary of the sheriff in 1910 was set at $10,000 per annum.

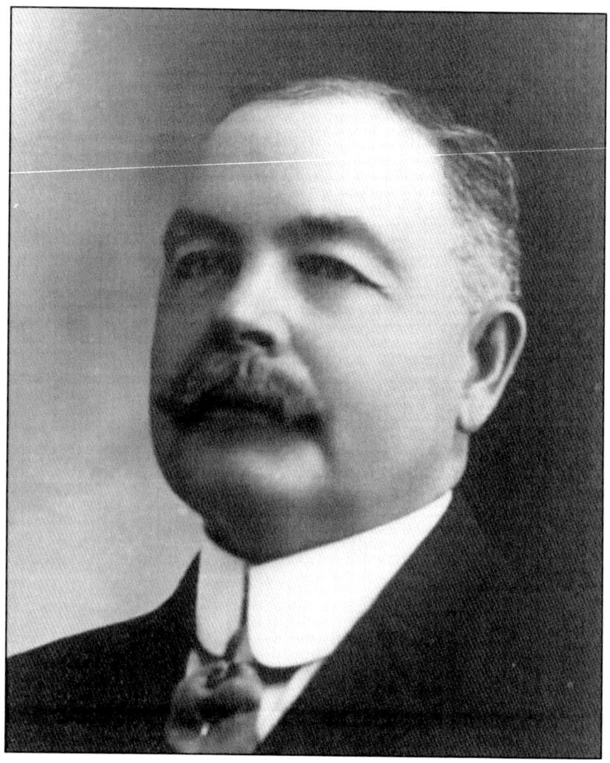

William J. Doyle was born in Katonah on October 3, 1863, and was well established in a general-merchandise business with his brothers Francis and David Doyle before entering public service. In 1900, Sheriff Samuel Miller selected William Doyle as one of his three regular deputies. His continued to serve under Sheriffs James Merritt, Charles Lane, and Henry Scherp. During his career, he made a transcontinental journey to return a fugitive to Westchester from California and undertook many other hazardous assignments. He was selected as under sheriff by Scherp, whose untimely death left Doyle as sheriff. Doyle went on to win election to the office in November 1911.

Charles E. Nossetter served as sheriff of Westchester County from 1918 to 1920. It was during his tenure that the group of special deputy sheriffs mentioned by Sheriff William Doyle in 1914 was transformed into the Sheriff's Emergency Force. Following the end of World War I, there was some debate regarding the need to maintain such a large posse, as well as the ability to quickly mobilize them. Nossetter appeared before the Westchester County Board of Supervisors to argue that the group should not be disbanded. In order to test the ability of the unit, Nossetter and the board arranged for a surprise drill. The entire group was assembled and ready for duty in less than one hour. The board of supervisors was impressed with the results of the exercise and passed a resolution to officially sanction the Sheriff's Emergency Force as a peacetime unit of the Sheriff's office.

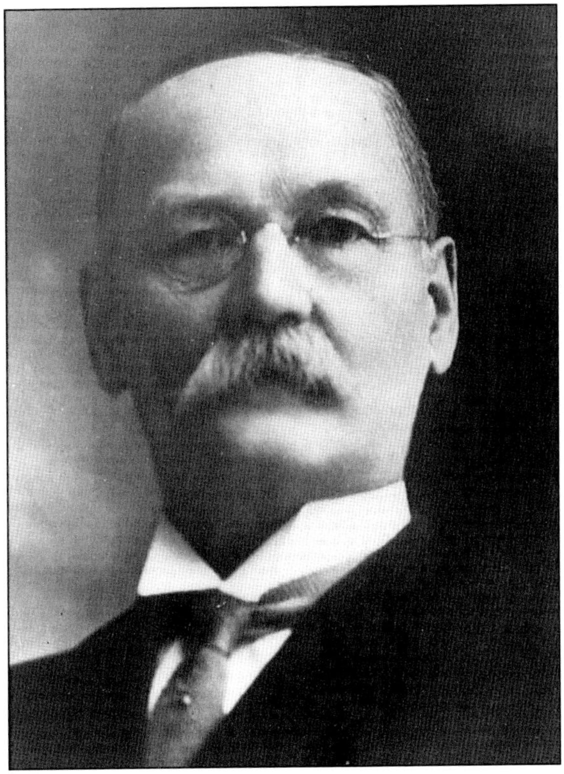

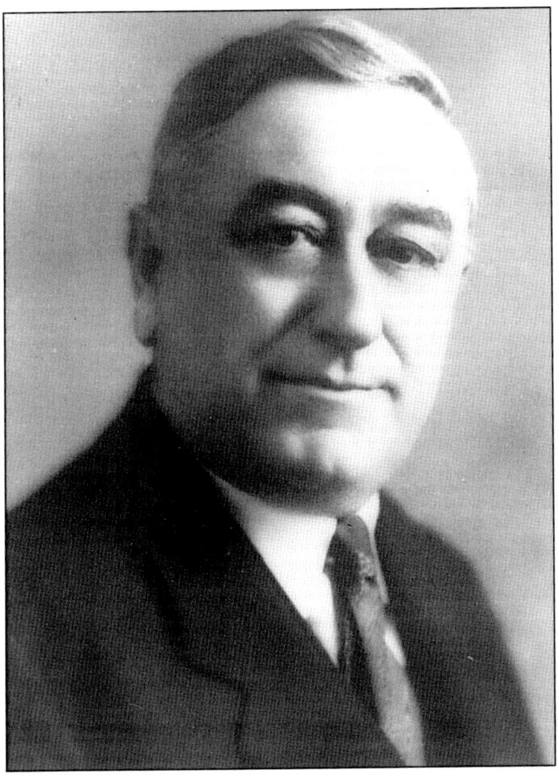

Arthur S. Maudlin of Yonkers held the office of sheriff from 1924 to 1926. One of the major contributions that he made to law enforcement in Westchester County was, with the cooperation of 46 other police agencies, to establish four zones within which police officials committed themselves to immediately notify each police agency in their designated zone whenever a crime occurred. The zones established by Maudlin divided Westchester into northern, central, southeastern, and southwestern response areas that included parts of Putnam County, Connecticut, and New York City. He also offered to make Deputy Sheriff Raymond Hill available to instruct one or two members of every police force in Westchester County in the science of fingerprint collection and comparison.

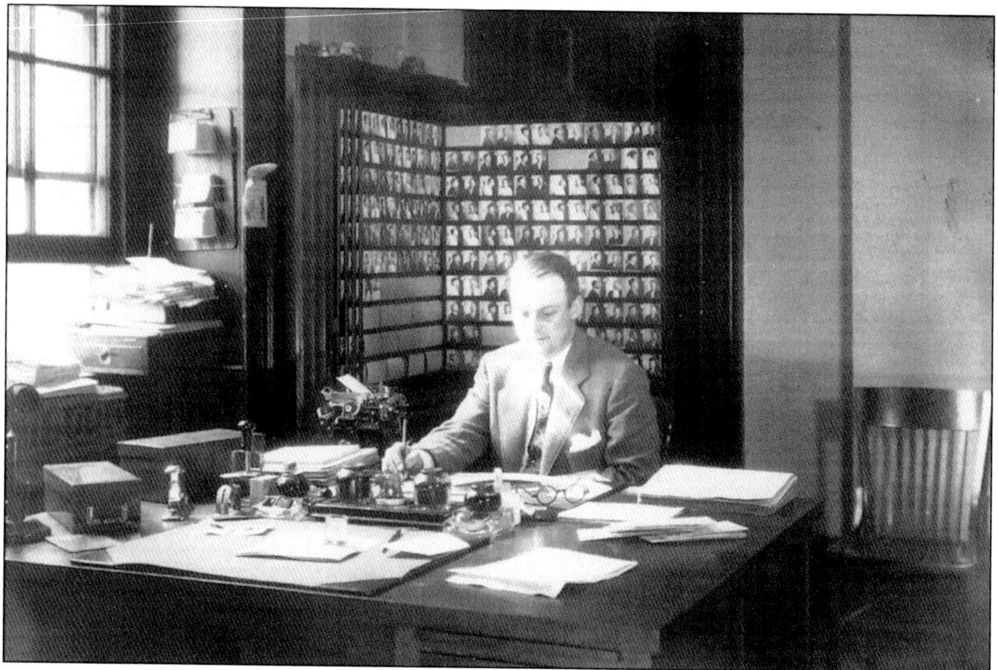

This photograph, taken inside the office of the sheriff at the Westchester County Courthouse in White Plains *c.* 1920, shows the sheriff's "Rogues Gallery" of mug shots neatly displayed behind the desk of the deputy sheriff.

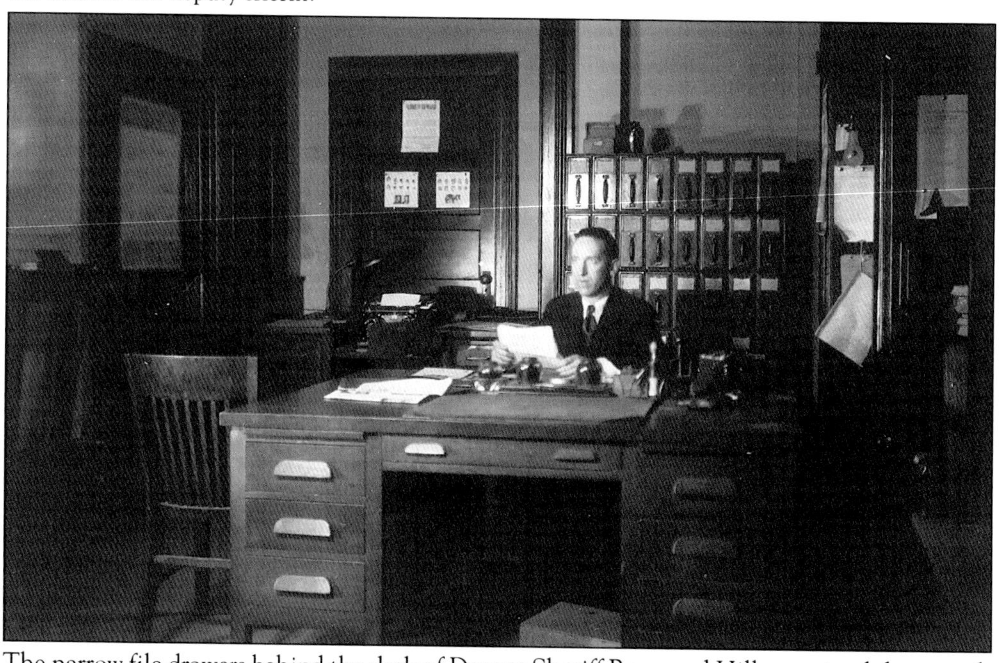

The narrow file drawers behind the desk of Deputy Sheriff Raymond Hill contained the records of the Bertillon measurements collected from all of the subjects processed by the sheriff's department. Bertillon measurements were precise measurements between various anatomical points that were used as a means of positively identifying a suspect or convict. The deputy is believed to be Raymond Hill.

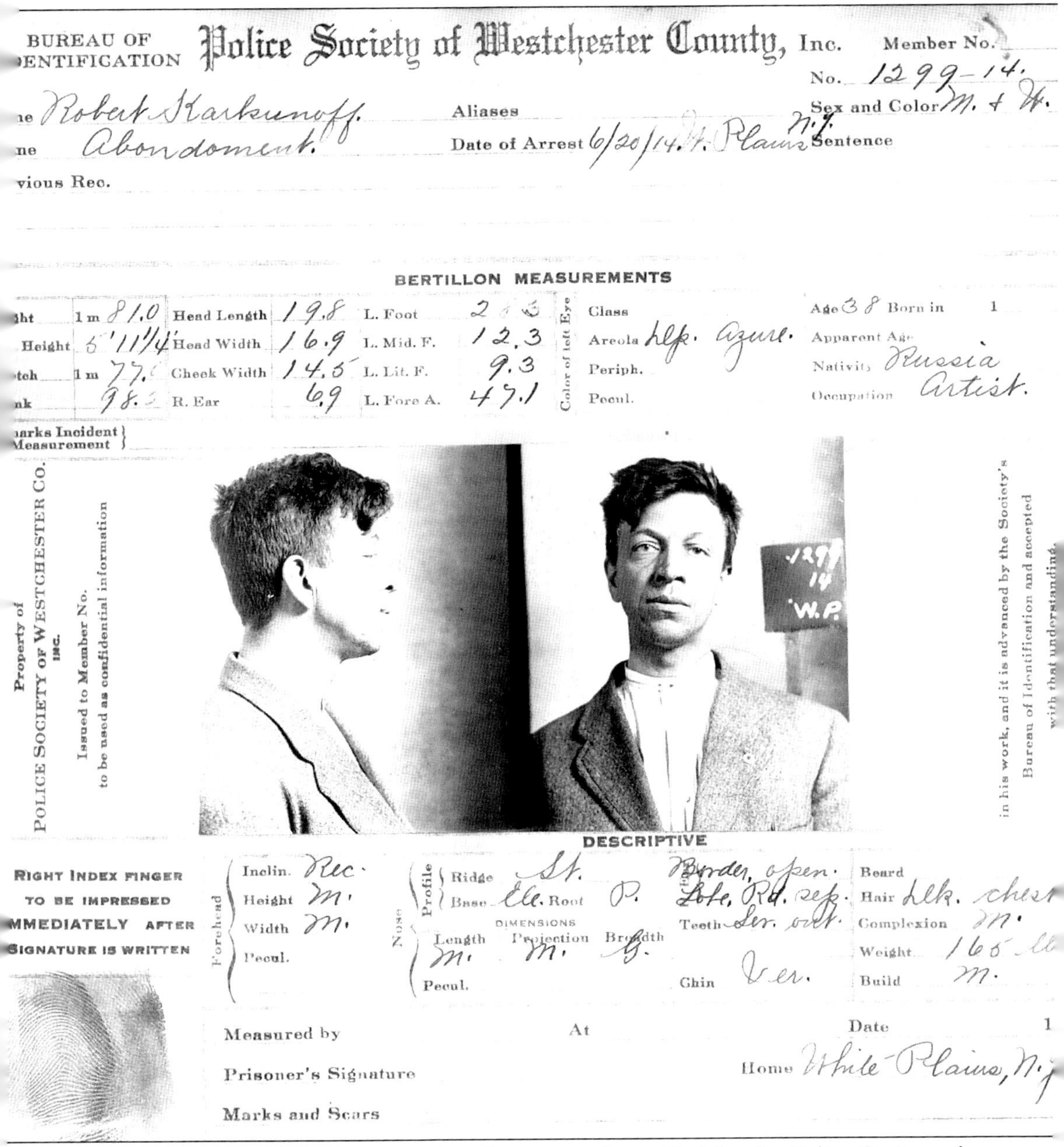

BUREAU OF IDENTIFICATION **Police Society of Westchester County,** Inc. Member No.

No. 1299-14.

Name Robert Karkunoff. Aliases Sex and Color M. & W.

Crime Abondoment. Date of Arrest 6/20/14. W. Plains N.Y. Sentence

Previous Rec.

BERTILLON MEASUREMENTS

Height	1 m 81.0	Head Length	19.8	L. Foot	28.5	Color of left Eye	Class	Age 38	Born in
Height	5' 11¼"	Head Width	16.9	L. Mid. F.	12.3		Areola Lfp. azure.	Apparent Age	
Stretch	1 m 77.	Cheek Width	14.5	L. Lit. F.	9.3		Periph.	Nativity Russia	
Trunk	98.	R. Ear	6.9	L. Fore A.	47.1		Pecul.	Occupation Artist.	

Remarks Incident to Measurement

Property of POLICE SOCIETY OF WESTCHESTER CO. INC.

Issued to Member No. to be used as confidential information

1299 14 W.P.

in his work, and it is advanced by the Society's Bureau of Identification and accepted with that understanding.

DESCRIPTIVE

RIGHT INDEX FINGER TO BE IMPRESSED IMMEDIATELY AFTER SIGNATURE IS WRITTEN

Forehead: Inclin. Rec. Height M. Width M. Pecul.

Nose: Profile: Ridge St. Base Ele. Root P. Dimensions: Length M. Projection M. Breadth G. Pecul.

Ear: Border, open. Lobe, Rd. sep. Teeth Ser. out. Chin Ver.

Beard Hair Blk. chest. Complexion M. Weight 165 lb. Build M.

Measured by At Date

Prisoner's Signature Home White Plains, N.Y.

Marks and Scars

This is an example of the prisoner identification card provided by the Police Society of Westchester County to its members. It had space to record Bertillon measurements, personal information, arrest information, and a mug shot on the front of the card. The back of the card had space to collect fingerprint data. The Fingerprint and Bertillon Bureau of Identification of Westchester County was first established by the Police Society of Westchester County on November 24, 1913. Irvington millionaire M.S. Beltzhoover provided $5,000 for the purchase of equipment following a series of robberies along the Hudson River communities of Westchester County. The Police Society of Westchester County maintained the records through 1914, after which the bureau of identification was attached to the Westchester County Office of the Sheriff.

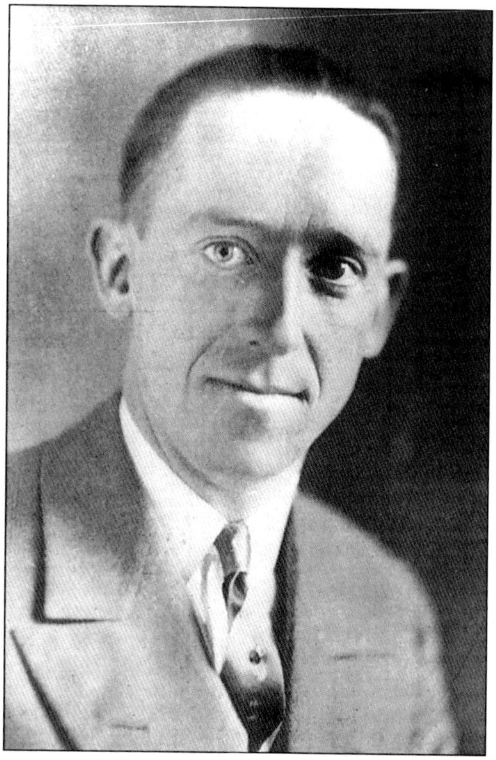

Deputy Sheriff Raymond Hill was widely respected as the foremost fingerprint expert in Westchester County.

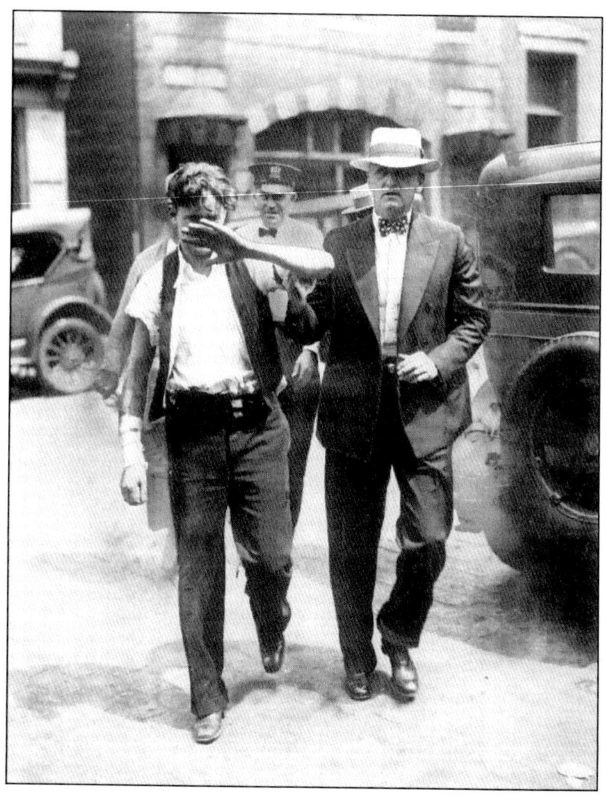

Deputy Sheriff Raymond Hill was also an energetic and resourceful investigator as evidenced by the role he played in many major investigations throughout his long career. This photograph, taken in 1929, shows Hill bringing in Joseph Heal, one of five suspects wanted in the shooting of a roadhouse keeper in Irvington on Hudson, the suspects were also accused of firing on the police.

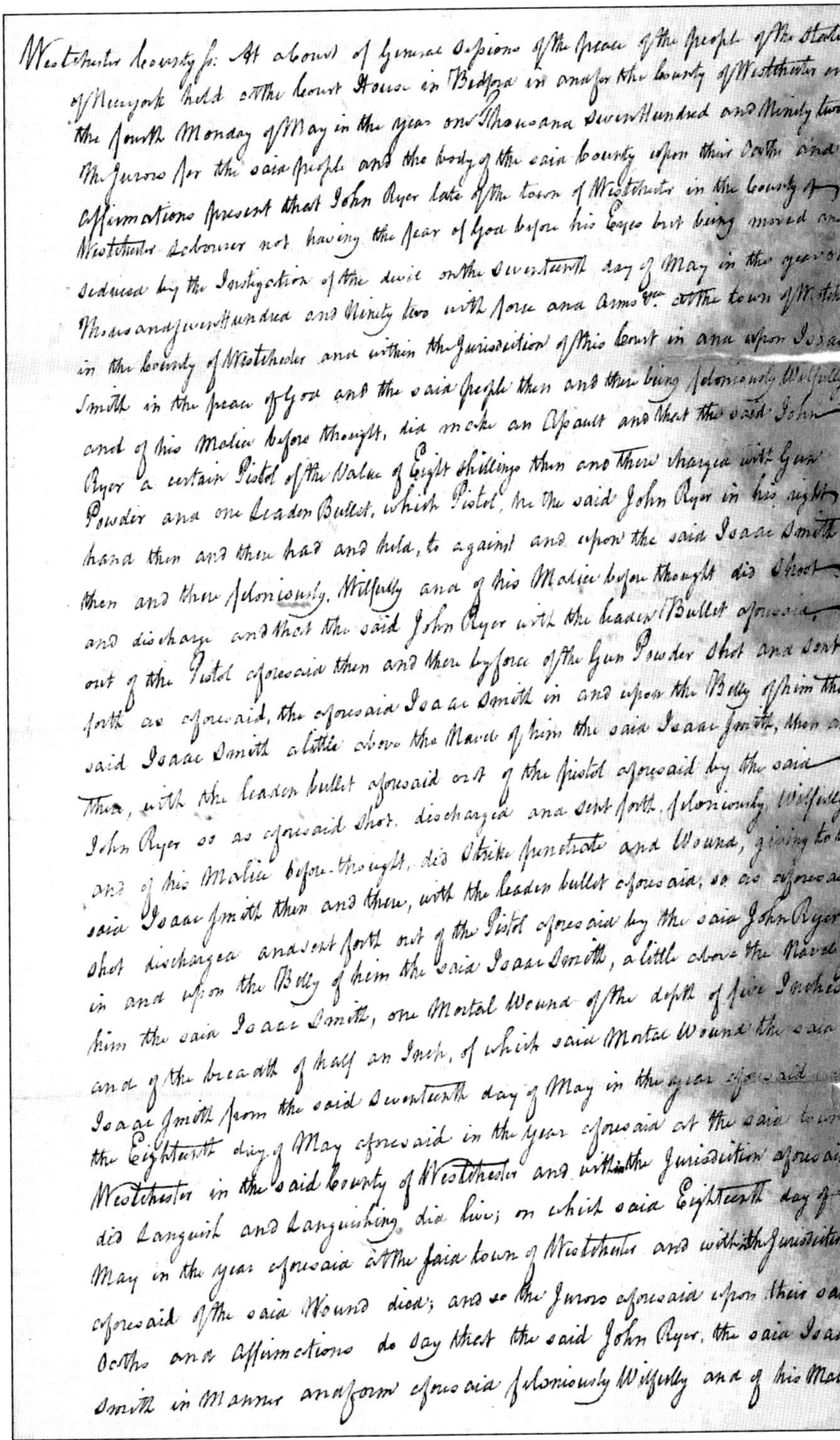

Westchester County ss: At a Court of General Sessions of the Peace of the People of the State
of Newyork held at the Court House in Bedford in and for the County of Westchester on
the fourth Monday of May in the year one Thousand Seven Hundred and Ninety two
The Jurors for the said People and the body of the said County upon their Oaths and
Affirmations present that John Ryer late of the town of Westchester in the County of
Westchester Labourer not having the fear of God before his Eyes but being moved and
seduced by the Instigation of the devil on the Seventeenth day of May in the year one
Thousand seven Hundred and Ninety two with force and Arms &c. at the town of Westchester
in the County of Westchester and within the Jurisdiction of this Court in and upon Isaac
Smith in the peace of God and the said People then and there being feloniously Willfully
and of his Malice before thought, did make an Assault and that the said John
Ryer a certain Pistol of the Value of Eight shillings then and there charged with Gun
Powder and one Leaden Bullet, which Pistol, he the said John Ryer in his right
hand then and there had and held, to against and upon the said Isaac Smith
then and there feloniously, Willfully and of his Malice before thought did Shoot
and discharge and that the said John Ryer with the leaden Bullet aforesaid
out of the Pistol aforesaid then and there by force of the Gun Powder Shot and sent
forth as aforesaid, the aforesaid Isaac Smith in and upon the Belly of him the
said Isaac Smith a little above the Navel of him the said Isaac Smith, then and
There, with the leaden bullet aforesaid out of the pistol aforesaid by the said
John Ryer so as aforesaid Shot, discharged and sent forth feloniously, Willfully
and of his Malice before thought, did Strike penetrate and Wound, giving to the
said Isaac Smith then and there, with the leaden bullet aforesaid, so as aforesaid
shot discharged and sent forth out of the Pistol aforesaid by the said John Ryer
in and upon the Belly of him the said Isaac Smith, a little above the Navel of
him the said Isaac Smith, one Mortal Wound of the depth of five Inches
and of the breadth of half an Inch, of which said Mortal Wound the said
Isaac Smith from the said Seventeenth day of May in the year aforesaid until
the Eighteenth day of May aforesaid in the year aforesaid at the said town of
Westchester in the said County of Westchester and within the Jurisdiction aforesaid
did Languish and Languishing did live; on which said Eighteenth day of
May in the year aforesaid at the said town of Westchester and within the Jurisdiction
aforesaid of the said Wound died; and so the Jurors aforesaid upon their said
Oaths and Affirmations do say that the said John Ryer, the said Isaac
Smith in Manner and form aforesaid feloniously Willfully and of his Malice

This is the original indictment charging John Ryer with the willful murder of Deputy Isaac Smith. Ryer shot Smith in a tavern in the town of Westchester, which was a part of the county of Westchester until it was annexed by New York City in 1874. (WCHS.)

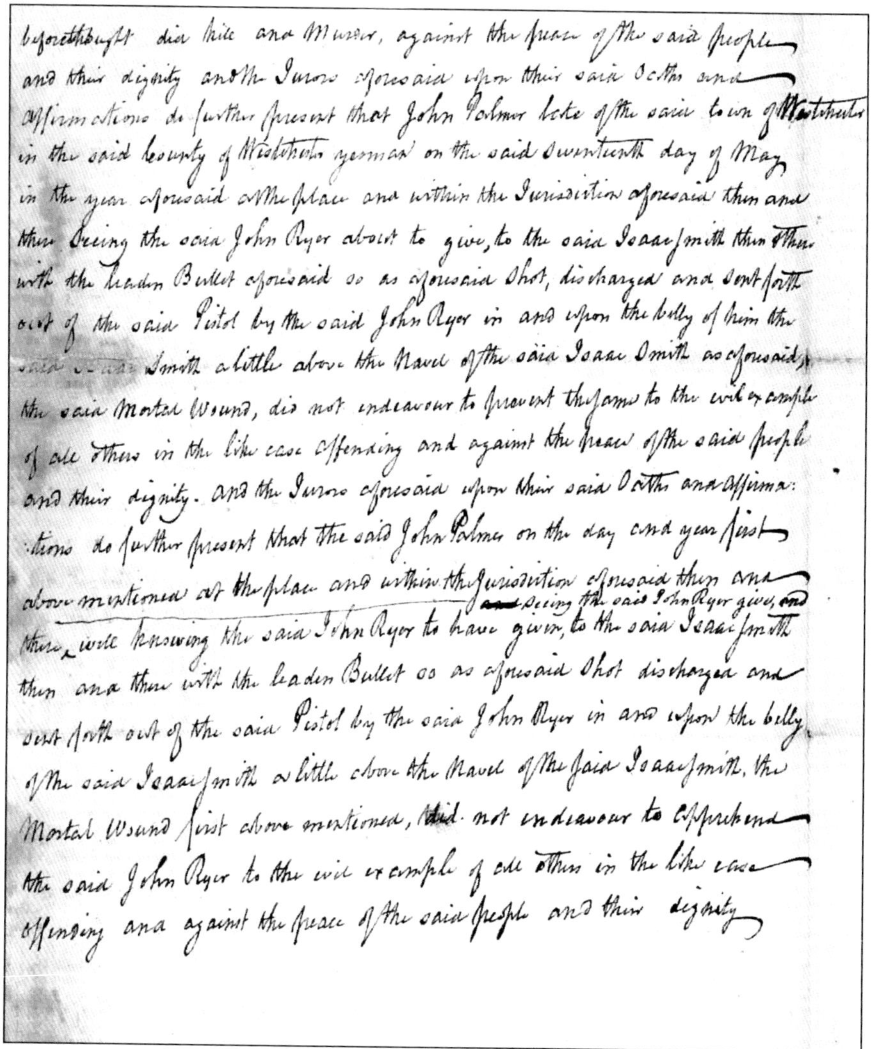
beforethought did kill and Murder, against the peace of the said people
and their dignity and the Jurors aforesaid upon their said Oaths and
Affirmations do further present that John Palmer late of the said town of Westchester
in the said County of Westchester yeoman on the said Seventeenth day of May
in the year aforesaid at the place and within the Jurisdiction aforesaid then and
there seeing the said John Ryer about to give, to the said Isaac Smith then & there
with the leaden Bullet aforesaid so as aforesaid Shot, discharged and sent forth
out of the said Pistol by the said John Ryer in and upon the belly of him the
said Isaac Smith a little above the Navel of the said Isaac Smith as aforesaid,
the said Mortal Wound, did not endeavour to prevent the same to the evil example
of all others in the like case offending and against the peace of the said people
and their dignity. And the Jurors aforesaid upon their said Oaths and Affirma:
:tions do further present that the said John Palmer on the day and year first
above mentioned at the place and within the Jurisdiction aforesaid then and
seeing the said John Ryer give, and
there well knowing the said John Ryer to have given, to the said Isaac Smith
then and there with the leaden Bullet so as aforesaid Shot discharged and
sent forth out of the said Pistol by the said John Ryer in and upon the belly
of the said Isaac Smith a little above the Navel of the said Isaac Smith, the
Mortal Wound first above mentioned, did not endeavour to apprehend
the said John Ryer to the evil example of all others in the like case
offending and against the peace of the said people and their dignity

John Ryer was a loyalist supporter who had actively fought against the Americans during the Revolution. On May 17, 1792, he went to Levi Hunt's Inn, where, after several hours of drinking and gambling, he became disorderly. When William Hunt, a town constable, went to the inn to investigate, John Ryer threatened him with a flintlock pistol and Hunt left the tavern. Later, Deputy Sheriff Isaac Smith attempted to arrest Ryer for breach of the peace and called upon those present to assist him. His call for assistance went unanswered, and Ryer shot Smith before making his escape. Smith died the next day leaving behind a wife and three children. Ryer fled to Canada but was captured in St. John, New Brunswick, on April 5, 1793. He was returned to Westchester County and tried for murder. On October 2, 1793, Ryer was hanged for his crime behind the county courthouse in White Plains. It was Sheriff Samuel Haight of Westchester who was charged with carrying out the order of the court. (WCHS.)

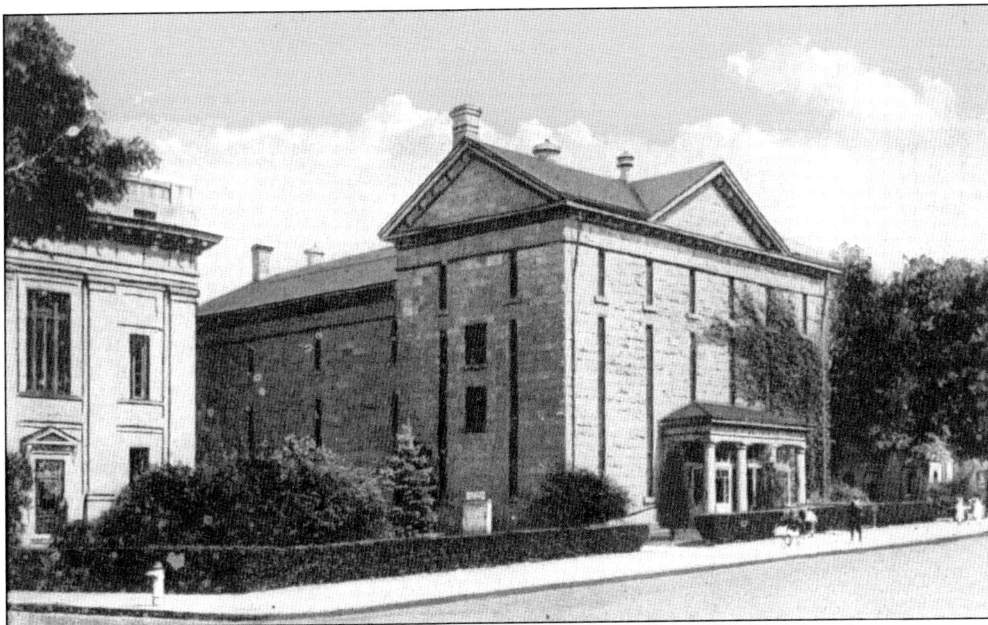

The old county jail, on Martine Avenue in White Plains, was built in 1856–1857, enlarged in 1883, and enlarged again in 1898. The building continued in use as a jail until 1932, when the new county jail at Eastview was opened. The building was used to store records until it was demolished in 1957. Throughout this time, it was the responsibility of the sheriff to oversee the operation of the jail. (WCHS.)

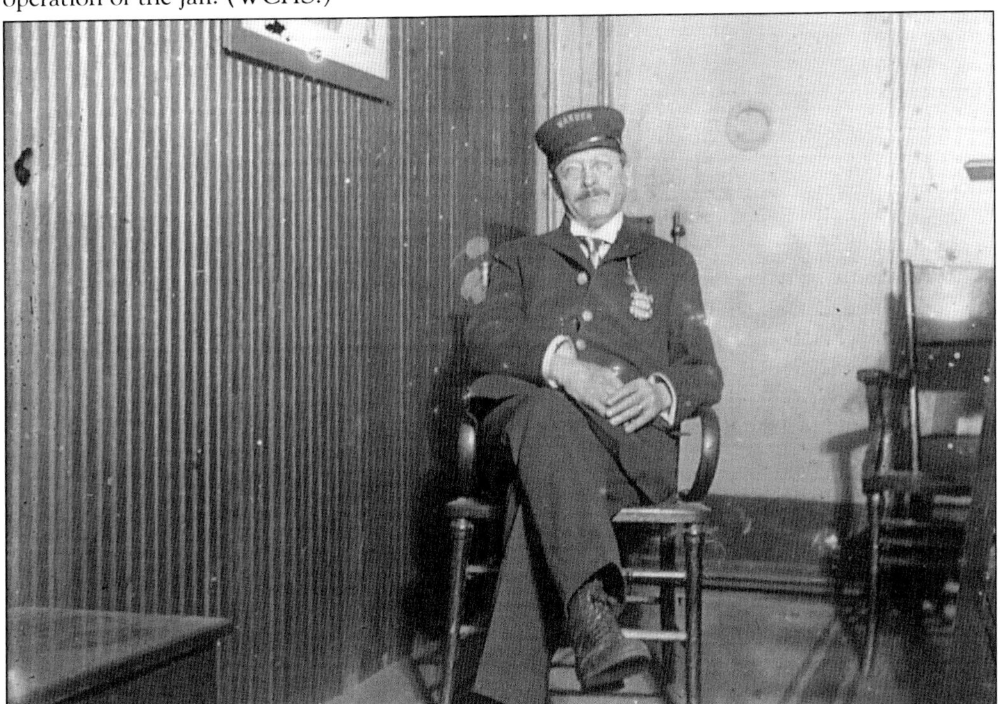

This photograph from 1911 shows the deputy sheriff-warden seated in the old county jail in White Plains.

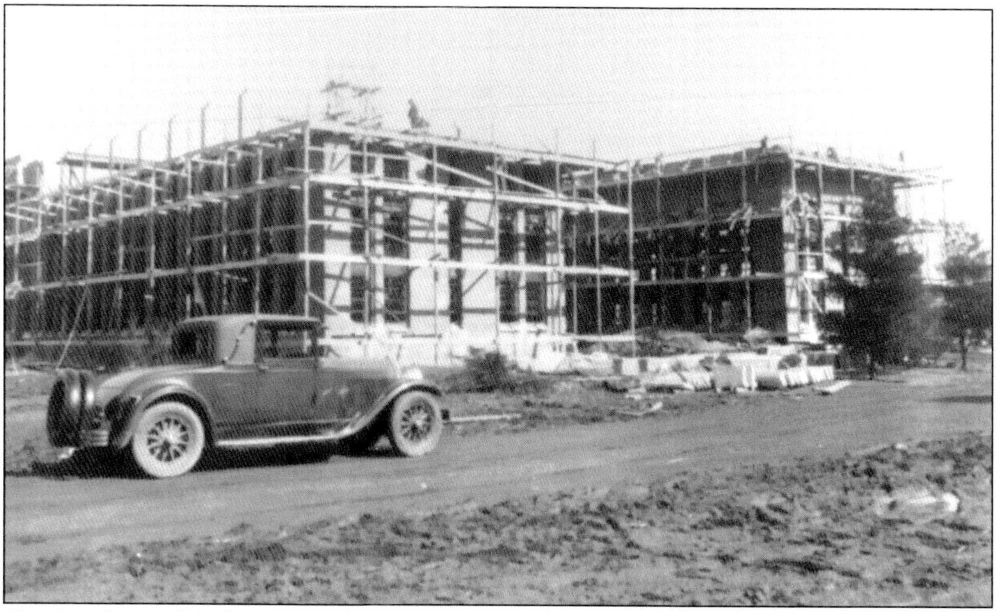

This March 2, 1931 photograph shows the new county jail at Eastview under construction. The area then known as Eastview is more commonly known today as the Grasslands Reservation.

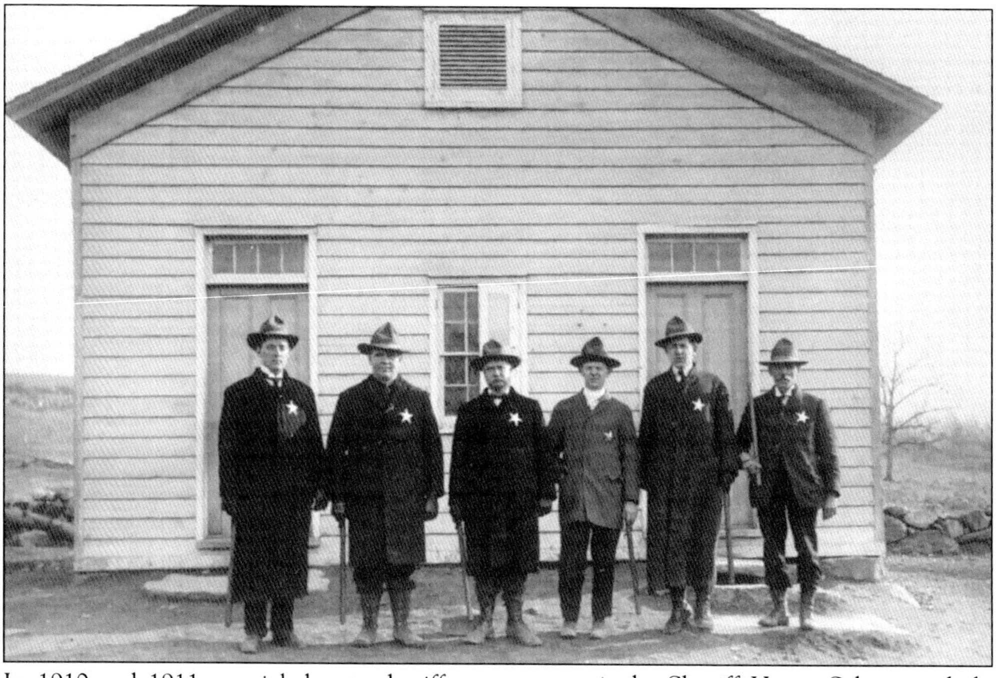

In 1910 and 1911, special deputy sheriffs were sworn in by Sheriff Henry Scherp to help maintain order during construction of the Catskill Aqueduct in Westchester County. The poor conditions under which the immigrant laborers lived and worked while employed on the aqueduct project often resulted in outbreaks of violence. Groups of men were often deputized throughout the history of Westchester County to deal with civil unrest and other threats to the community. The original members of the Westchester County Park Patrol Force were also deputized before they received statutory authority as police officers.

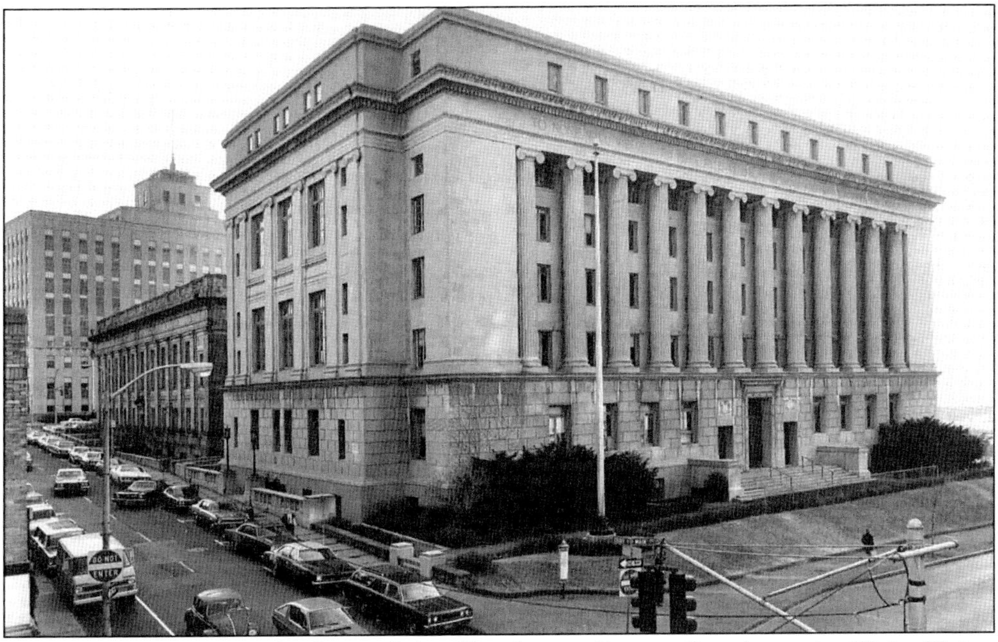

This photograph shows the front of the Westchester County Courthouse in White Plains. The courthouse was built during the years 1915 to 1917. It continued in use until 1975, when the move to the present county courthouse, which was dedicated on December 17, 1973, was completed. (WPHS.)

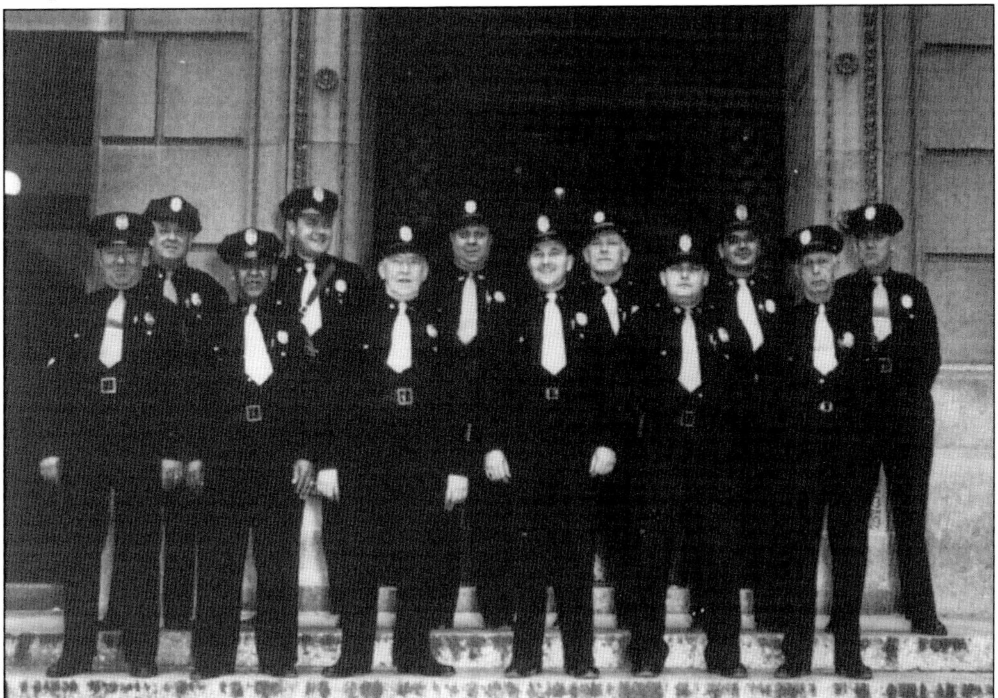

These deputy sheriffs, including John O'Brien (fourth from left), were assigned to courthouse duty *c.* 1940. They pose on the steps of the 1917 courthouse.

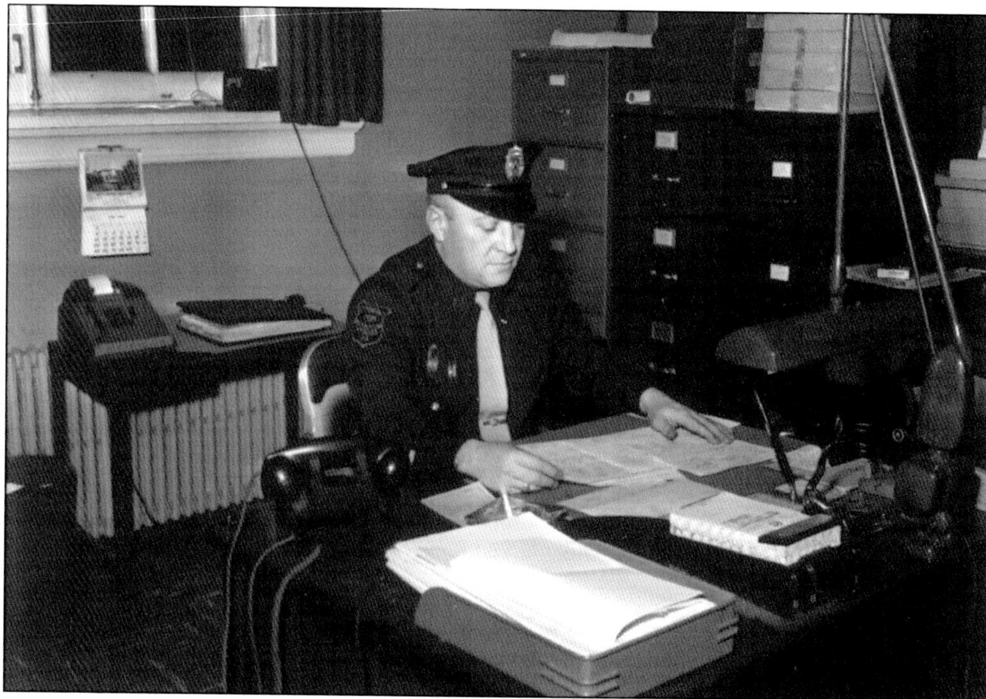

A uniformed deputy sheriff was assigned to the sheriff's outer office in the Westchester County Courthouse to assist the public and to provide security.

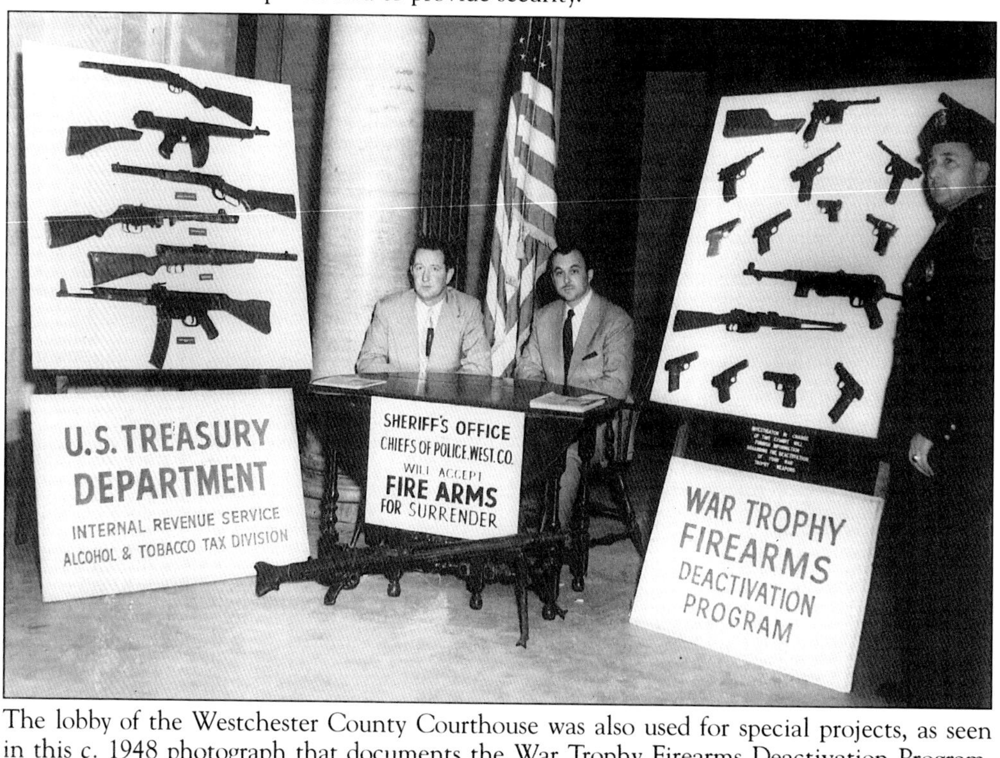

The lobby of the Westchester County Courthouse was also used for special projects, as seen in this c. 1948 photograph that documents the War Trophy Firearms Deactivation Program, which was designed to remove dangerous weapons from the community.

Deputy Sheriff Bernard Gale poses c. 1950 in uniform.

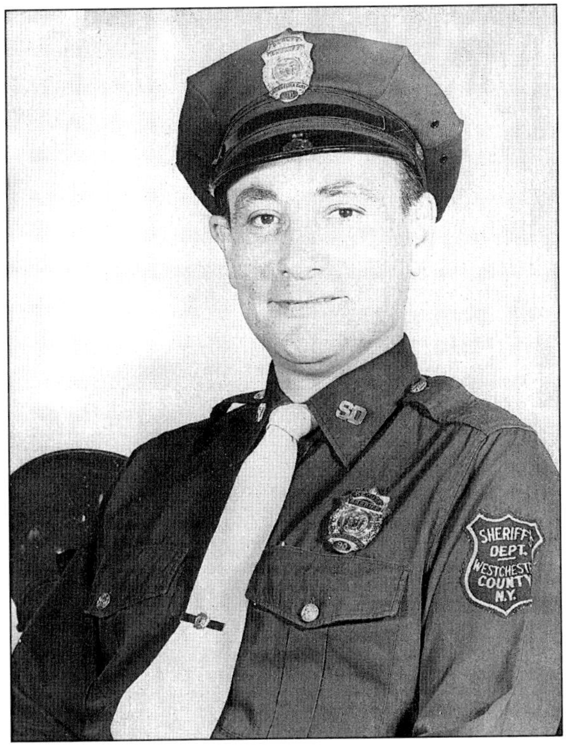

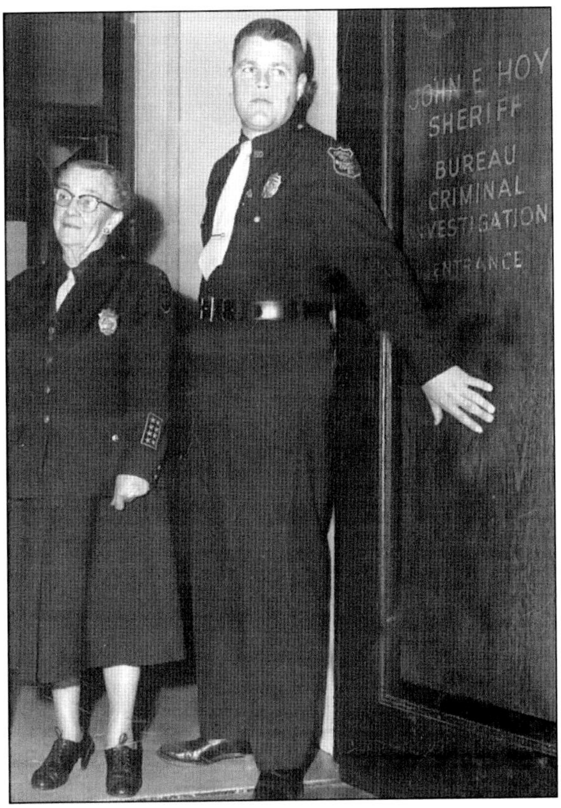

Deputy Sheriff John O'Brien and an unidentified deputy sheriff enter the office of Sheriff John E. Hoy *c*. 1951.

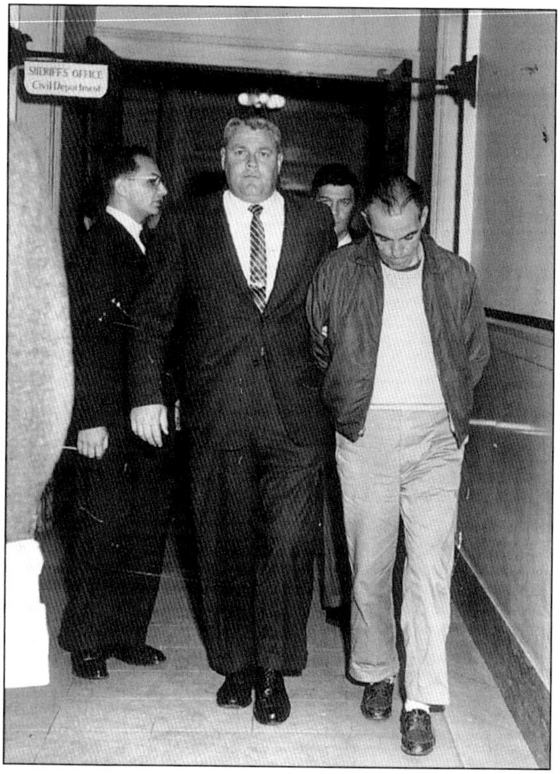

Investigator John O'Brien (center) escorts a prisoner inside the courthouse *c*. 1960.

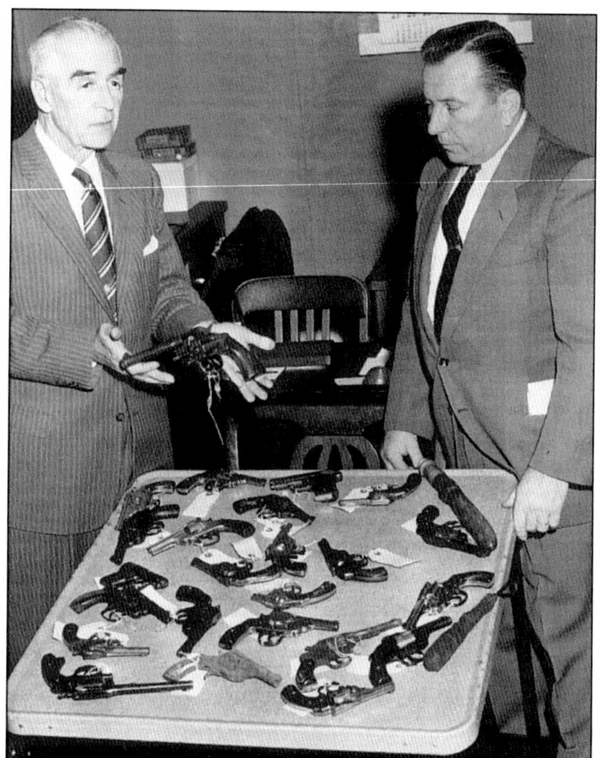

John E. Hoy (left) served as sheriff of Westchester County from 1951 to 1967. He was responsible for expanding the investigative role of the office of the sheriff in Westchester County. In this 1959 photograph, he displays a seized revolver while Paul Black, investigator, looks on.

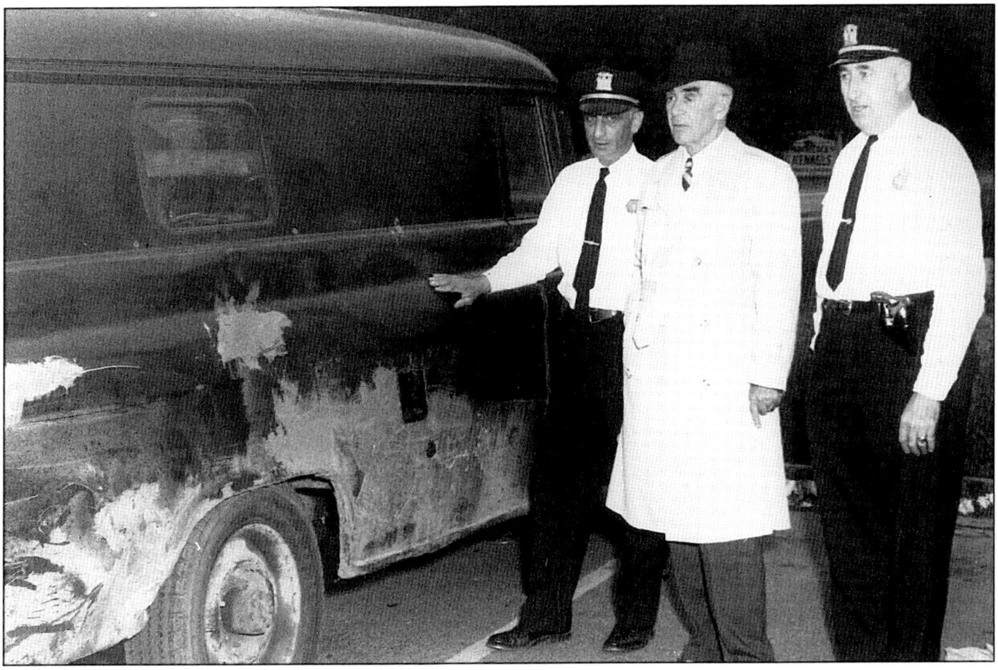

Sheriff John Hoy (center) examines a vehicle with senior members of his staff.

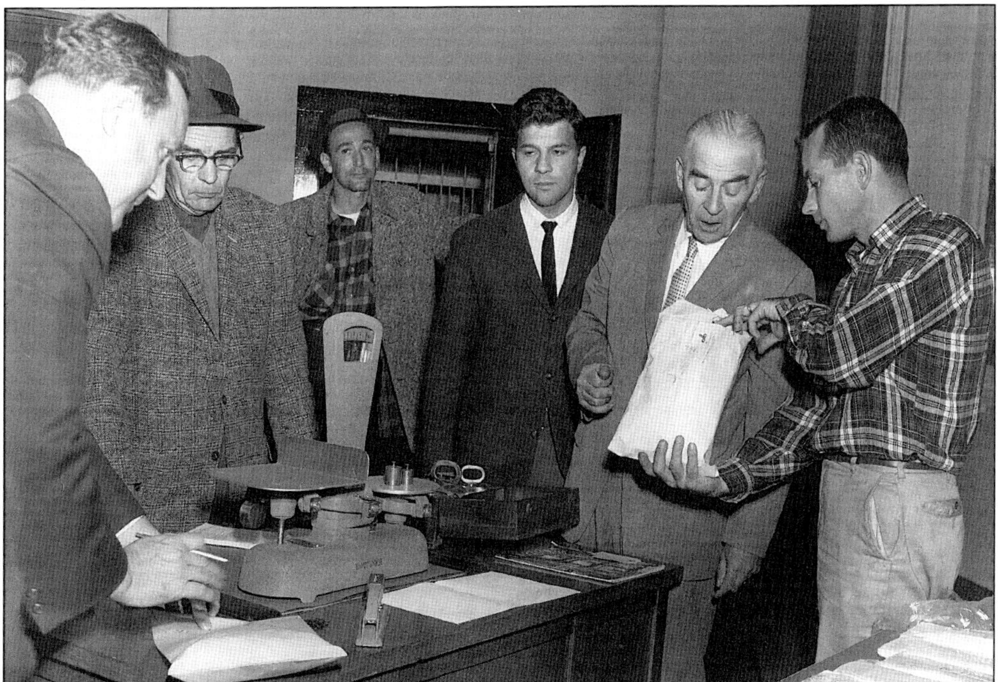

Sheriff John Hoy (second from right) inspects the evidence in a major drug arrest. Among those with him are Frank Salvaggi (fourth from right) of the Federal Narcotics Bureau; John Dolce (third from right), current commissioner of the White Plains Police Department; and Frank Conklin (far right), investigator.

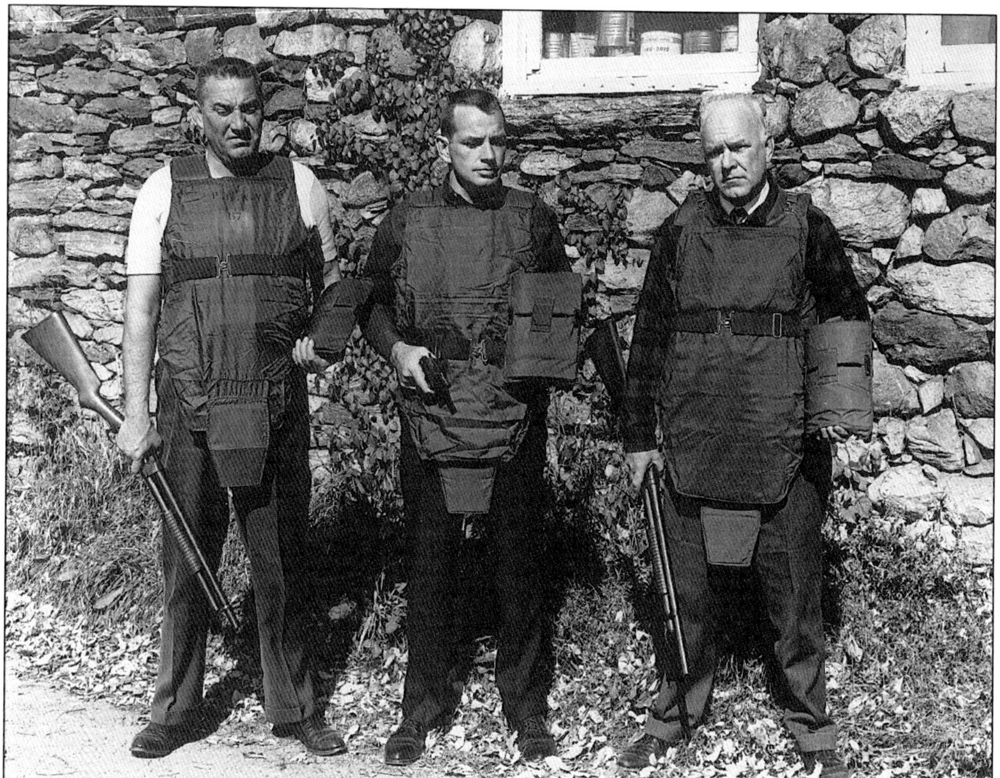

Three investigators of the Westchester County Sheriff's Department are equipped with shotguns and body armor for use in high-risk operations c. 1960. They are, from left to right, Kirk Vend, Frank Conklin, and Arthur Thela.

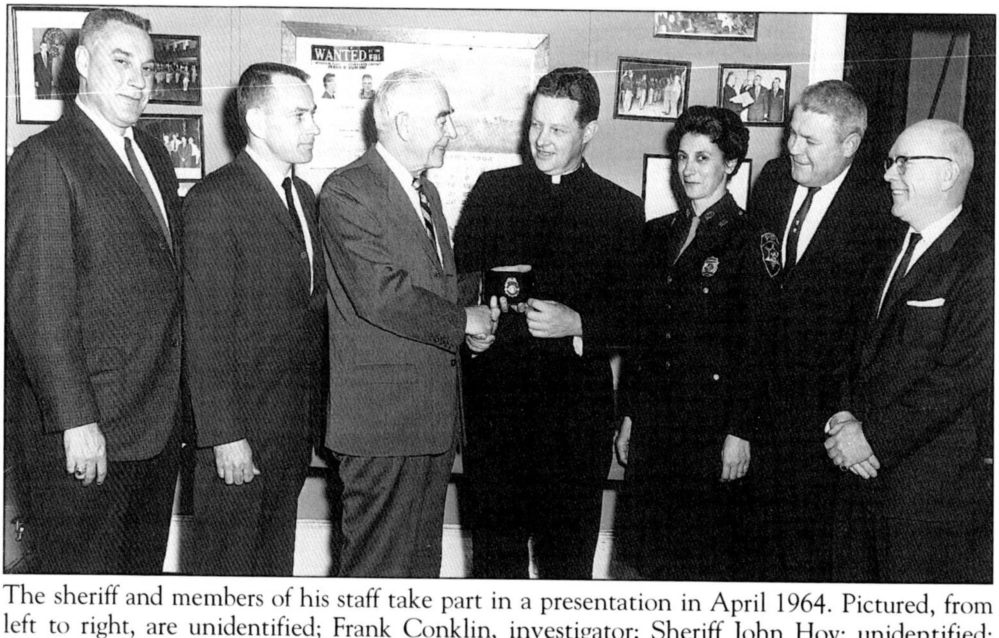

The sheriff and members of his staff take part in a presentation in April 1964. Pictured, from left to right, are unidentified; Frank Conklin, investigator; Sheriff John Hoy; unidentified; Deputy Sheriff Frances Anderson; and John O'Brien and Arthur Thela, investigators.

In 1961, Sheriff John Hoy (third from right) held a press conference at the Westchester County Courthouse to explain the new mutual aid plan for Westchester County police departments. The mutual aid plan was designed to facilitate the rapid deployment of police personnel from one Westchester County jurisdiction to another in response to an emergency situation. The plan was an outgrowth of Sheriff Arthur Maudlin's 1924 plan, which divided Westchester County into four police zones. The mutual aid response plan remains in effect today.

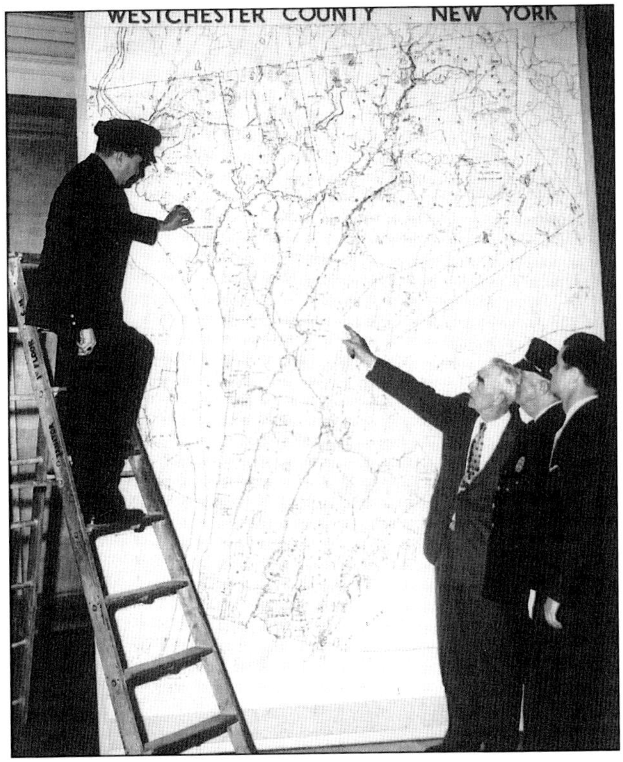

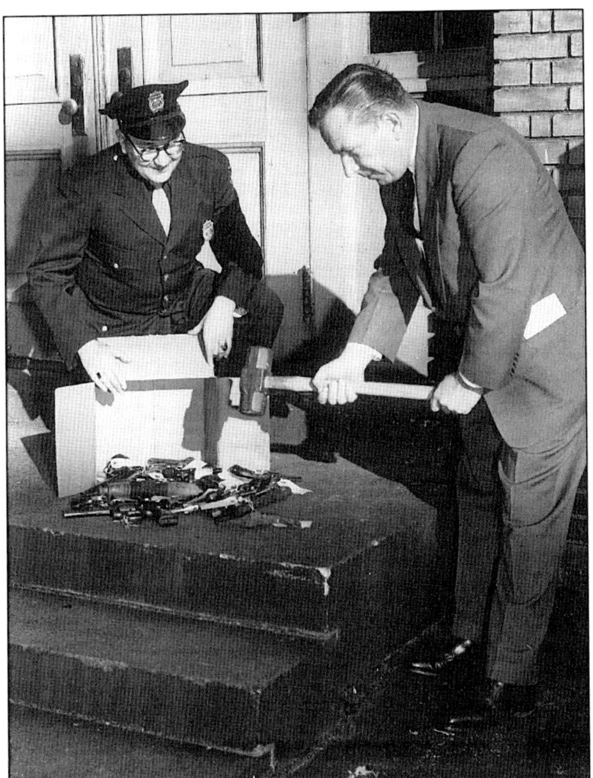

Investigator Paul Black (right) destroys seized weapons with a sledgehammer while Deputy Sheriff John Adams, secretary to Sheriff John Hoy, looks on. This photograph was taken in White Plains on December 16, 1959.

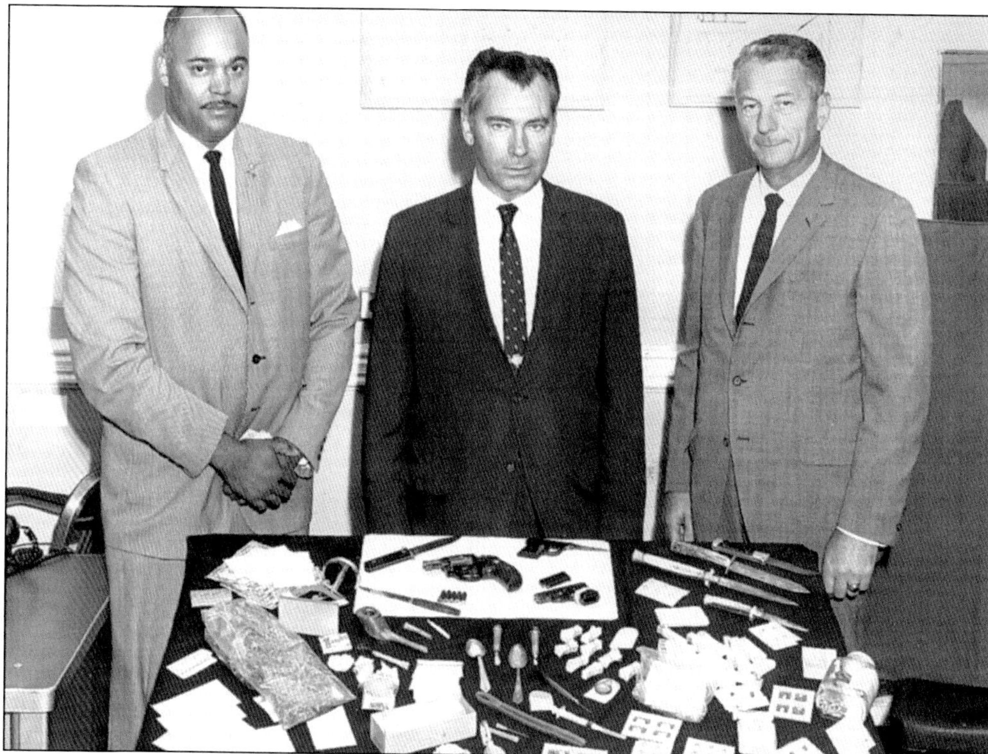

Daniel F. McMahon (center) served as Westchester County sheriff from 1968 to 1973. Prior to his election as sheriff, he served as a U.S. assistant attorney and as commissioner of the Yonkers Police Department. In 1974, Gov. Malcolm Wilson appointed him a court of claims judge, a post he retained until his retirement from public life in 1985. With him, examining evidence seized during the course of a narcotics investigation, are Charles R. Jackson (left), senior criminal investigator, and Under Sheriff Eugene A. Fenelon.

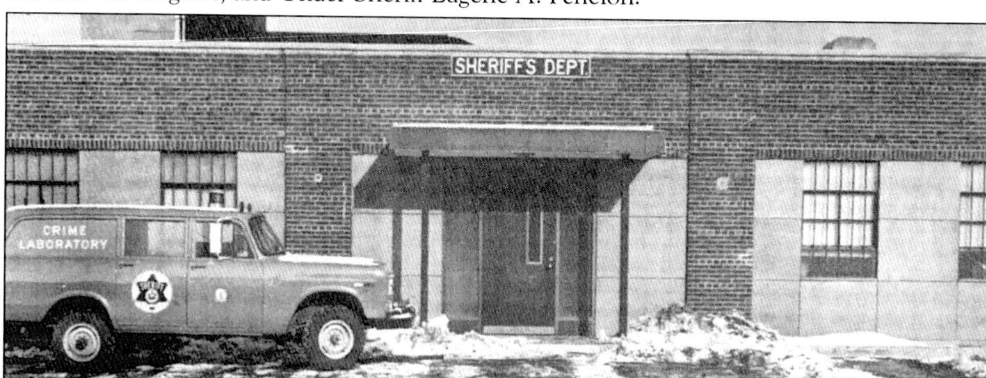

Sheriff Daniel McMahon was strongly committed to the improvement of the Westchester County Sheriff's Department and immediately expanded the criminal investigation division with a focus on narcotics enforcement. This necessitated the creation of a crime lab, located in Eastview across from the jail, which opened in 1969, and the acquisition of a mobile crime lab vehicle to support the increased investigative effort. During McMahon's tenure, the responsibility for the operation of the jail was transferred to the newly created Westchester County Department of Corrections.

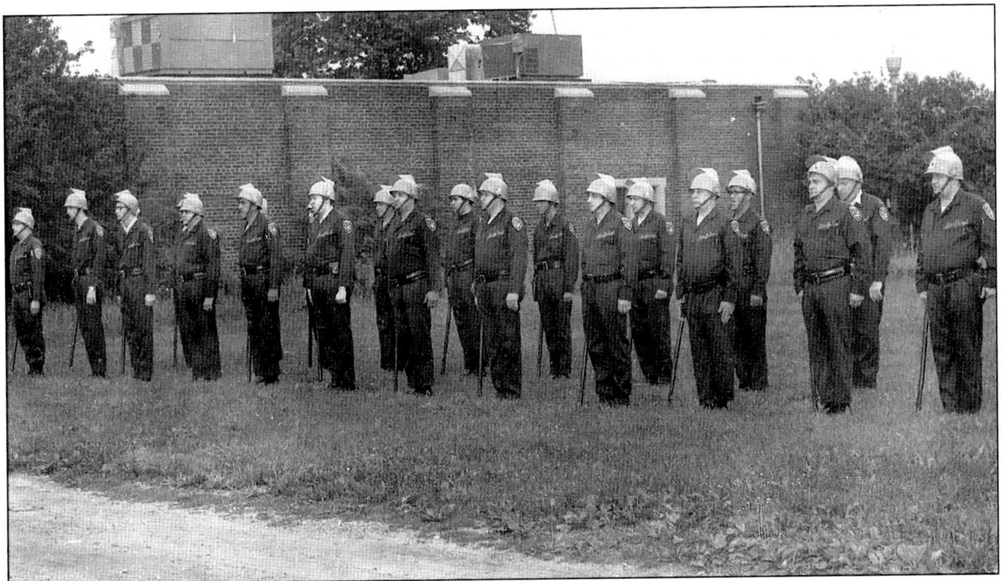

In response to an increasing number of incidents of civil unrest, Sheriff Daniel McMahon created a riot squad in 1968. This unit is shown here conducting training on the grounds of the Grasslands Reservation in Eastview.

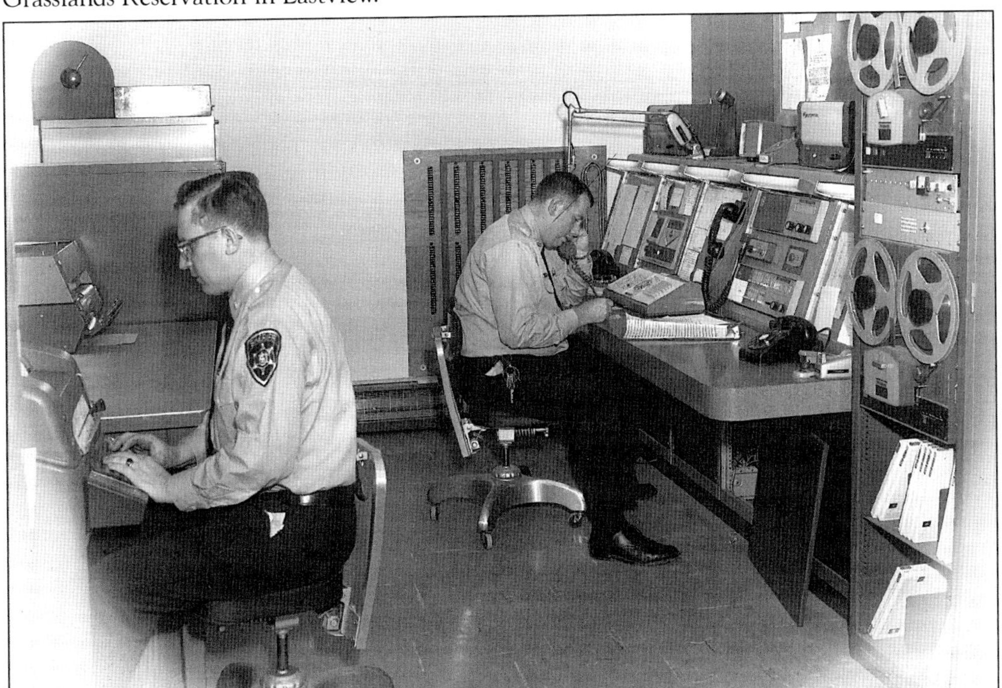

This photograph from January 10, 1971, shows the communications center for the sheriff's department, staffed by Deputy Sheriffs Jack Singer (left) at the teletype and Jeff King at the radio console. Sheriff Daniel McMahon sought to improve police communications during his term of office and established a county-wide hotline that went into operation on June 13, 1968. The dedicated telephone system allowed a caller to speak to all of the involved police agencies simultaneously.

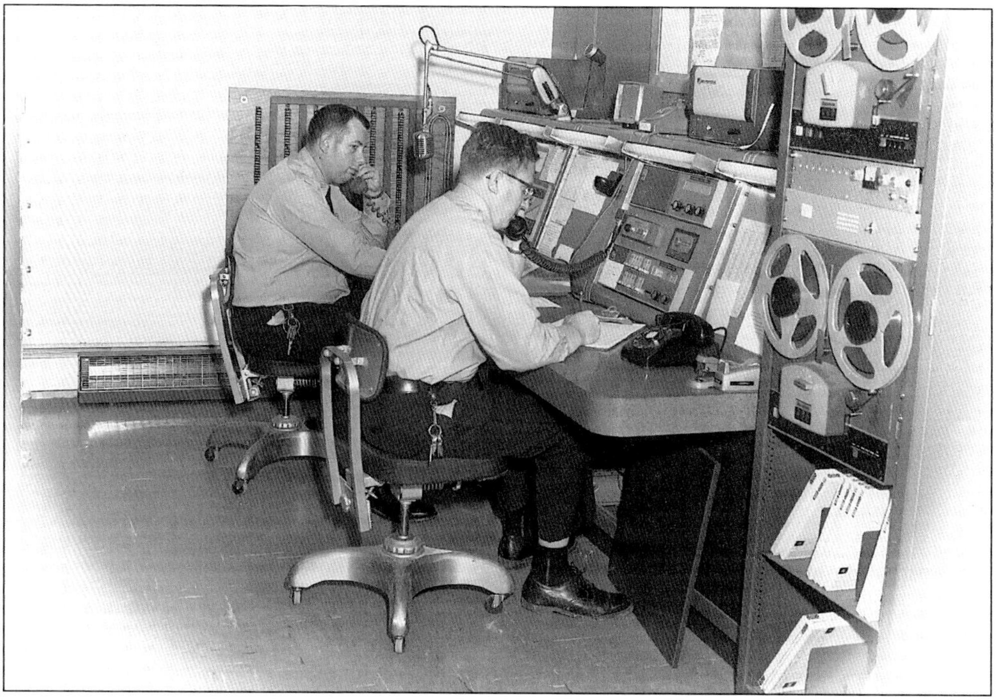

Deputy Sheriffs Jeff King and Jack Singer take calls in the communications center of the sheriff's department.

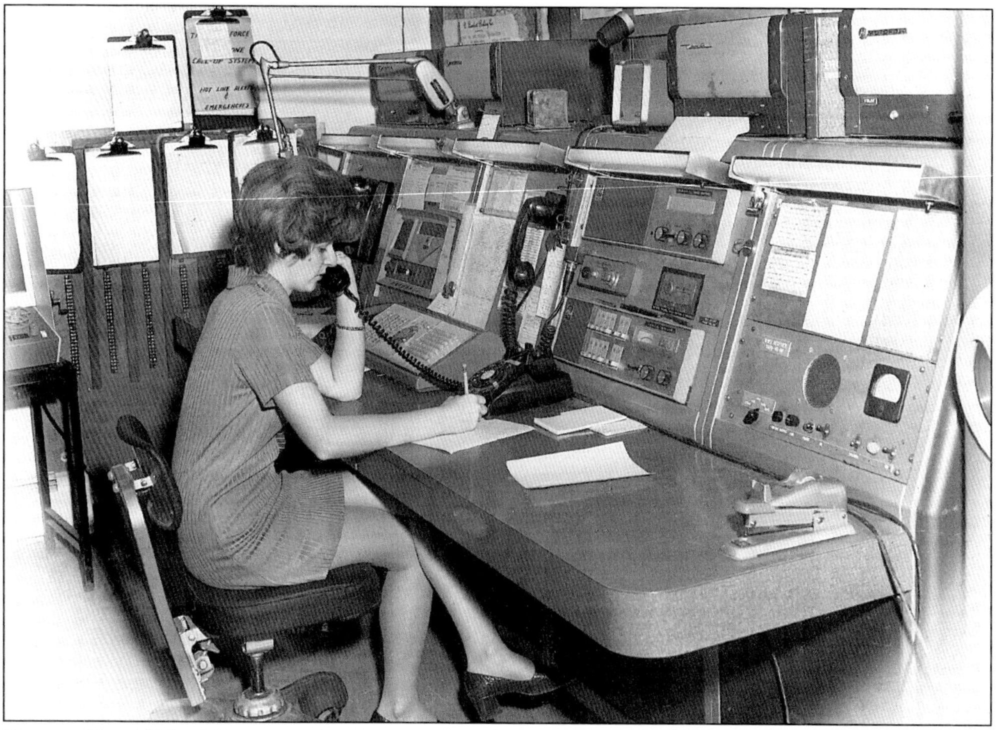

Deputy Sheriff Terri Potanovich takes a call at the radio console located in the sheriff's building at Eastview.

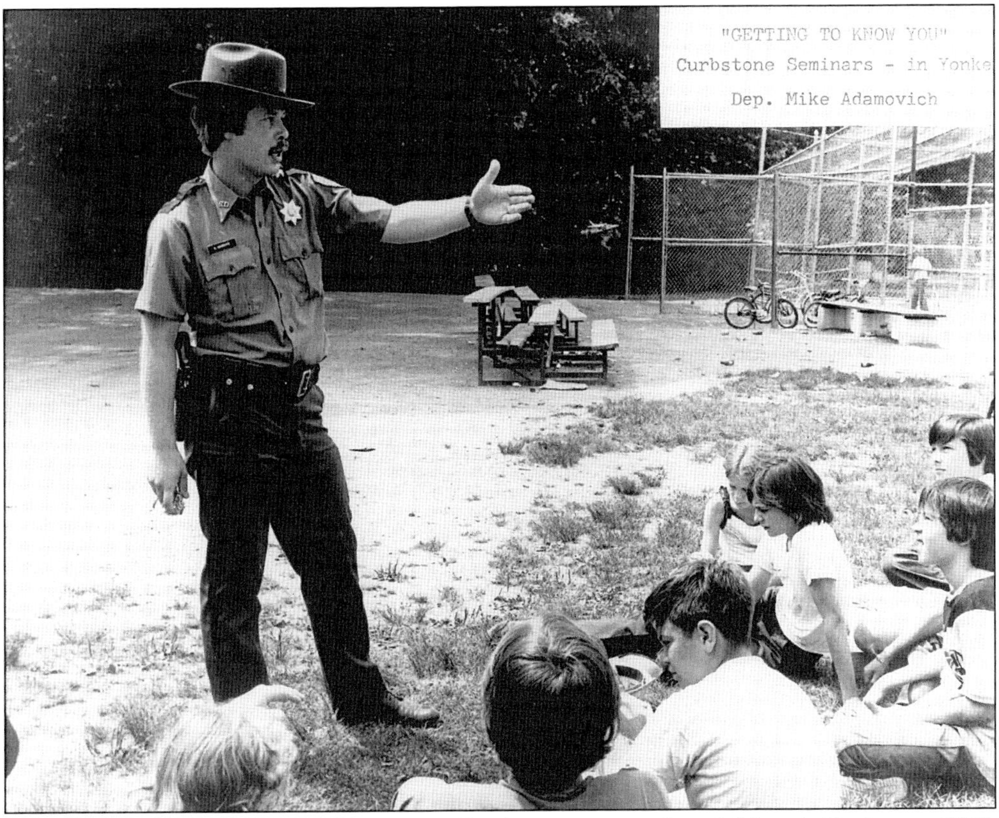

Deputy Sheriff Mike Adamovich presents a "curbstone seminar" to children in Yonkers c. 1975. This program was designed to foster better relations between the law enforcement agency and the community while educating children on personal safety issues.

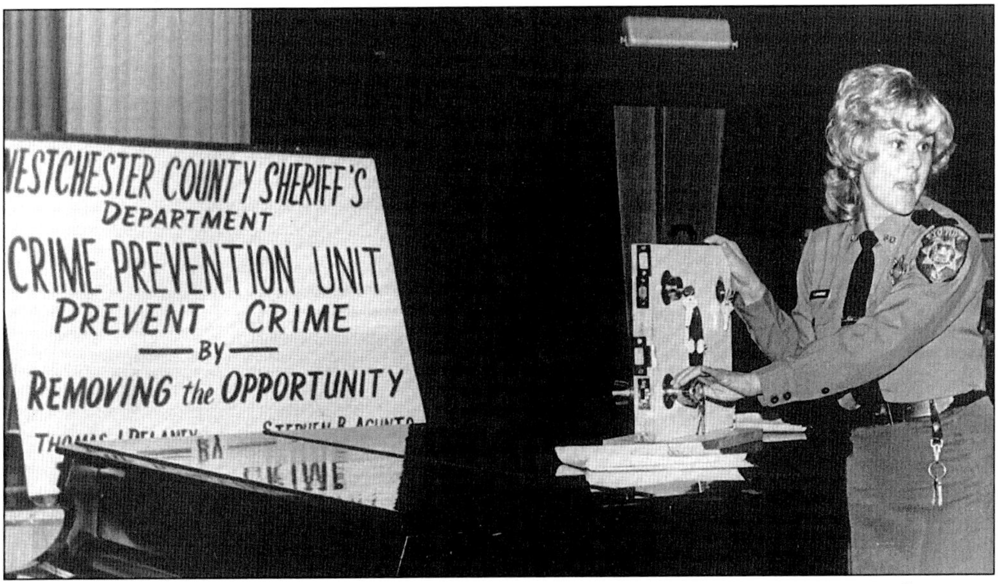

Deputy Sheriff Vivian Bayreuther gives a crime prevention seminar to a group of citizens c. 1975. Sheriff Thomas J. Delaney (1974–1979) initiated outreach programs such as this one.

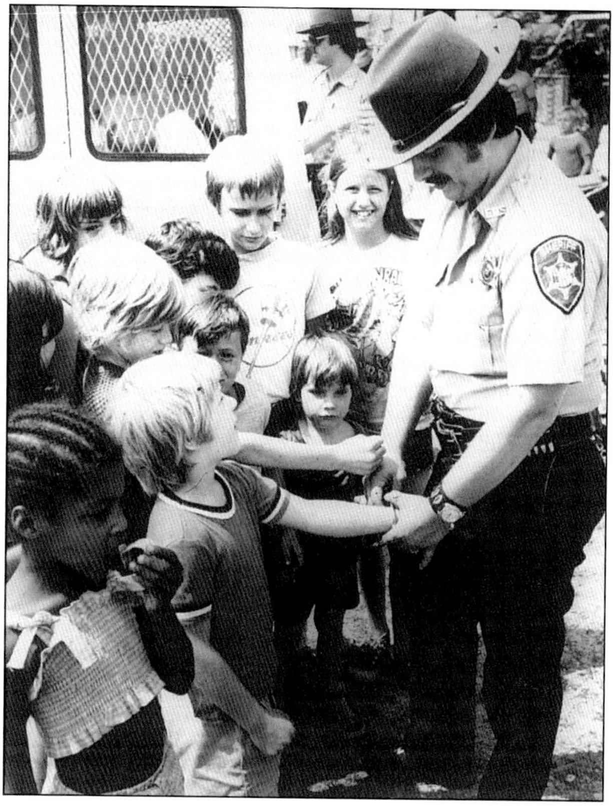

Deputy Sheriff Dolph Tutoni demonstrates handcuffing techniques to children as part of a crime prevention and community outreach program *c.* 1975.

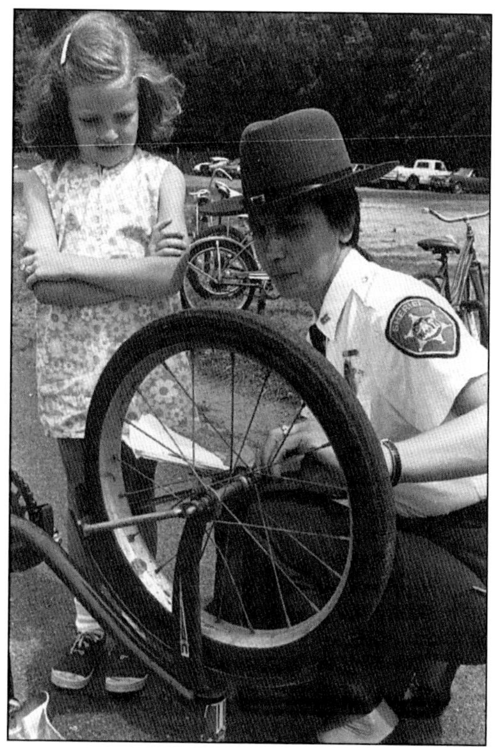

Deputy Sheriff Frances Anderson goes over bicycle safety with a child *c.* 1975. Deputy Sheriff Stephen Acunto was responsible for organizing and administering the various crime prevention programs initiated by Sheriff Thomas Delaney.

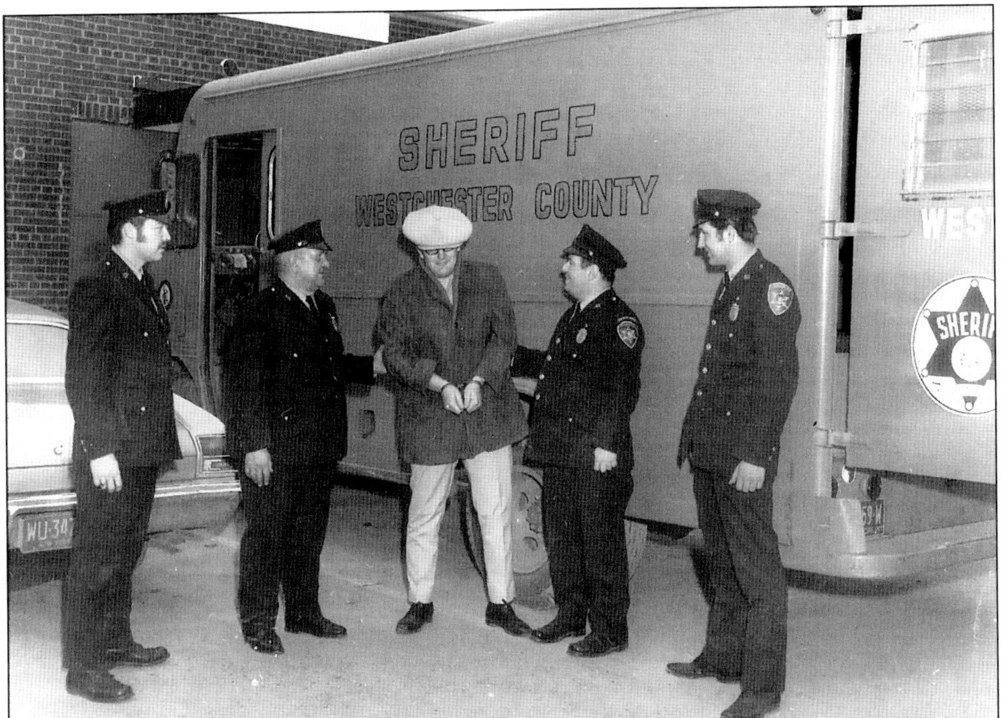

With the prisoner-transport van waiting, five deputy sheriffs have their picture taken outside the sheriff's office at Eastview c. 1970. They are, from left to right, James Gardner, Gus Wasylenko, Frederic Arone (posing as a prisoner), Len Nowack, and Roger Rokicki.

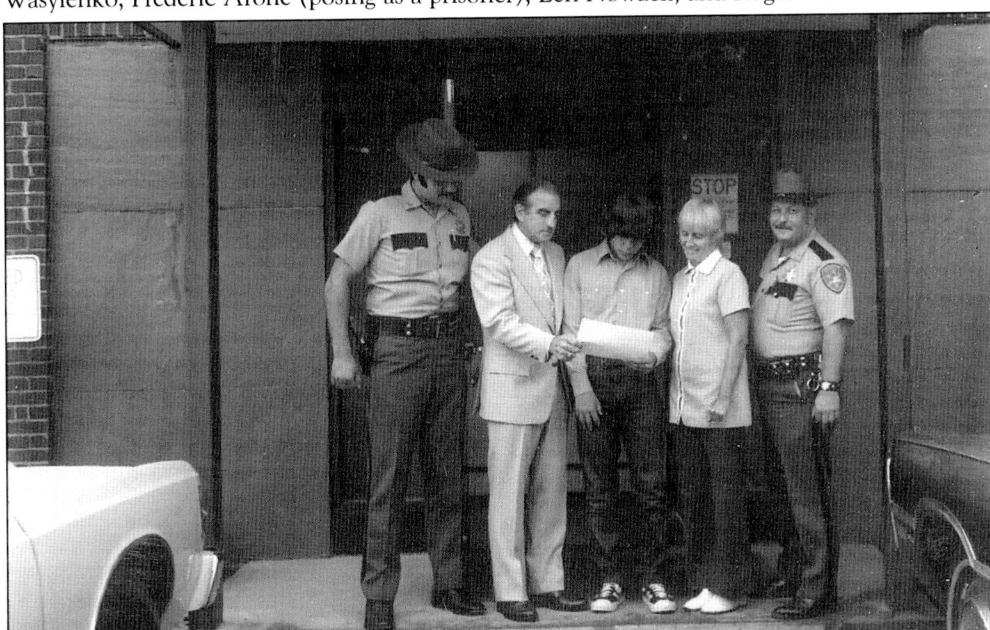

In front of the sheriff's building in Eastview c. 1975, three deputy sheriffs discuss a crime prevention program with a young man and a woman. The three are, from left to right, Vincent Ragaini, Stephen Acunto, and Len Nowack.

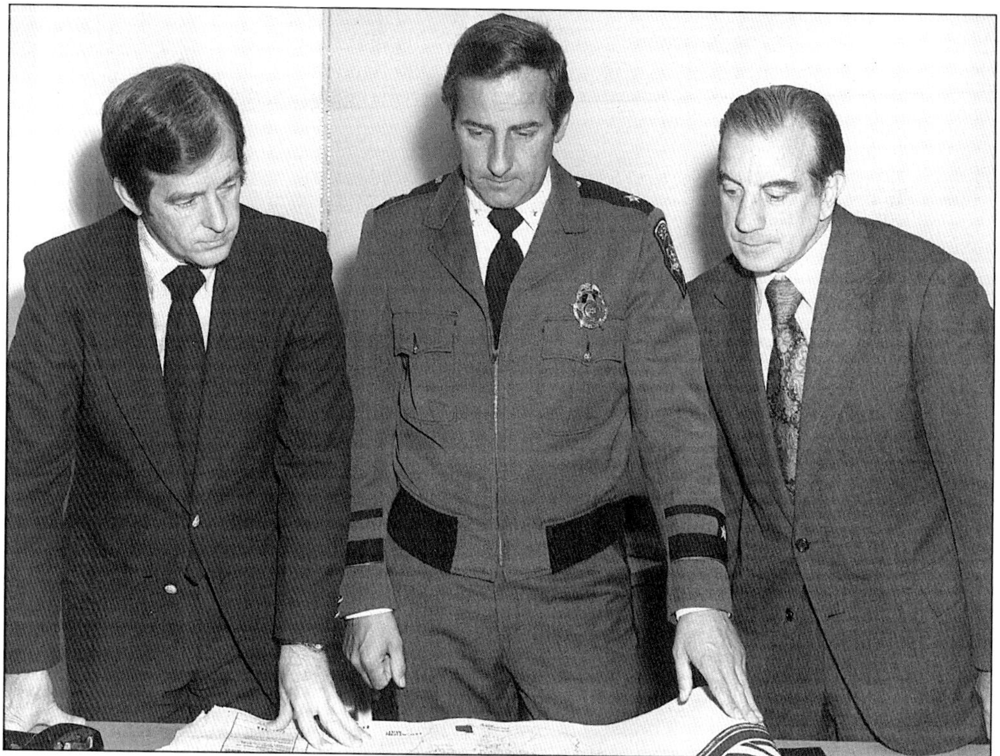

Reviewing construction plans *c.* 1975 are, from left to right, unidentified; John DeLeo, chief of investigations; and Stephen Acunto, deputy sheriff.

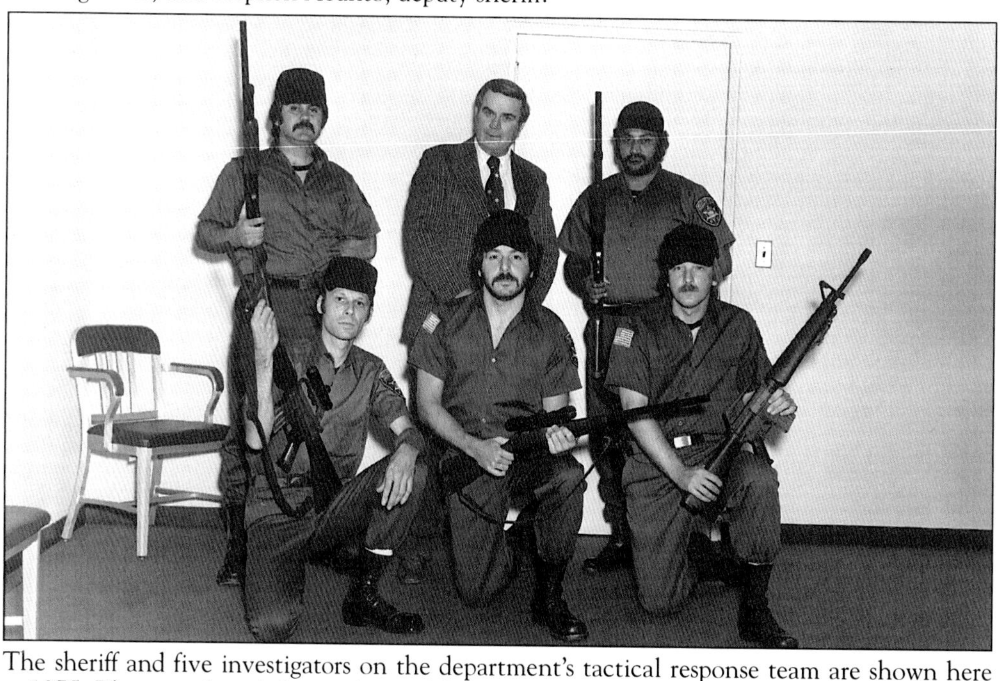

The sheriff and five investigators on the department's tactical response team are shown here *c.* 1975. They are, from left to right, as follows: (front row) Ken Zajack, Ernest Colaneri, and Ken Cowen; (back row) Ron Poherence, Sheriff Thomas Delaney, and Angel Feliciano.

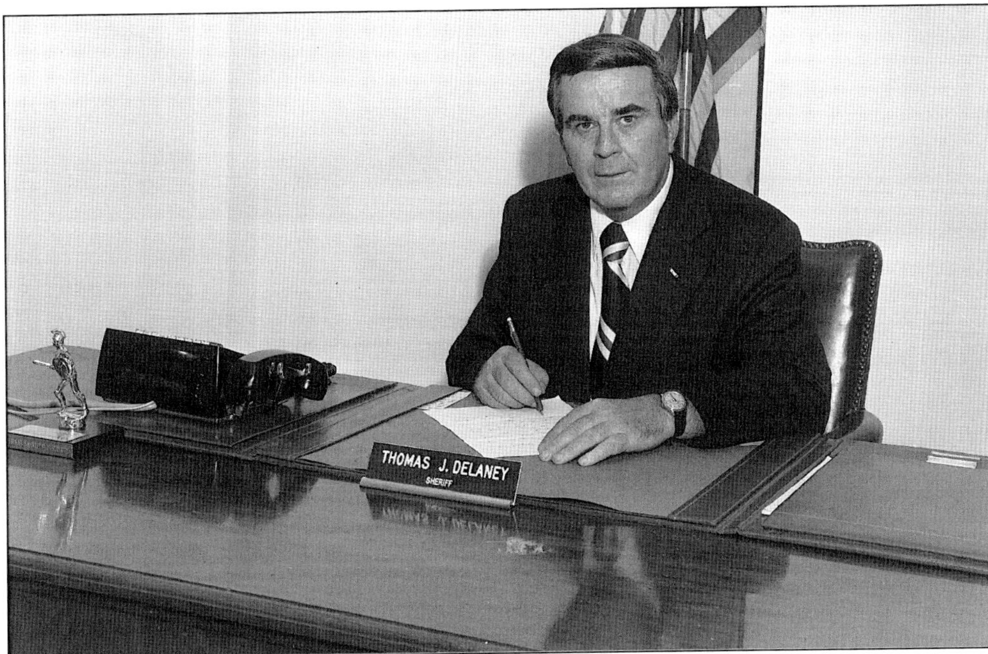

Sheriff Thomas J. Delaney was the last sheriff of Westchester County prior to the merger with the Westchester County Parkway Police, on July 1, 1979. He became the first commissioner-sheriff of the newly created Westchester County Department of Public Safety.

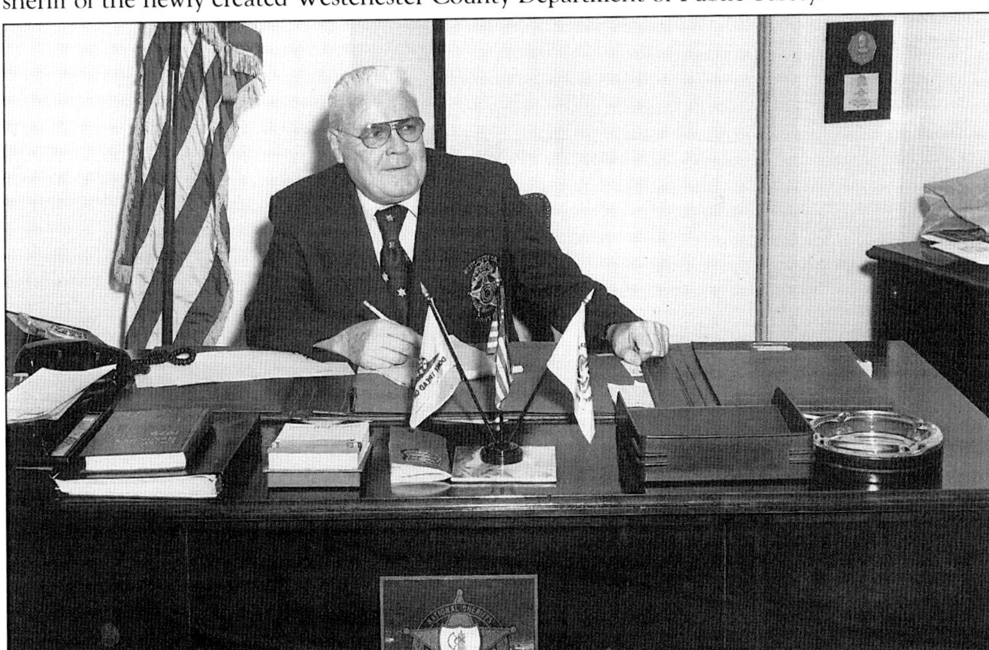

John O'Brien served as under sheriff to Sheriff Thomas Delaney. The office of under sheriff dates back to 1847; however, it was largely an honorary title until 1899, when the legislature passed an act that significantly changed the operation of the office of the Westchester County sheriff. O'Brien later served as the second commissioner-sheriff of the Westchester County Department of Public Safety.

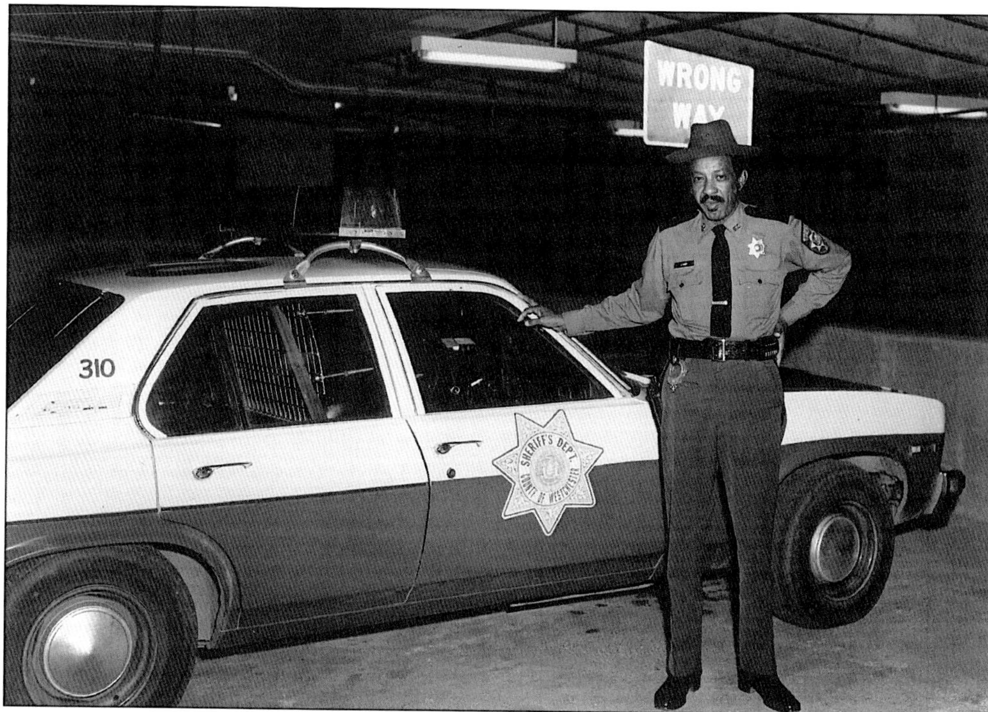

Deputy Sheriff John Hicks stands next to a white-over-red 1976 Chevrolet Nova in the Westchester County Courthouse garage. His uniform consists of dark gray pants and a light gray shirt.

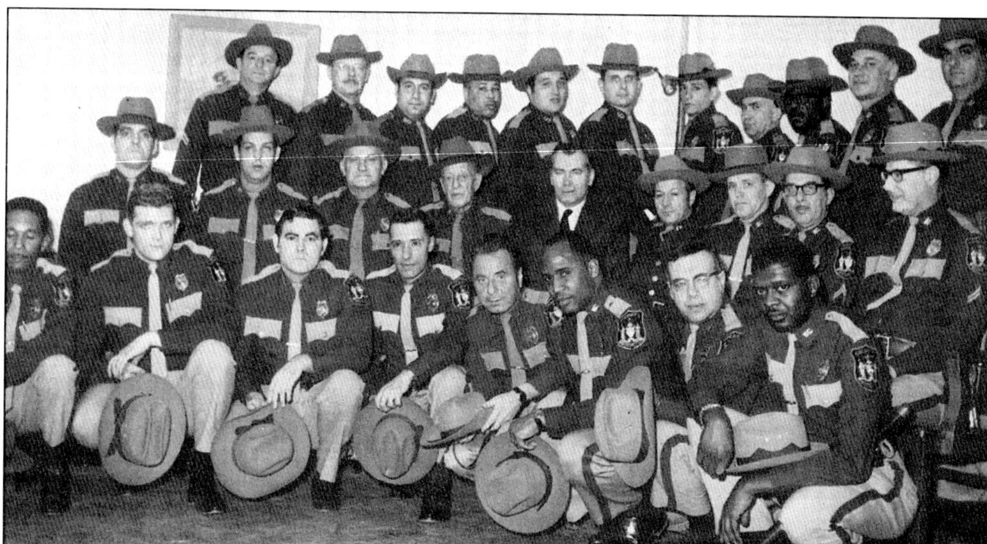
The Sheriff'sEmergency Force has existed under various names since World War I. A volunteer organization, it has provided excellent service to the people of Westchester throughout its existence. Among those appearing in this 1968 photograph are the following: (front row) John Dillon (second from left), current chief of the Public Safety Emergency Force; (middle row) Chief John Randazzo (fourth from left); Sheriff Daniel McMahon (fifth from left); and Col. Harold Kimball (sixth from left).

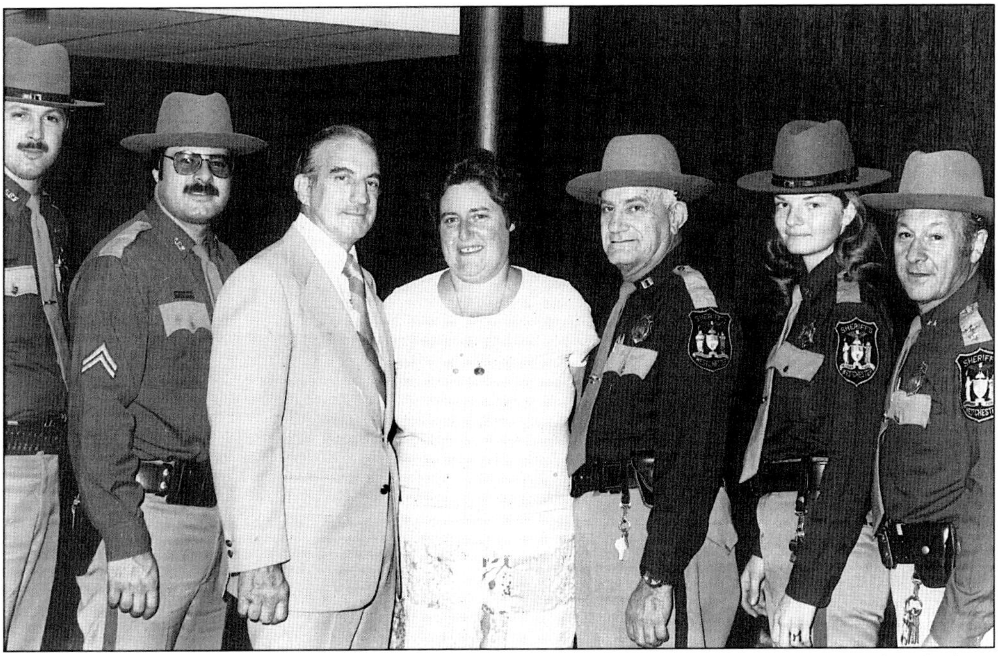

In this *c.* 1975 photograph are five members of the Sheriff'sEmergency Force (in uniform), from left to right, Andrew Philips, Craig Glassman,Captain Viviano, unidentified, and Chief John Randazzo. With them are Deputy Sheriff Stephen Acunto and an unidentified woman.

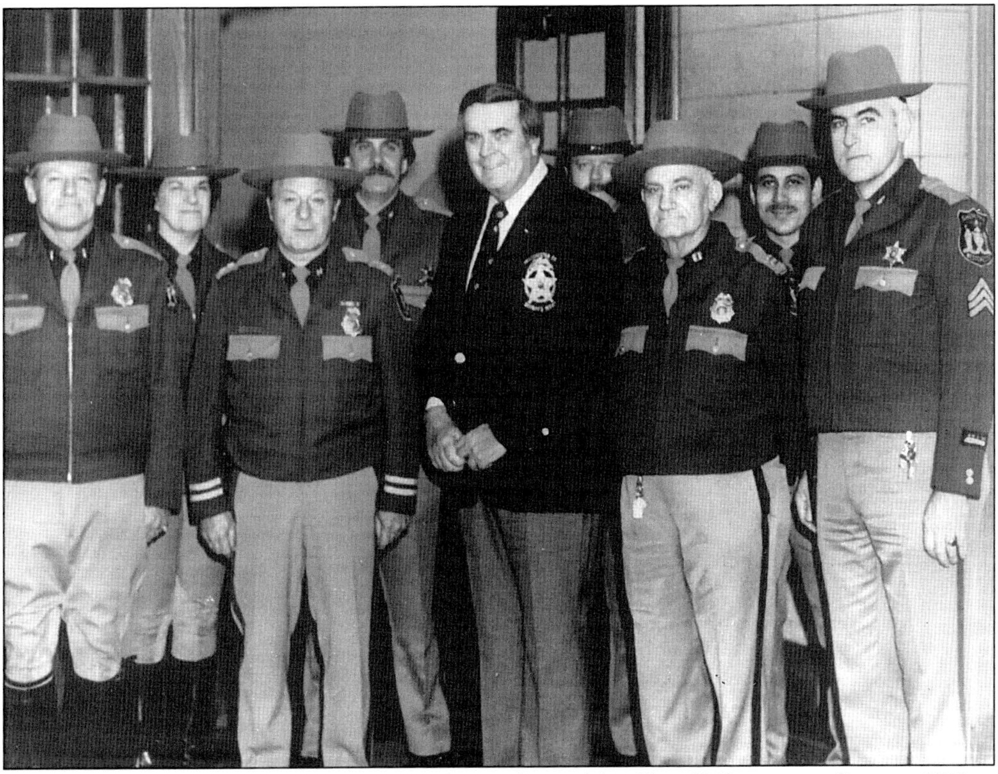

Sheriff Thomas Delaney (center) poses with members of the Sheriff'sEmergency Force *c.* 1975.

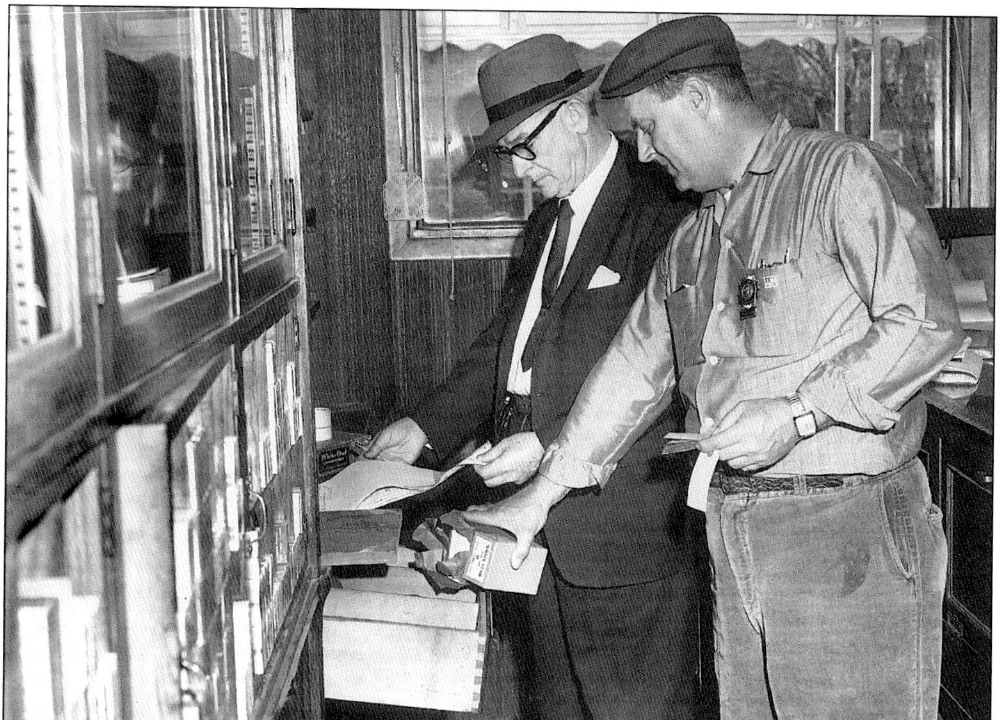

This photograph documents a raid made on a gambling operation on March 26, 1962, by members of the sheriff's department and the office of the district attorney. Deputy Sheriff Joseph J. Reid (left) and John McKeon, the district attorney's investigator look through the evidence.

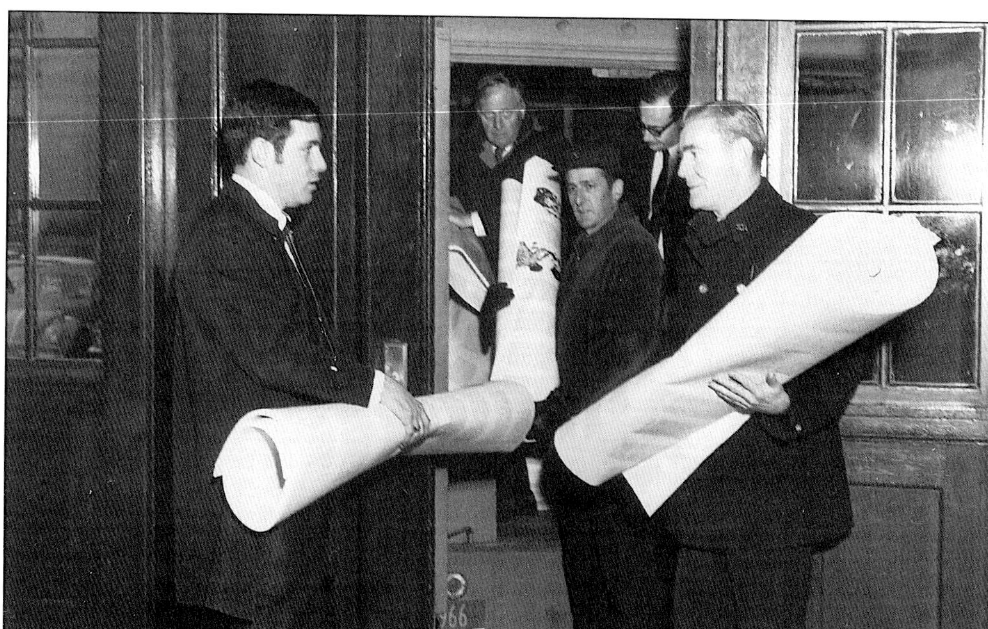

This photograph documents a pornography raid c. 1970. Pictured are three deputy sheriffs: Ernest Colaneri (left), James Fleming (second from left), and John Cunningham (right).

Two

THE WESTCHESTER COUNTY PARKWAY POLICE: 1926–1979

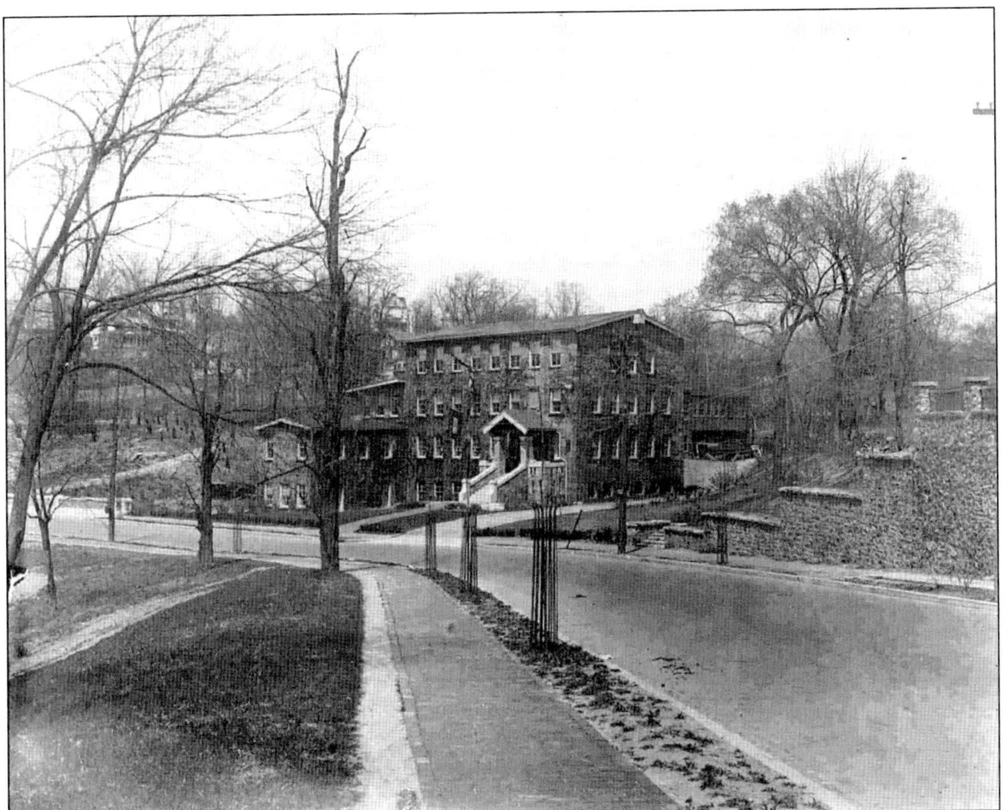

This is a view of the original Westchester County Parkway Police headquarters, located on Pondfield Road in Bronxville. This building, formerly known as Swain's Mill, was acquired by the Bronx River Parkway Commission and was converted during the construction of the parkway. Headquarters remained here until June 1953, when relocated to the present site in Hawthorne. (WCHS.)

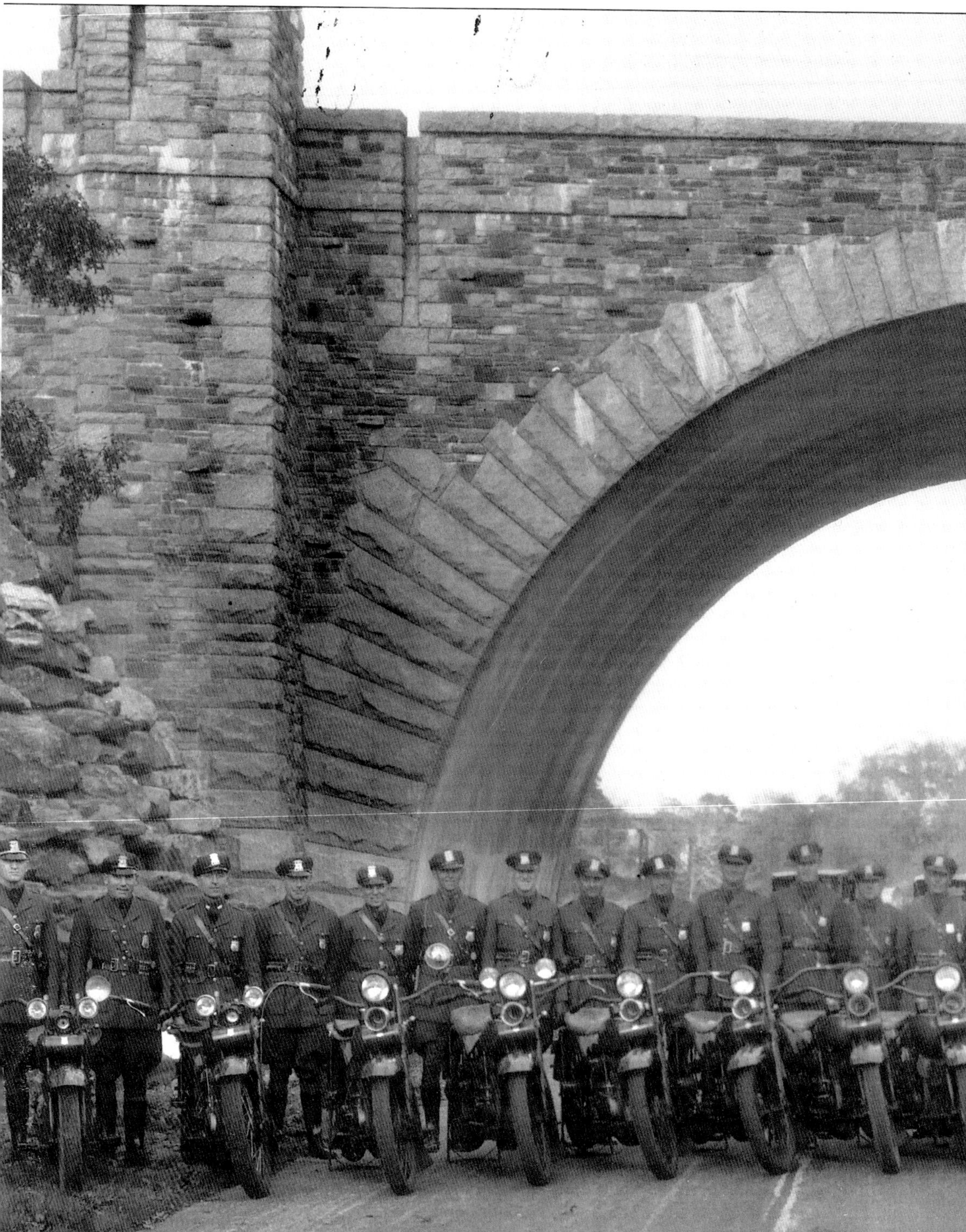

This view shows the Westchester County Parkway Police at the New Haven Railroad viaduct over the Hutchinson River Parkway in Mount Vernon *c.* 1930. The Hutchinson River Parkway

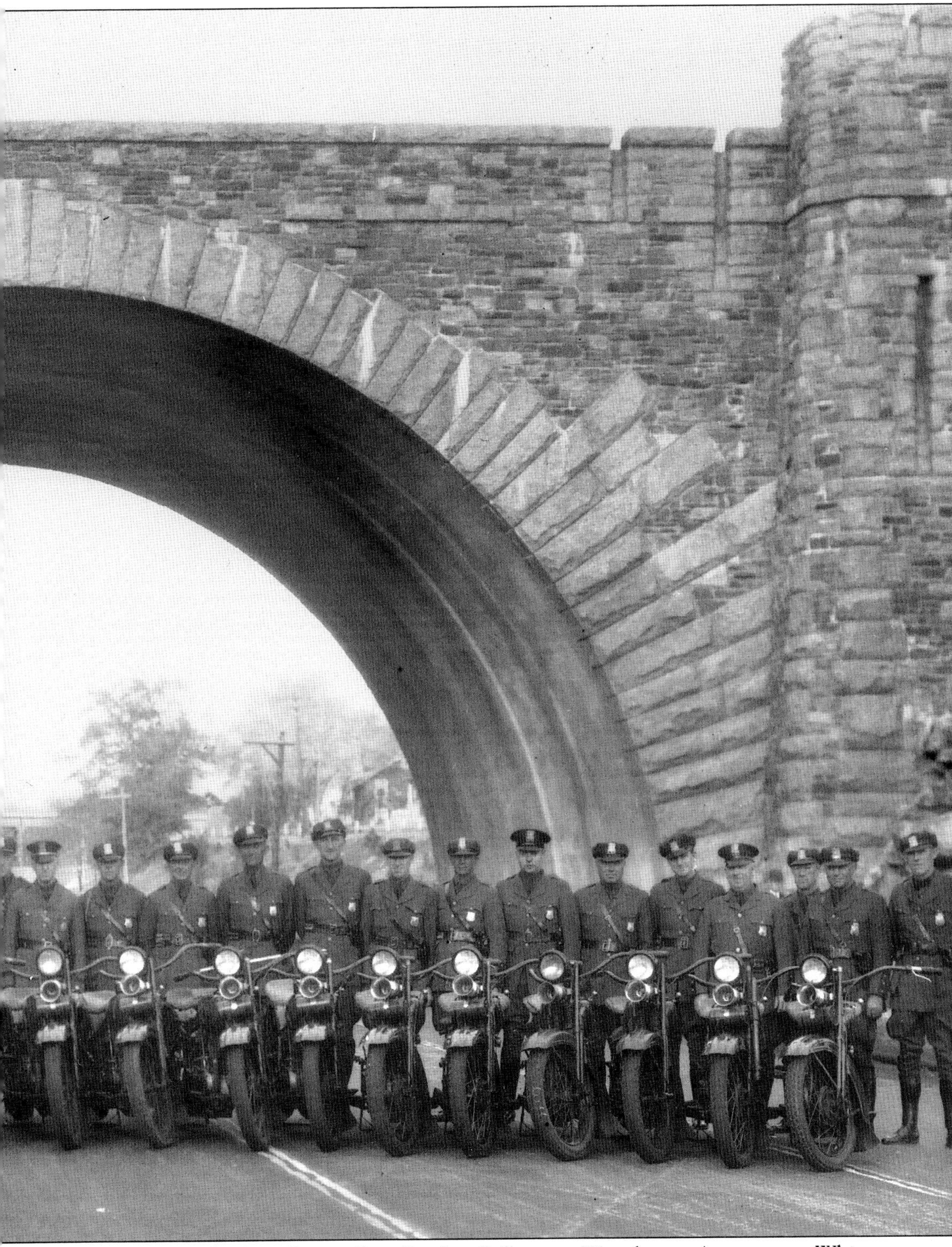

was opened to traffic from Boston Post Road in Pelham to Westchester Avenue near White Plains during 1928.

Behind the Blotter

A History of the Westchester County Parkway Police Department

By Robert Robischon

"Future generations will doubtless assume that the restored valley never needed restoration and that the Bronx Parkway Drive, to provide for restricted traffic, was the sole object for the creation of the parkway. Such, however, was not the case. The inception of the idea for the establishment of the parkway was founded more upon a need for the cure of unsanitary conditions than to provide facilities for pleasure traffic."

These prophetic words are to be found in the final report with which the Bronx River Parkway Commission concluded, on Dec. 31, 1925, a total of eighteen years of labor in building up the key lands which set the foundation for the vast Westchester Park and Parkway system. Already, at that date, the Commission had seen the newer Westchester County Park Commission organized in 1922 to take over the expansion of its labors with the opening of the first sections of the Bronx River Parkway traffic routes.

In the short period of a decade and a half this prophecy has been justified. How few motorists on the vast Westchester Parkway system, how few campers in the reservations or picnickers in the Parks, enjoying facilities which are regulated by the Westchester County Parkway Police, realize that this all is the outgrowth of a movement initiated nearly a quarter of a century ago with the primary purpose of abating unsanitary conditions along the old Bronx River for the protection of the health of bordering Westchester and the Metropolis to the south. Any history of the development, growth, and works of the Westchester County Parkway Police, therefore, might well begin with a backward glance beyond the date of its inception.

In this background will be found the source of a tradition which already, in a department as young as the Westchester Parkway Police, has made itself felt as an inspiration to service beyond the letter of the law, feeling that police work transcends enforcement and extends into the realm not only of prevention but also education and public welfare.

Organized in July of 1907 under an act of the Legislature adopted earlier that year, the original Bronx Parkway Commission immediately set about to undertake a survey and make maps of the project before it, seeking funds for the purpose from New York City and Westchester County according to the provisions of the enabling law. The Commission also approached various owners of land along the course of the Bronx River, obtaining options and in several cases outright grants of land, among these notably being offer of a continuous strip two and one-half miles long between Scarsdale and White Plains, and 30 acres in the vicinity of Bronxville for local recreational areas. The Commissioners found most owners extremely

"Behind the Blotter—A History of the Westchester County Parkway Police Department," by Robert Robischon, originally appeared in the program for the ninth annual Entertainment and Reception for the Westchester County Parkway Patrolmen's Benevolent Association, held on September 21, 1940.

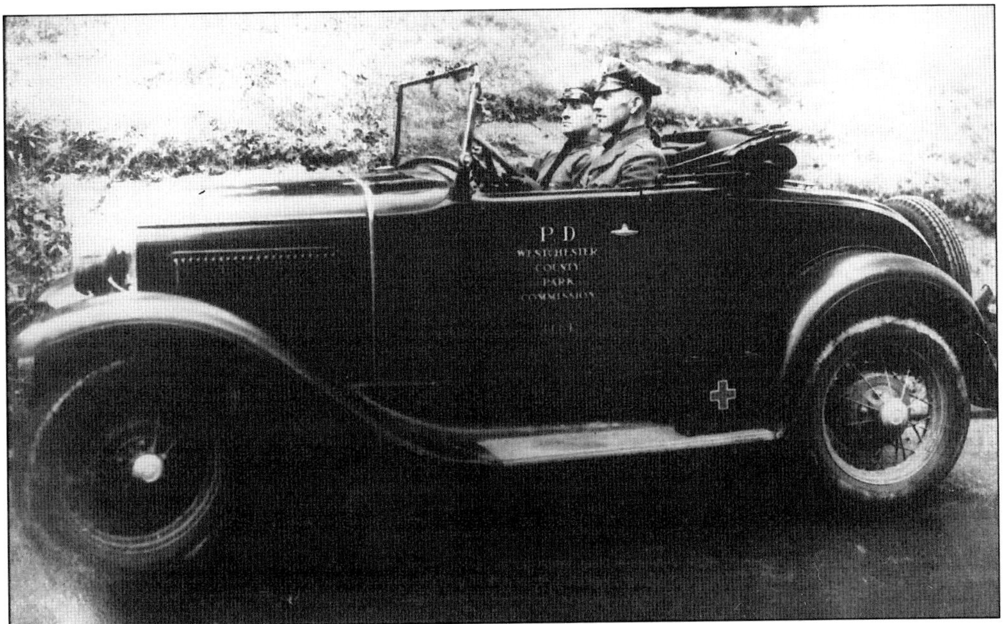

Two officers of what was then referred to as the Westchester County Park Commission Police Department patrol are seen here in a 1931 Chevrolet. The passenger is Albert Lang, who was hired as a special patrolman on July 1, 1930, at a rate of $5 per day. He was later hired as a patrolman on April 1, 1931, at a rate of $1,900 per annum. By May 1, 1932, he was earning $2,100 per annum with a 10 percent reduction due to the Depression, which gave him an actual salary of $1,890 per annum.

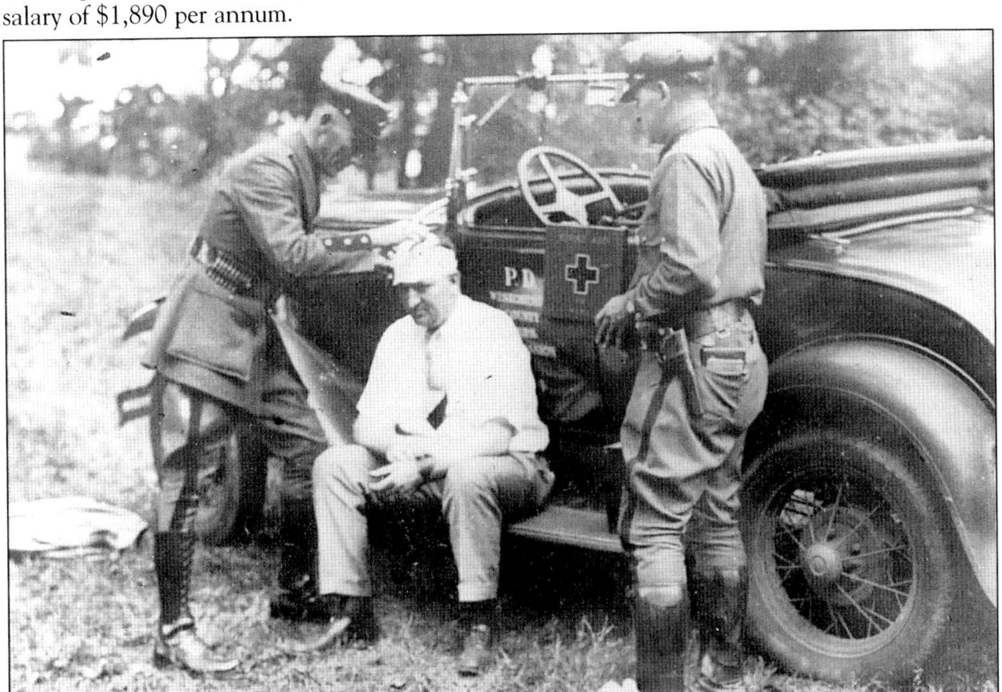

The same two officers seen above are shown demonstrating their first aid skills. Their uniforms include puttees and cross-draw holsters.

cooperative, either willing to give property or to sell at figures well below market value, because of the realization of the public benefit which would come from the protection of the river and dedication of the valley as a public parkway. Funds to proceed with the survey were not obtained until several years later, and it was not until 1913 that the Commissioners had both money and authority of the kind they desired to proceed with actual acquisition of land by purchase. In the meantime considerable donations of land had been accepted, the surveys had been completed, and the Bronx River Parkway project was well on its way. So there had been initiated a work which had been discussed as early as 1895, when a commission had been appointed to investigate the feasibility of a sewer along the valley of the Bronx River.

By 1917, when the World War put a temporary stop to further expansion of the Parkway project, practically all lands had been acquired necessary to the work, between the city line and Kensico Dam. In its report of that year the Commission points out that although the primary purpose was "to reclaim the Bronx River from its intolerable condition as an open sewer," there was a secondary purpose "to provide a parked driveway outlet for New York City's tens of thousands of pleasure cars."

Pointing to the necessity of cessation of construction because of the war, the report concludes "it is most fortunate that the necessary land has been acquired, so that the development of the project is assured and its completion is only a matter of time. In the meantime the lands and river have been restored to a clean and wholesome condition and the Reservation, even though not fully improved, is available for the enjoyment of the people."

It is here that was planted the seed from which eventually grew the present Westchester County Parkway Police. For the Commission found itself with property on its hands containing parks, paths, swimming places, and other recreational areas which needed patrolling both for the protection of property and of the public. No police department as such was created for the Parkway system for a number of years, however, police protection on the Parkway property depending upon a few special patrolmen who rode bicycles along the Parkway paths, and the visits of local policemen to park areas within their jurisdictions.

Meanwhile, construction of the Parkway drive was resumed after the World War, and by 1922 the Parkway was open to traffic between Woodlawn and Mount Vernon, and between Scarsdale and White Plains. It was in that year also that the Westchester County Parkway Commission was created, organizing on April 25 with the late W. Delavan Baldwin as its president. With traffic flowing heavily over the open sections of the Parkway, the law was amended to make violations of Parkway ordinances penal offenses, and authorizing appointment of patrolmen.

In 1925, with the Bronx River Parkway completed from Bronx Park to Kensico Dam, the Bronx Parkway Commission passed out of existence at the end of the year, under an amended Parkway law

"Behind the Blotter," by Robert Robischon, continues.

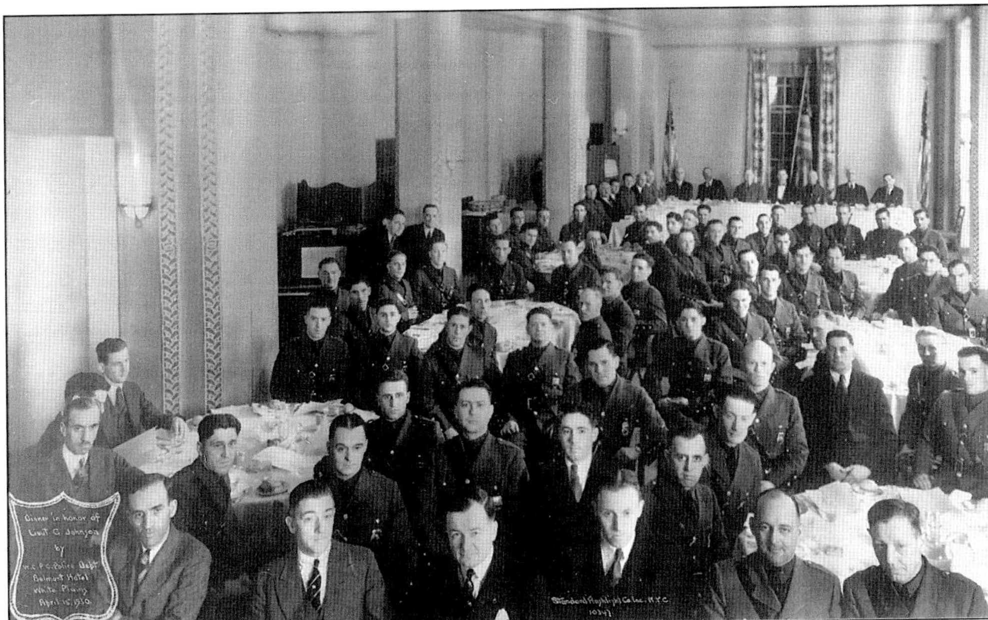

The Westchester County Park Commission Police Department holds a dinner in honor of Lt. G. Johnson. The event took place at the Belmont Hotel in White Plains on April 15, 1930.

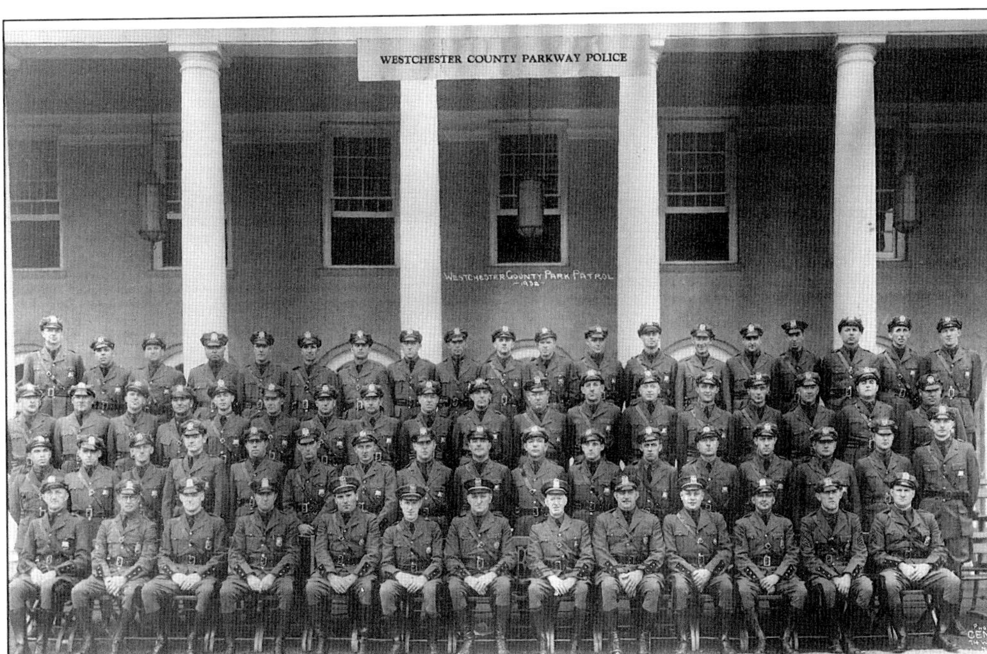

The Westchester County Park Patrol assembles in 1932 in front of the Tibbetts Park Bathhouse, located in Yonkers.

leaving the Parkway property within the Bronx with title vested in New York City, and the balance in Westchester with title vested in the county and its maintenance under the Westchester County Park Commission. In the interval since its organization in 1922, the County Commission already had embarked upon the initial stages of development of the entire system of Parkways and Parks within Westchester.

It was in early 1926, therefore, that there appeared the first semblance of a county Parkway police, when the Park Commission provisionally appointed men taken over from the Bronx Parkway Commission and organized what was then called the Westchester County Park Patrol Force. Under William J. Byrne as Park Keeper, these men included Frank J. McCabe, now Captain; August Helfrich, now Lieutenant; Martin J. Tewey, Rossiter W. McCoy and George Glintenkamp, now Sergeants; Cornelius J. Ormond and Vincent Zahradka, now Patrolmen; and Frederick Grune and Richard Hartford. With the establishment of a Civil Service list, on May 24, 1926, Chief Byrne was given a full appointment as Captain, with him appointments also going to McCabe, Helfrich, Tewey, McCoy, Glintenkamp, Ormond and Zahradka. In addition there was appointed Ralph E. Van Demark, who headed the eligible list and is now a Captain; Julius E. Jaeschker, now a Lieutenant; Russell Dunckel, now a sergeant in Greenburgh; and Patrolmen Alvah J. Tompkins, Joseph Campbell, William J. Zukowsky, and Anthony J. Pankwitts, the latter now in charge of the motorcycle shop. In addition Charles W. Fischer was on the original eligible list but refused appointment to become a sergeant on the Mount Pleasant constabulary, subsequently entering the Parkway force when the town's constabulary was disbanded.

Under these appointments, effective June 1, 1926, patrolmen on the Parkway Patrol Force received $1,900 per year, and the age limit for entering the department was from 25 to 35 years. At that time it was not necessary for a man to know how to ride a motorcycle to qualify for appointment, the department undertaking his instruction after he became a member. Today this accomplishment is a requirement, while the minimum age limit has been reduced to 21 years.

From this modest beginning of 15 men has grown the present Parkway Police Department, headed by Thomas F. Reynolds as Director, with one chief clerk, two captains, three lieutenants, seven sergeants, one detective sergeant and three detectives, 73 patrolmen, one mechanic, and one janitor; a total of 94 men. Physical equipment of the department includes 20 automobiles and 28 motorcycles, and a fully equipped emergency police car, donated to the department in 1938 by the Westchester County Parkway Patrolmen's Benevolent Association.

Growth of the department during the past decade and a half has been gradual and in relation to the expansion of the system of Parks and Parkways, until today the force has under its jurisdiction 65 miles of Parkways and over 18,000 acres of land. The duties of

"Behind the Blotter," by Robert Robischon, continues.

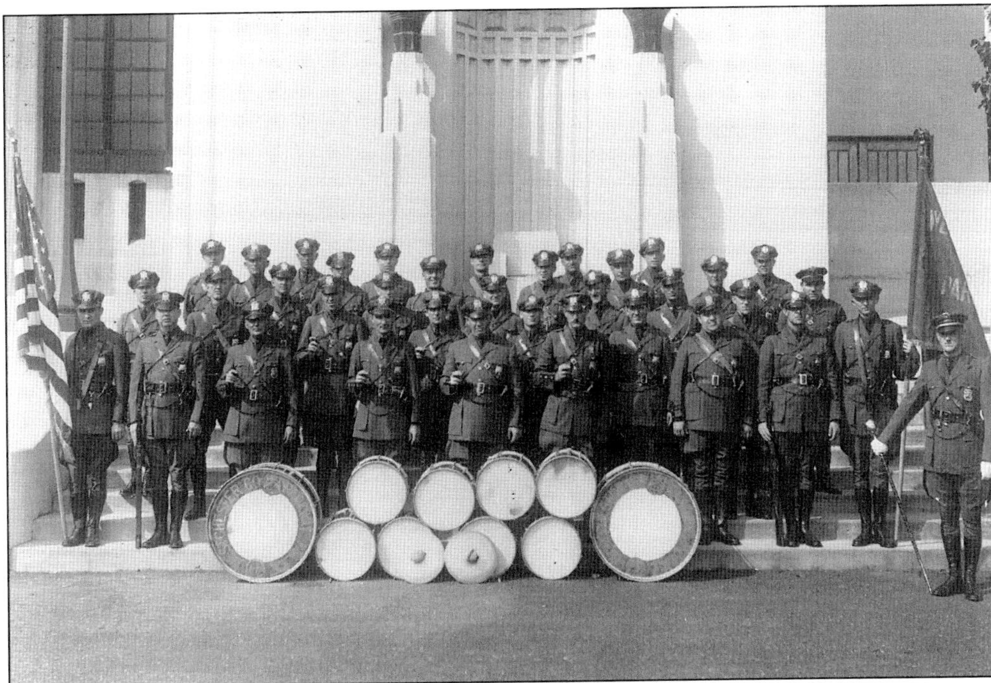

The Westchester County Parkway Police Fife and Drum Corps poses in front of the Westchester County Center in White Plains. The fife and drum corps was established on July 1, 1933. Among the officers pictured is Vincent Anthony (back row, sixth from left).

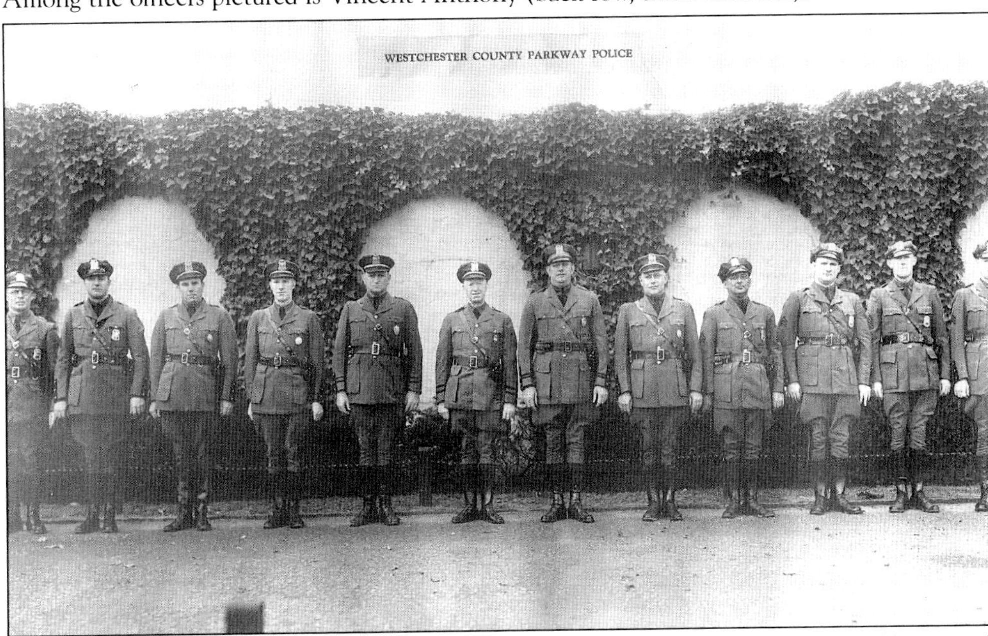

Officers of the Westchester County Parkway Police stand in the area of the Tibbetts Park Bathhouse. The group includes six sergeants, three lieutenants, two captains, and a chief. In the center is Chief William J. Byrne, flanked by Capts. Frank J. McCabe (left) and Ralph E. Van Demark. Also identified is Michael Morgan (third from right), who was promoted to sergeant on September 16, 1931.

the Parkway police include the patrolling of these miles of Parkways, and the supervision of all the beaches, swimming pools, golf courses, and other recreation areas included in the Park lands.

Today the supervision of these areas is divided into two precincts. The Western Precinct, under command of Captain McCabe, takes in the Bronx River Parkway from Scarsdale Road to the New York City line, the Cross County Parkway from the Fleetwood Bridge to the Saw Mill River Parkway, the Saw Mill River Parkway from the city line to Chappaqua, Tibbetts Brook Park, Kingsland Point Park, Woodlands Lake now known as V. Everit Macy Park, Crugers Park, Ward Poundridge Reservation, the Blue Mountain Reservation, and the Sprain Lake Golf Course. In the Eastern Precinct, under command of Captain Van Demark, is the Bronx River Parkway from Scarsdale Road north to the Kensico Dam, the County Center, the Central Westchester Parkway, the Hutchinson River Parkway from the city line at Pelham Bay to the Connecticut line, the Cross County Parkway from the Fleetwood Bridge to the Hutchinson River Parkway, Glen Island, Wilson Woods, and the Maple Moor and Saxon Woods Golf Courses.

Into this vast area, in addition to the routine problems of patroling the Parkways for traffic control and the apprehension of traffic violators or the assistance of motorists in distress, have come all the varieties of crime with which any large police force would have to deal. Besides providing excellent arteries for regular motor traffic, the Parkways have on occasion been chosen by hold-up men and other criminals as avenues of escape from their crimes, and it has been the duty of the Parkway police on such occasions to keep vigilant watch and seek to apprehend such criminals.

It has been the misfortune, through the years, for some of the Parkway patrolmen to meet their death on the Parkways in the exercise of their duties in pursuing the speeder or the fleeing criminal. On this honor roll are the names of Raymond Tehan, Clifton Cypher, George W. Segnit, Michael Erdley and Manuel Borgos.

Others have found occasion to distinguish themselves in the pursuance of perilous adventures in overtaking and apprehending such violators. For those who perform unusual accomplishments in the line of such duty there are three classes of awards. The first of these, for meritorious service, brings a citation with merit points under the Civil Service Act counting for advancement. Similarly, the award for commendable service carries a somewhat larger point award, while the exceptional service award carries the Department Medal as well as a substantial point award.

First to earn such citation was Patrolman Charles T. Smith, who on February 10, 1931, while patrolling the Saw Mill River Parkway, received an alarm to watch for holp-up men who had robbed a jewelry store in Beacon. Observing their car speeding down the Parkway, he gave chase to Van Cortlandt Park, where after a gun battle he captured one of the trio. The two others were killed a few hours later by New York City police.

(Continued on second following page.)

"Behind the Blotter," by Robert Robischon, continues.

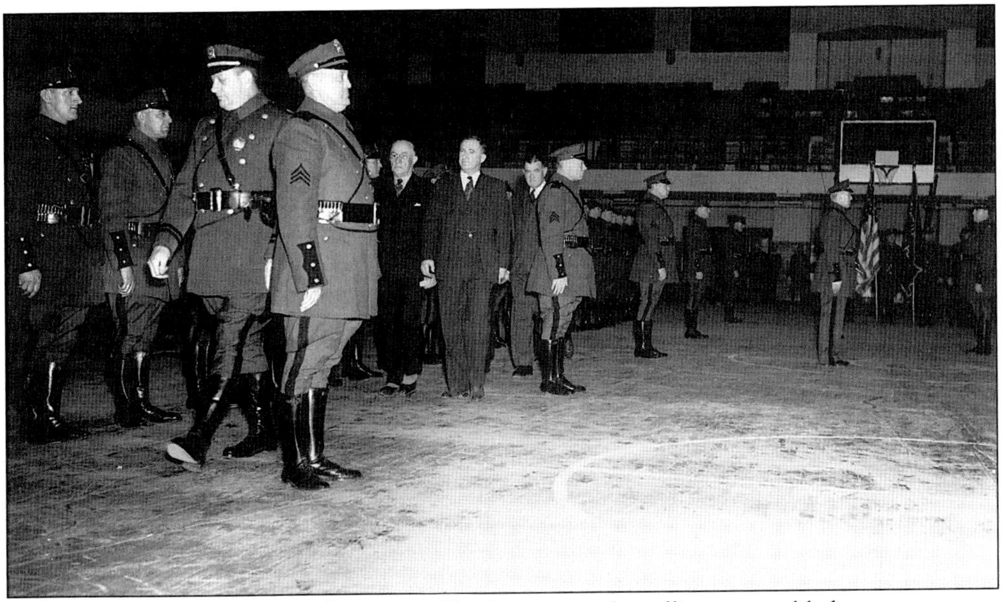

Capt. Ralph Van Demark and county officials inspect the officers assembled at a ceremony at the Westchester County Center in White Plains. At this event, the Westchester County Parkway Patrolmen's Benevolent Association presented a fully equipped police emergency truck to the county of Westchester. Sgt. Thomas Delahanty stands in the foreground.

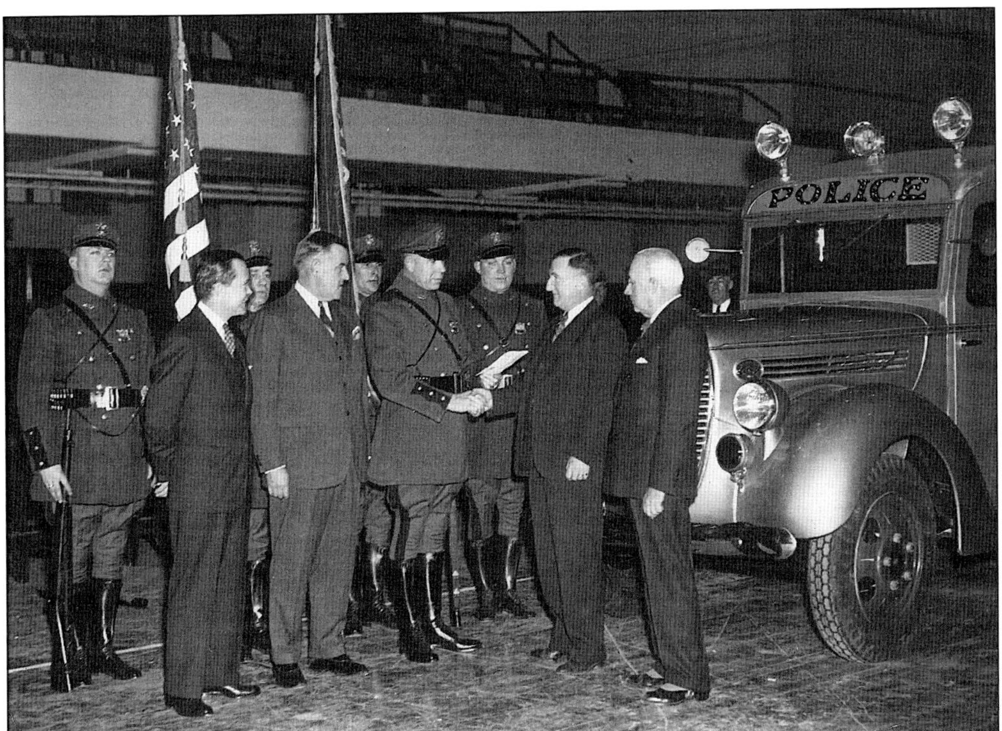

Here members of the Westchester County Parkway Patrolmen's Benevolent Association present the police emergency truck to county officials.

The next to gain distinction was Patrolman Charles E. White, who on September 17, 1932, apprehended a gang of thugs who had just committed a hold-up at the Continental Bakery in Mount Vernon. Meeting them on the Bronx River Parkway as they were turning into Bronx River Road, he engaged them in a gun battle, killing one and capturing two, although he had been grazed by a bullet.

On August 2, 1938, Detective Eugene Curran captured at gun point two armed bandits, wanted for a series of crimes including hold-ups of petting parties and other persons in the Parks.

Within the year past, Patrolmen Samuel J. Lewis and Alfred H. Crumm distinguished themselves when, on May 12, 1939, while patrolling the Bronx River Parkway they received an alarm to watch for four armed bandits who had held up a gasoline station. Spotting the hold-up car, they gave chase in their patrol car at 80 miles per hour and captured the fleeing quartet after an exchange of shots.

One of the most recent changes in the Parkway Police Department was effected this Spring, shortly after appointment to the Park Commission of Col. John Stilwell, vice-president of the Consolidated Edison Company and president of the National Safety Council. Col. Stillwell is in direct charge of the department within the Commission, with Mr. Reynolds as Director.

This change has seen the men of the department doff their former uniforms of olive drab, to don a more colorful and distinguishing garb of military cut. This new uniform has an outside coat of deep blue with slashes of French grey on the sleeve. The coat is worn over a shirt of navy blue, while the trousers of French grey have a wide navy tripe. Puttees and shoes are black leather, the visored cap having a French grey crown.

As a corollary to the growth of the department, the men within it soon began to feel the need of a membership organization which could carry out the various benevolent activities which were assumed from time to time on a voluntary basis. As a result, in 1931 there was formed the Westchester County Parkway Patrolmen's Benevolent Association, Inc., the principle function of which is to help members and their families in time of need, and to pay a death benefit. In keeping with its nature as a patrolmen's organization, although all members of the force may belong, officers must all be of the rank of patrolman. Its presidents since formation have been Rossiter McCoy, Thomas Delahanty, Frank Mueller, Arthur Stevens, William J. Slater, and the present incumbent, Charles T. Smith.

From time to time this organization has undertaken to assist in worthy projects outside of its own membership field. One of the most notable instances of such action came in 1938, when the members recognized the need of the force for a fully equipped emergency car, but likewise realized that the county was not in a position to include such an item of equipment in the budget at a time when expenditures were being held to a minimum.

As a result, the Association purchased and donated to the County for use on the Parkways and in the Parks a modern police emergency truck, fully equipped for rescue or riot work. This equip-

"Behind the Blotter," by Robert Robischon, continues.

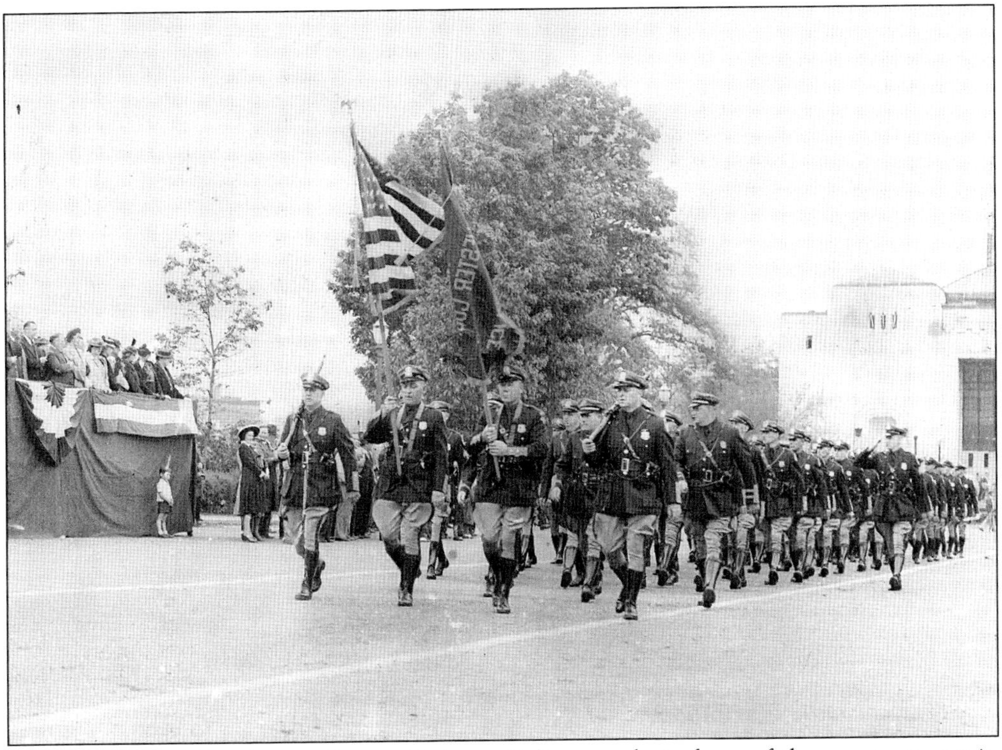

Members of the Westchester County Parkway Police parade in front of the county center in their new uniforms in the spring of 1940. The uniforms consisted of deep-blue jackets with slashes of French gray on the sleeve, navy blue shirts, French gray trousers with a navy blue stripe, a visored cap with a French gray crown, and black leather shoes and puttees. The uniform is the same today except for the puttees and the cut of the pants.

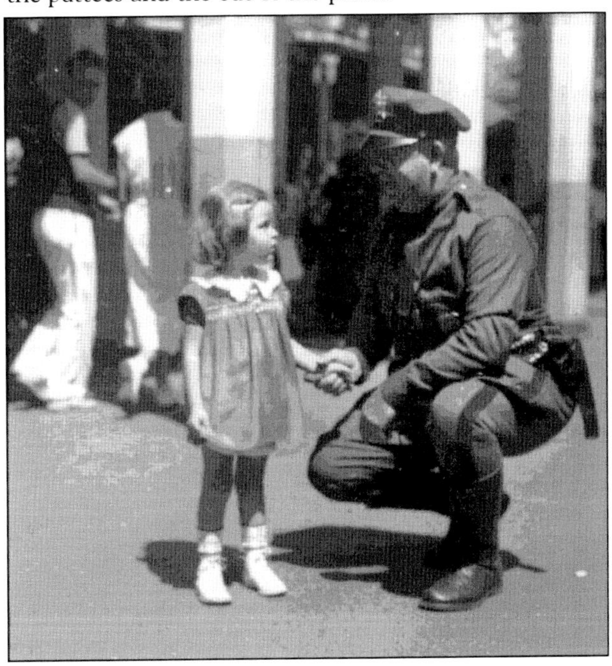

An office of the Westchester County Parkway Police assists a young girl at Playland c. 1929.

ment, some of it donated by interested firms and individuals, includes among many other items an acetylene torch, fire fighting materials, picks, shovels and crow bars, tear gas gun and bombs, and block and tackle for lifting and hauling. Available not only to the Parkway police but also on call for any town or village department which needs its services, this car has already proven its worth on numerous occasions. In rescue and resuscitation, for first aid at bad accidents, and in riot prevention it has demonstrated its effectiveness. In last Winter's heavy snowstorm, for instance, it was the means of saving many persons marooned in their cars, either pulling the vehicles out of drifts, or where that was impossible taking the passengers to nearby towns and in some instances to their very homes.

Once yearly for the past nine years the Association has held an Entertainment and Ball, for which tickets are offered at a nominal price to the public. This is the only opportunity afforded those in Westchester who are in sympathy with the good work being done by the Association to contribute to its efforts, and for their ticket purchase they not only receive the satisfaction of aiding this cause, but also a good evening's entertainment.

The members of the Parkway Patrolmen's Association, therefore, hope that their efforts to better the circumstances of their more unfortunate members will meet with the approval of the public. For this cooperation and support they pledge untiring effort not only in the line of duty, but in a further devotion to everything which will make Westchester a better community, in keeping with the tradition which is the spirit and the continuing life of their organization.

"Behind the Blotter," by Robert Robischon, concludes.

Officer Frank J. Herlihy (right) poses with an unidentified New York state trooper at the former Hawthorne Circle on the Saw Mill River Parkway. Herlihy was appointed park patrolman on April 1, 1930. He was an outstanding athlete and an accomplished artist.

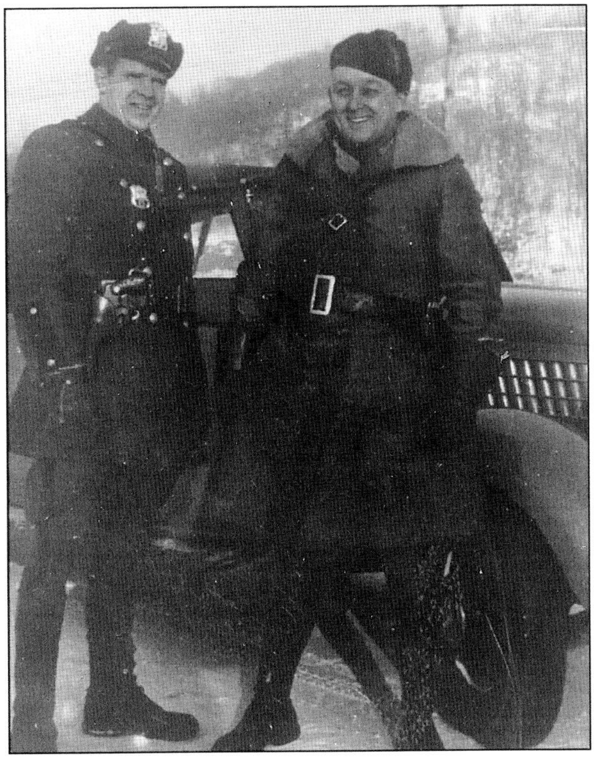

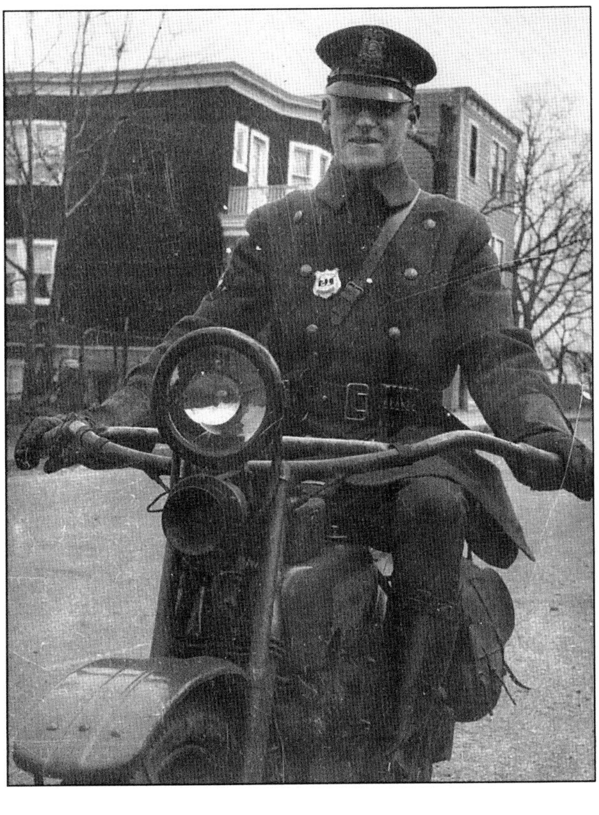

Officer Rossiter W. McCoy was one of the original nine members of the Bronx Parkway Patrol, who formed the original Westchester County Park Patrol Force. He was appointed a park patrolman on June 1, 1926. He is seen here on a World War I surplus motorcycle, wearing the original khaki uniform and badge of the Bronx Parkway Patrol. He was promoted to sergeant on September 16, 1931.

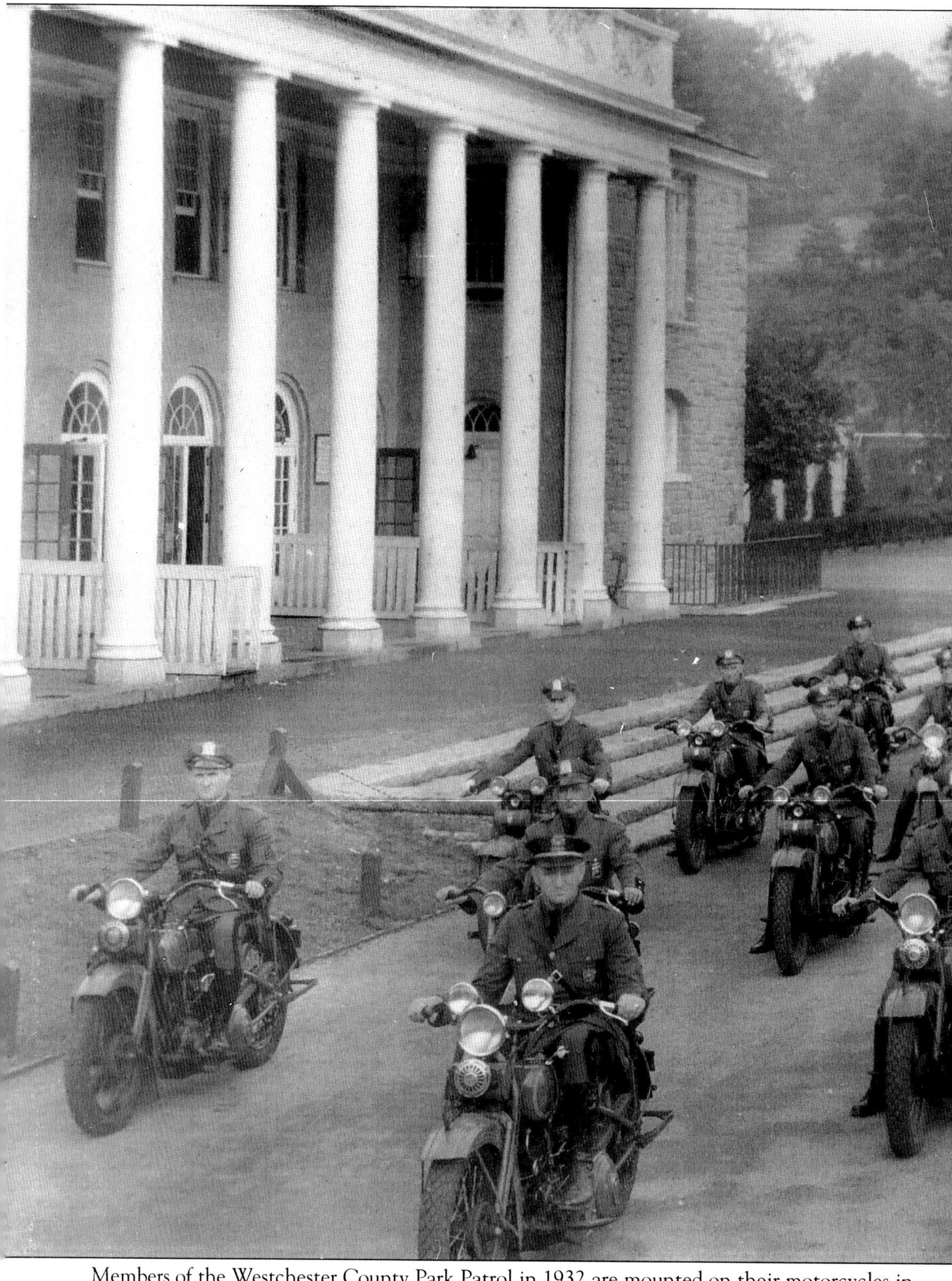

Members of the Westchester County Park Patrol in 1932 are mounted on their motorcycles in

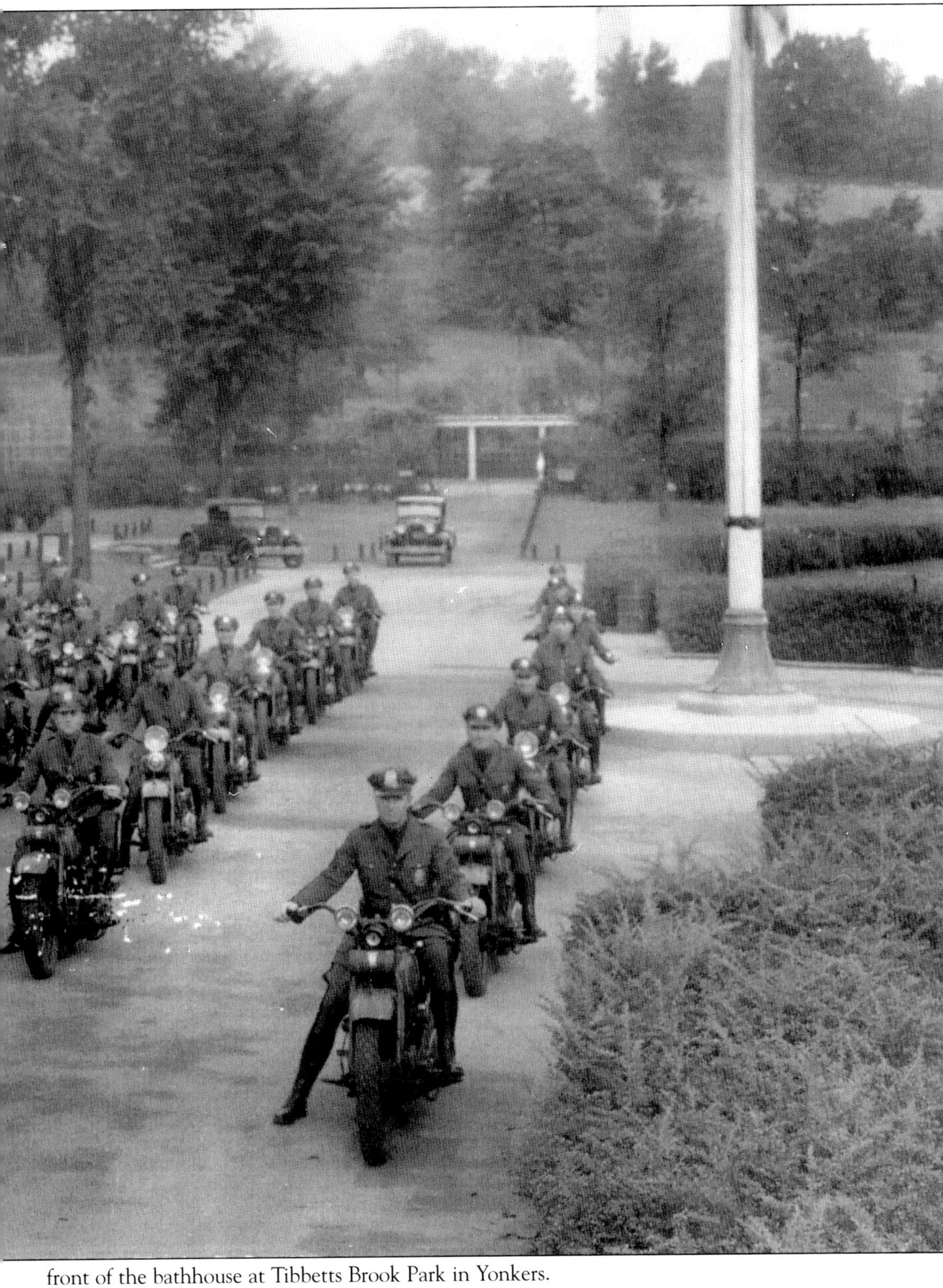

front of the bathhouse at Tibbetts Brook Park in Yonkers.

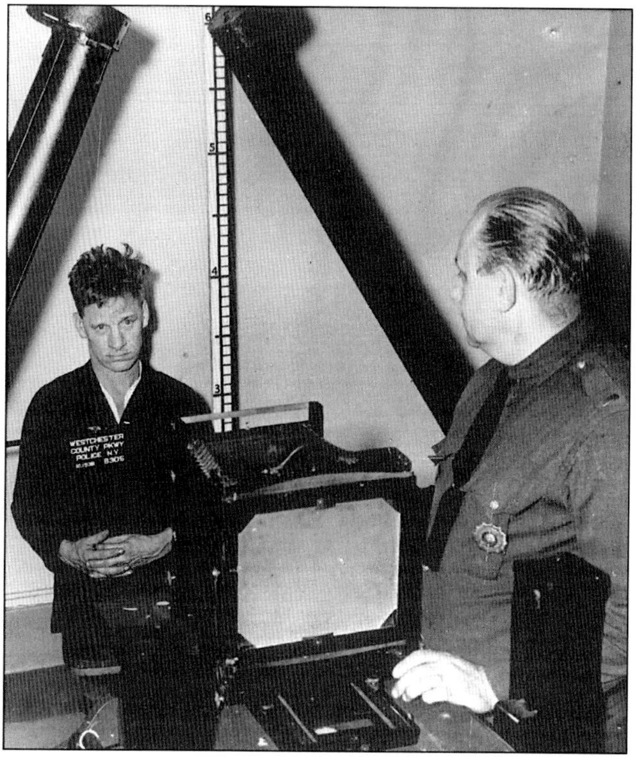

Using sophisticated camera equipment, Lt. August Helfrich (right) processes a prisoner on December 19, 1938.

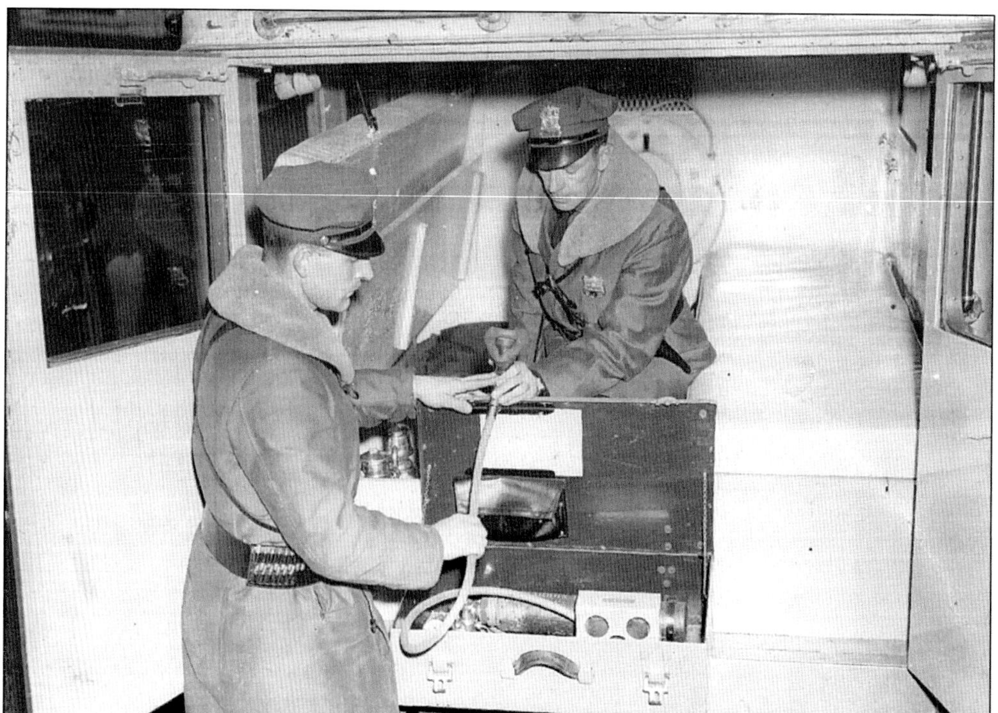

Officers George K. Becktoft and Allan J. Mansell inspect rescue equipment stored in the police emergency truck *c.* 1938.

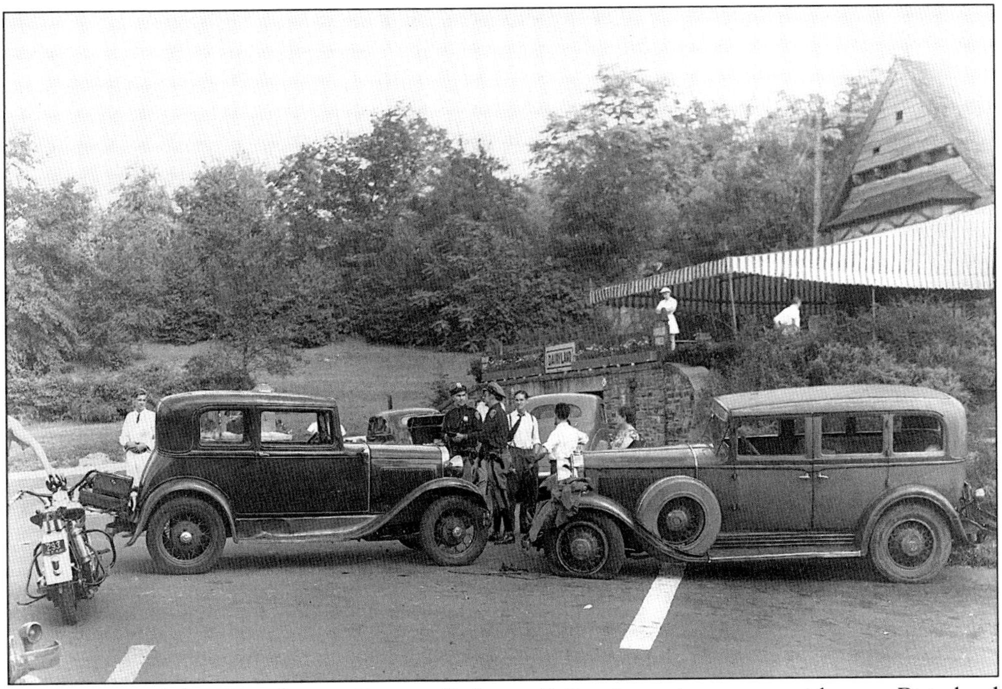

Two officers of the Westchester County Parkway Police investigate an accident at Dairyland c. 1940.

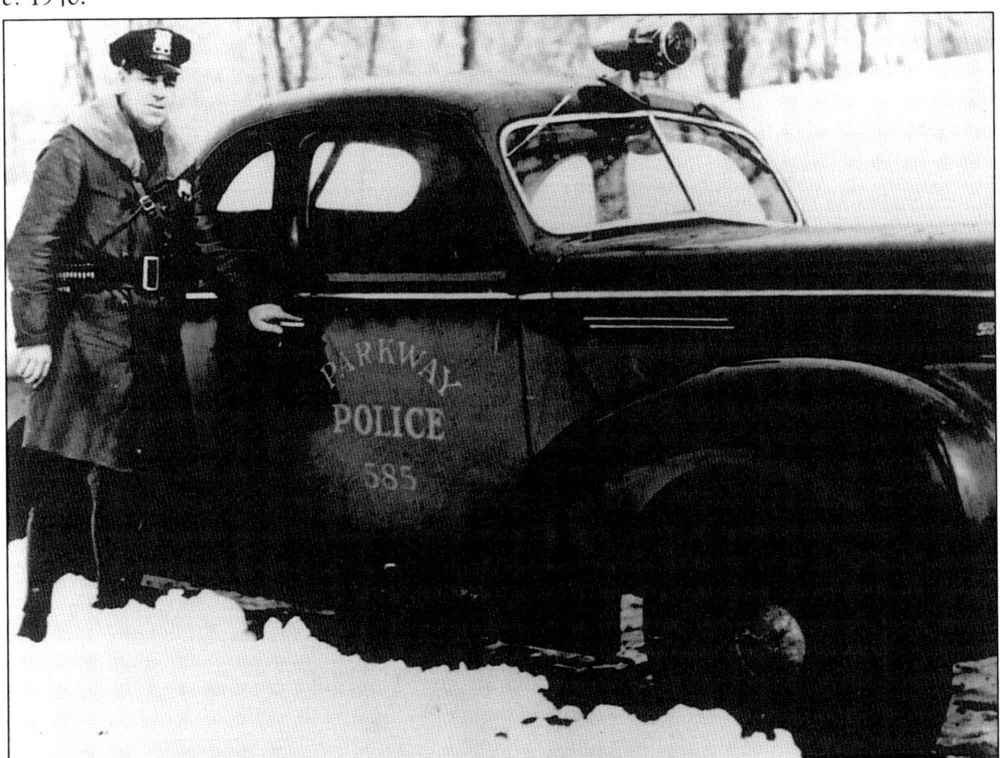

A patrolman of the Westchester County Parkway Police prepares to go out on patrol c. 1940.

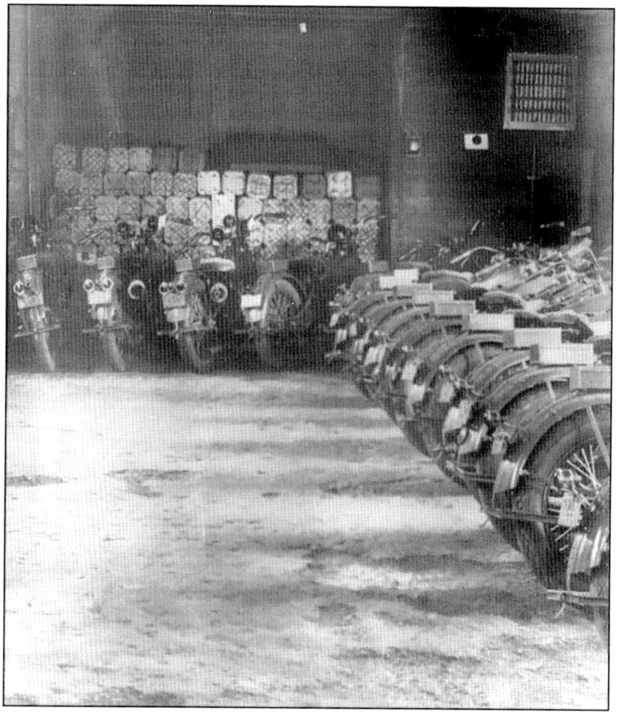

This interior view of the police garage at the Bronxville headquarters shows the department motorcycles in storage *c.* 1930.

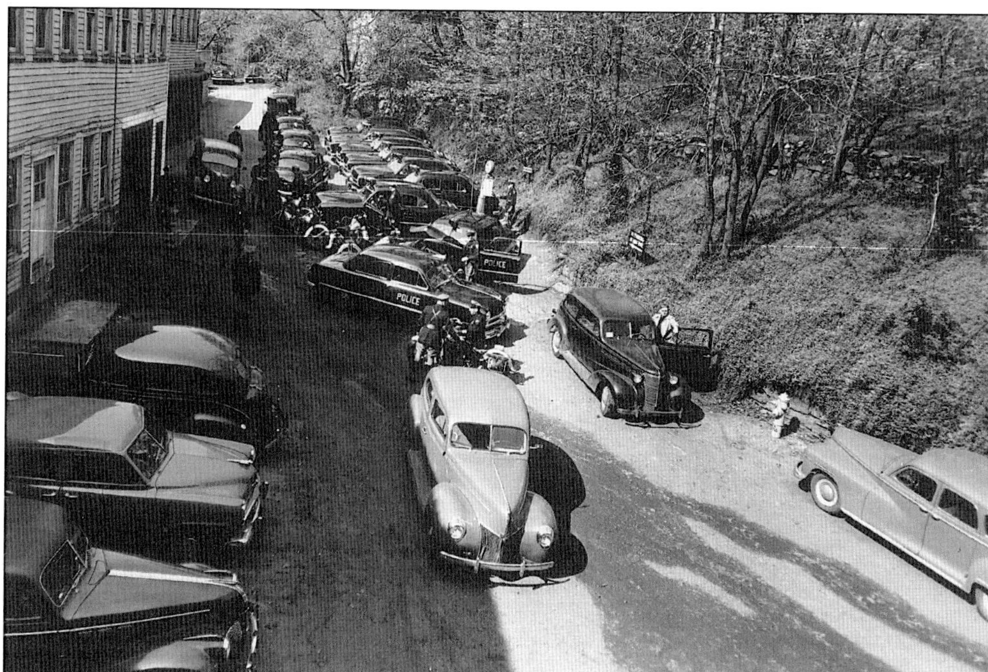

The scene behind the police garage at the Bronxville headquarters *c.* 1950 demonstrates the movement away from motorcycle patrol to automobile patrol. This change in the method of patrol was a response to the number of officers killed and injured while riding motorcycles. All nine of the parkway police officers who died in the line of duty between 1925 and 1960 died in motorcycle accidents.

Officer Raymond Tehan died on October 1, 1925, as a result of injuries he received in a line-of-duty motorcycle accident on September 27, 1925. He was a member of the Bronx Parkway Patrol at the time of his death at the age of 25.

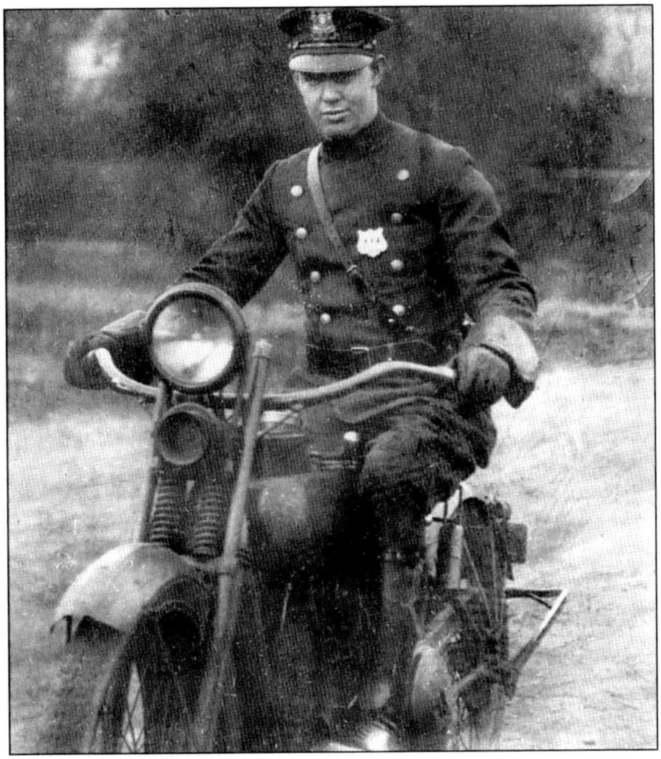

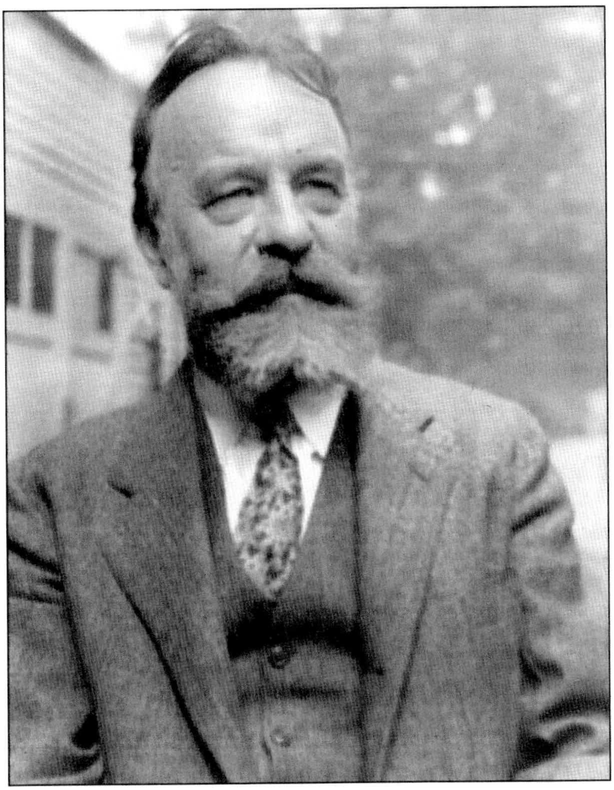

Herman W. Merkel, who was appointed general superintendent of the Westchester County Park Commission in 1926, served as the first superintendent of the Westchester County Park Commission Police Department. He was also a consulting forester to the Bronx Parkway Commission as early as 1913.

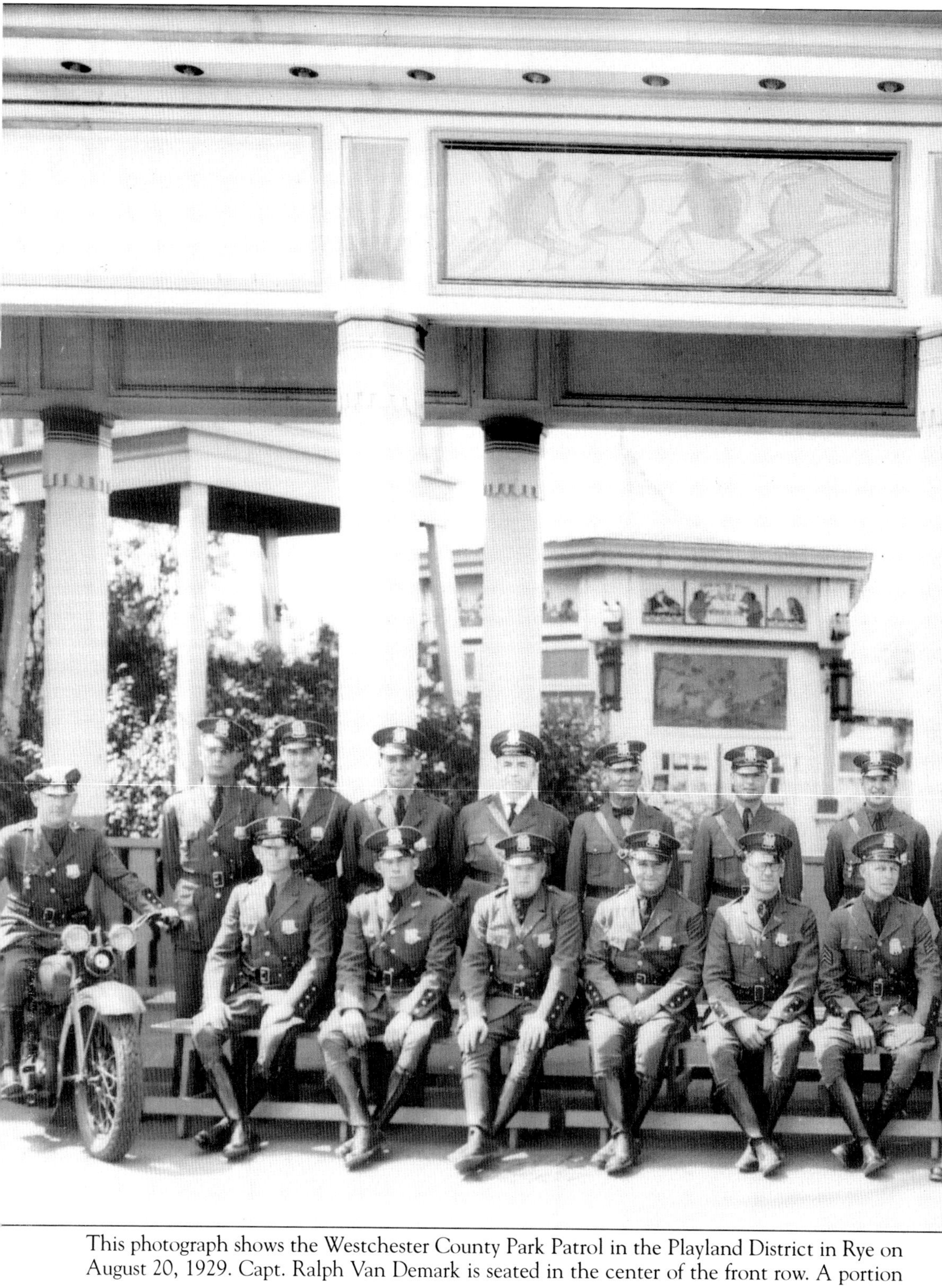

This photograph shows the Westchester County Park Patrol in the Playland District in Rye on August 20, 1929. Capt. Ralph Van Demark is seated in the center of the front row. A portion

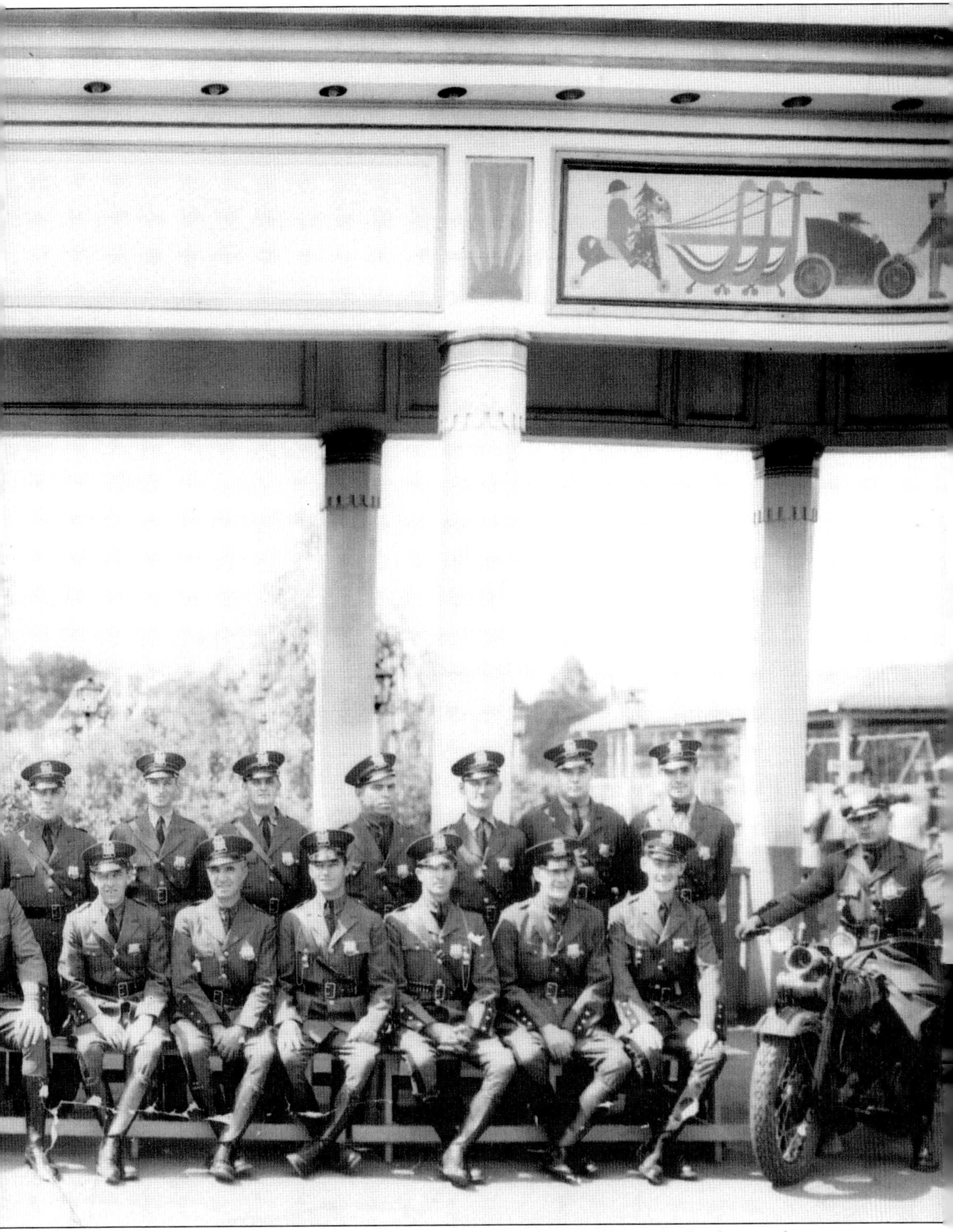

of the original colonnade and Kiddyland area at Playland is visible in the background.

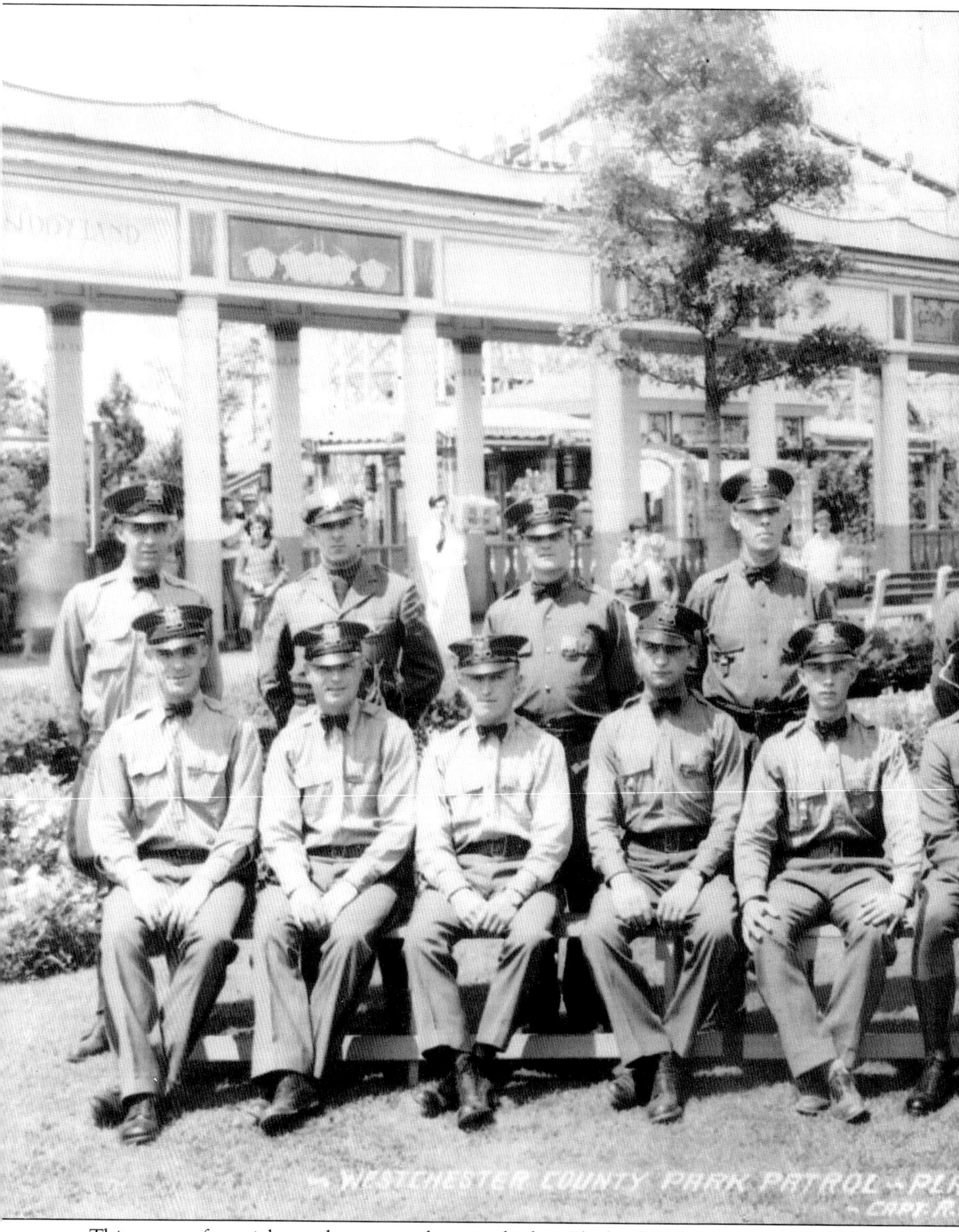

This group of special patrolmen was photographed at Playland Park in front of Kiddyland on August 8, 1929. John Rosko Sr. sits in the front row, third from the right. His son John J. Rosko

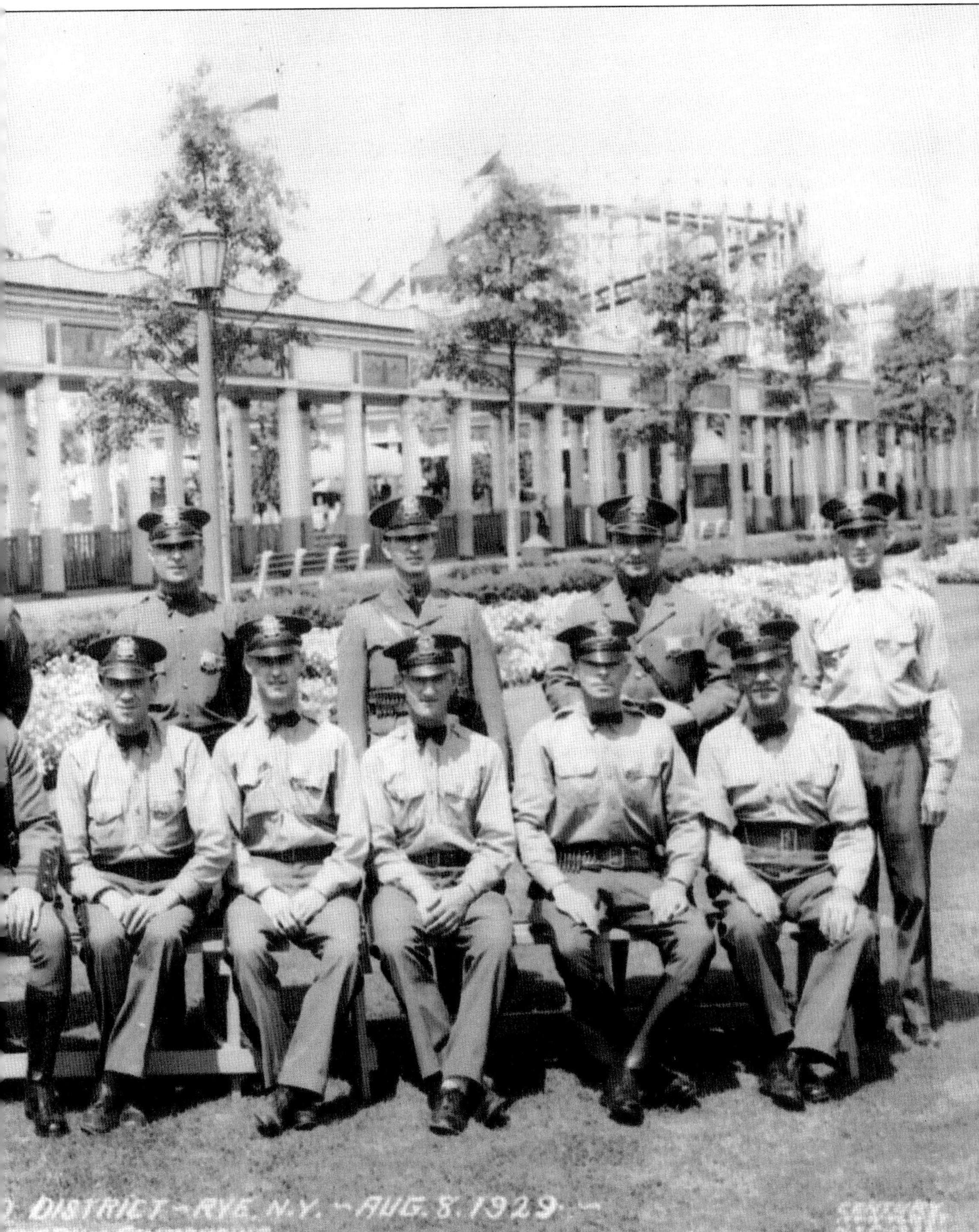

was also a member of the parkway police in later years.

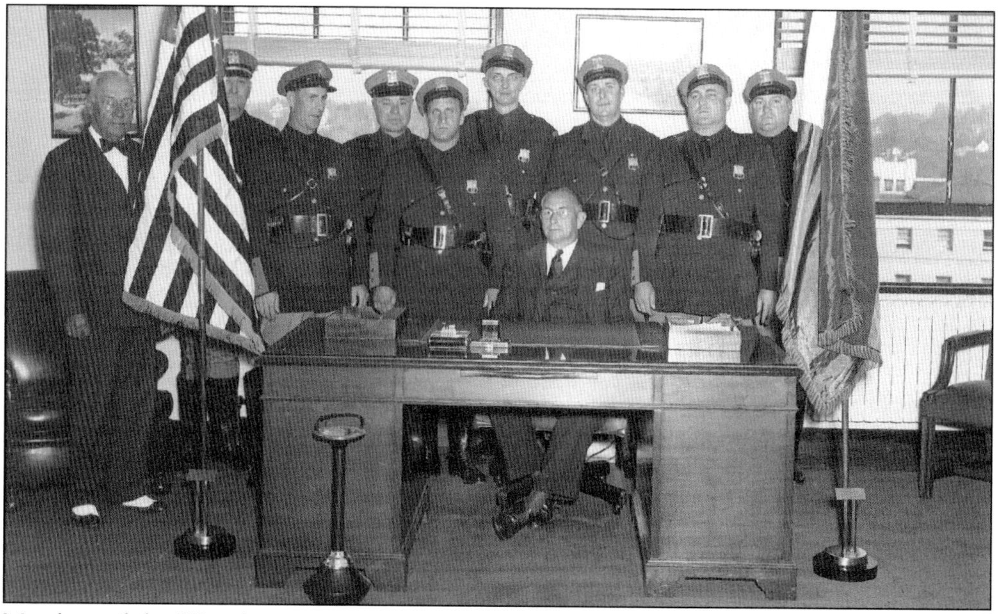

Members of the Westchester County Parkway Police meet with Herbert C. Gerlach, county executive, seated in his office in the county office building in White Plains on October 1, 1949. Present, from left to right, are Commissioner Orrie Kelly, Capt. Frank J. McCabe, and six patrolmen—I. Ericson, Cornelius Ormond, Ralph Tilley, William Cuniff, Walter Lutze, and Edward Boland.

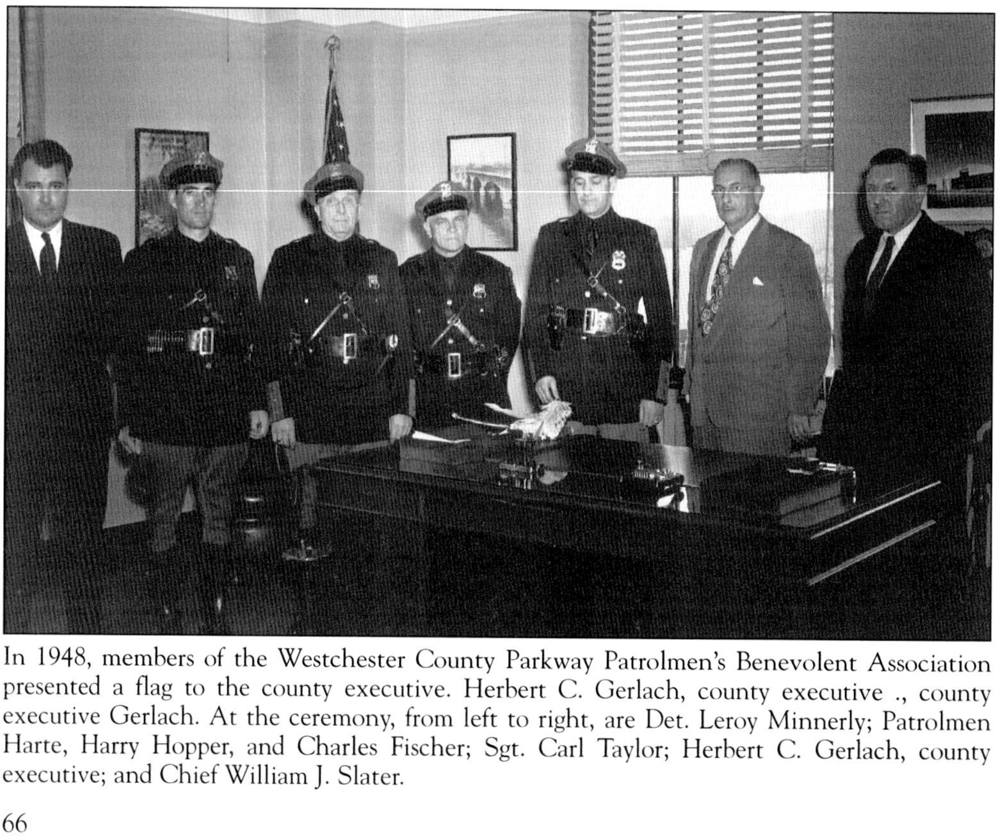

In 1948, members of the Westchester County Parkway Patrolmen's Benevolent Association presented a flag to the county executive. Herbert C. Gerlach, county executive ., county executive Gerlach. At the ceremony, from left to right, are Det. Leroy Minnerly; Patrolmen Harte, Harry Hopper, and Charles Fischer; Sgt. Carl Taylor; Herbert C. Gerlach, county executive; and Chief William J. Slater.

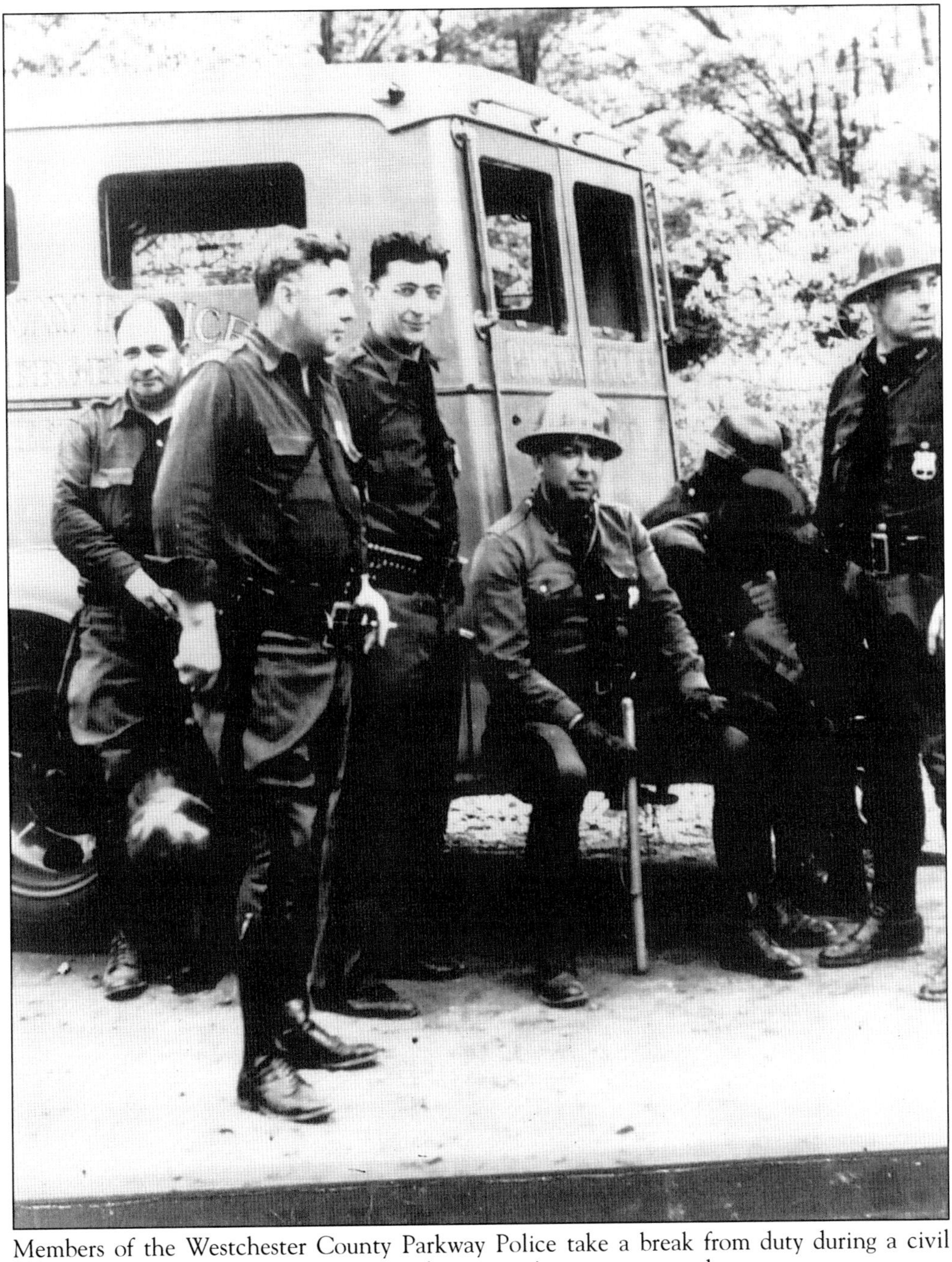

Members of the Westchester County Parkway Police take a break from duty during a civil disturbance c. 1940. Behind them is the department's emergency truck.

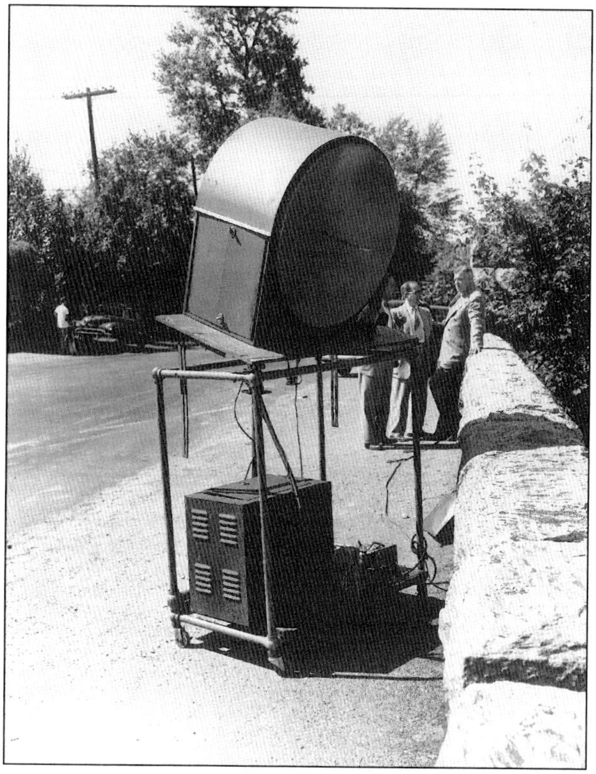

An early traffic radar unit is tested at King Street on the Hutchinson River Parkway.

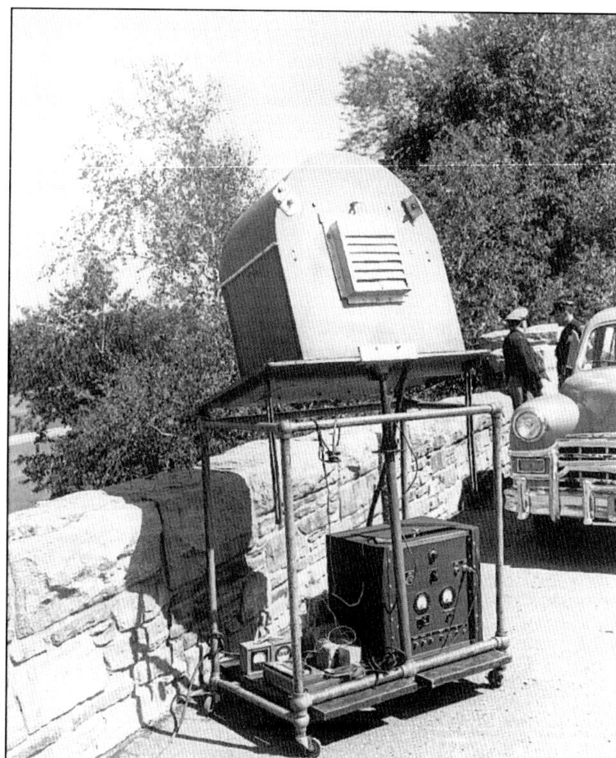

The two photographs on this page were taken on September 4, 1952. Two parkway police officers are visible in the background of this image.

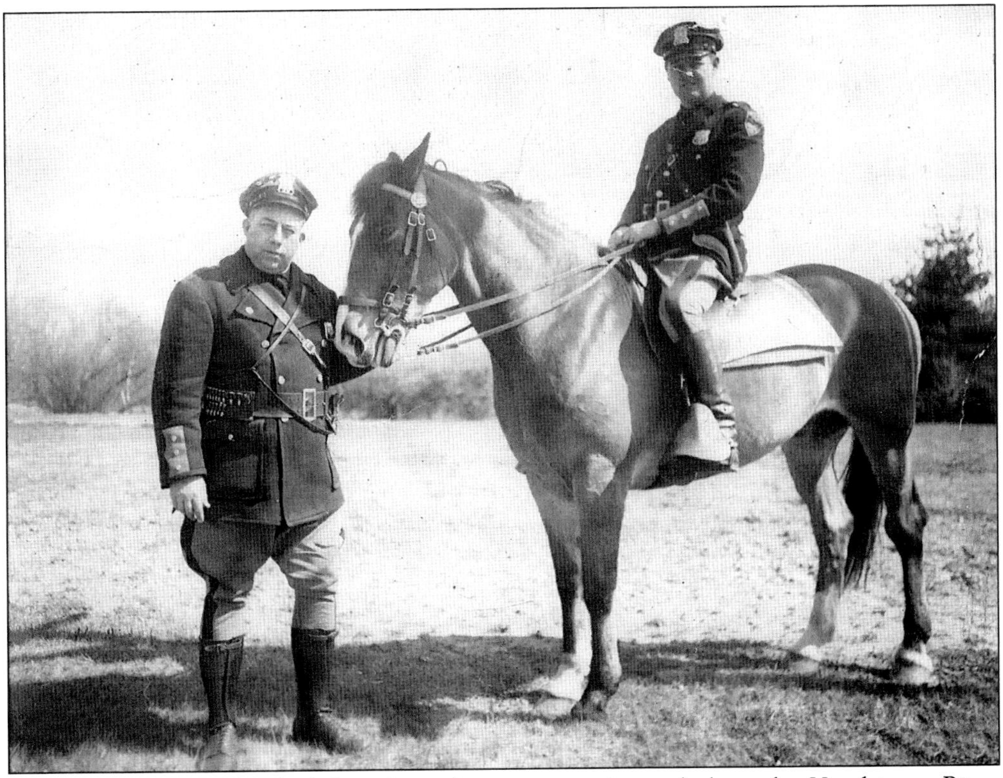

Officer William Cordes (right) performs horse-mounted patrol along the Hutchinson River Parkway in April 1951. Officer Frederick Vosatka Sr. stands by.

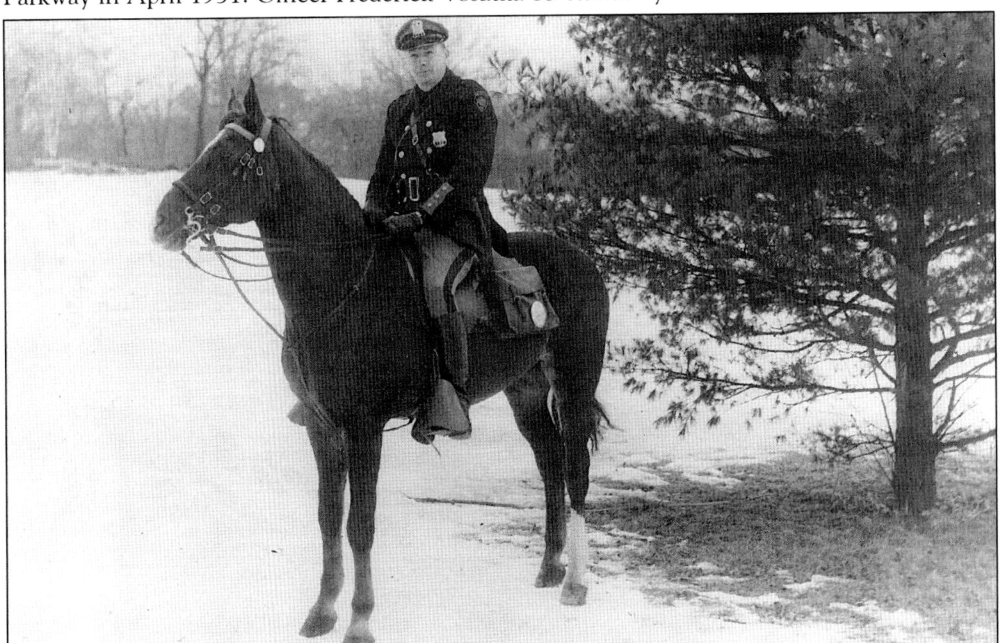

Officer John Sahaida was the last member of the Westchester County Parkway Police to perform horse-mounted patrols. He is seen here with his mount Sam c. 1970.

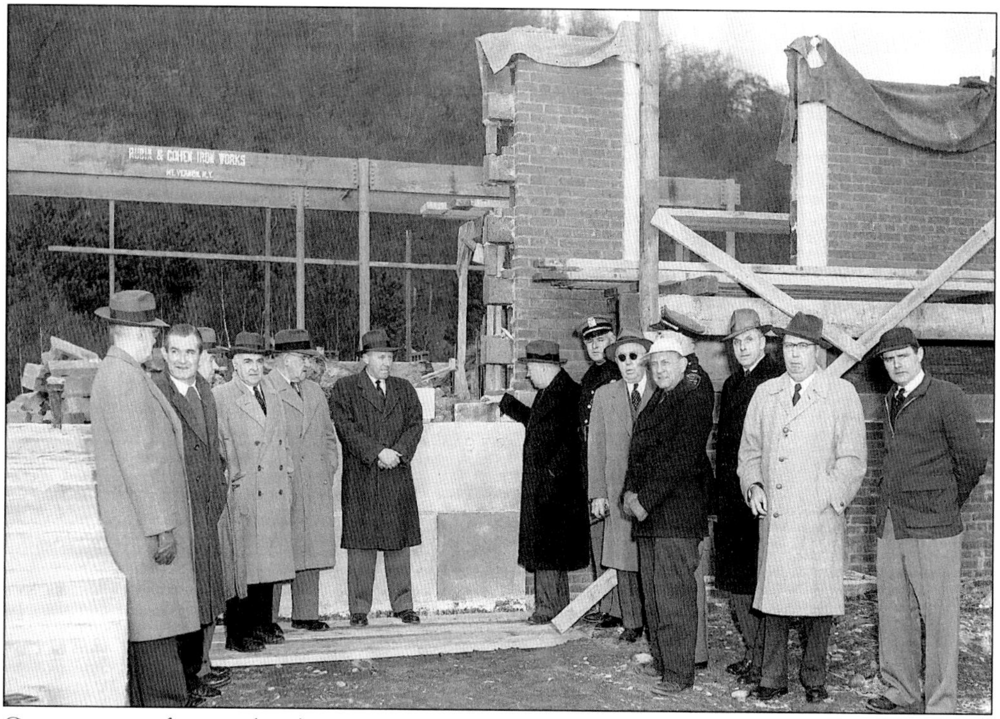

Construction of a new headquarters building in Hawthorne was begun in 1952. A group of dignitaries looks on as Commissioner Orrie Kelly places a time capsule into the cornerstone of the new building on December 20, 1952.

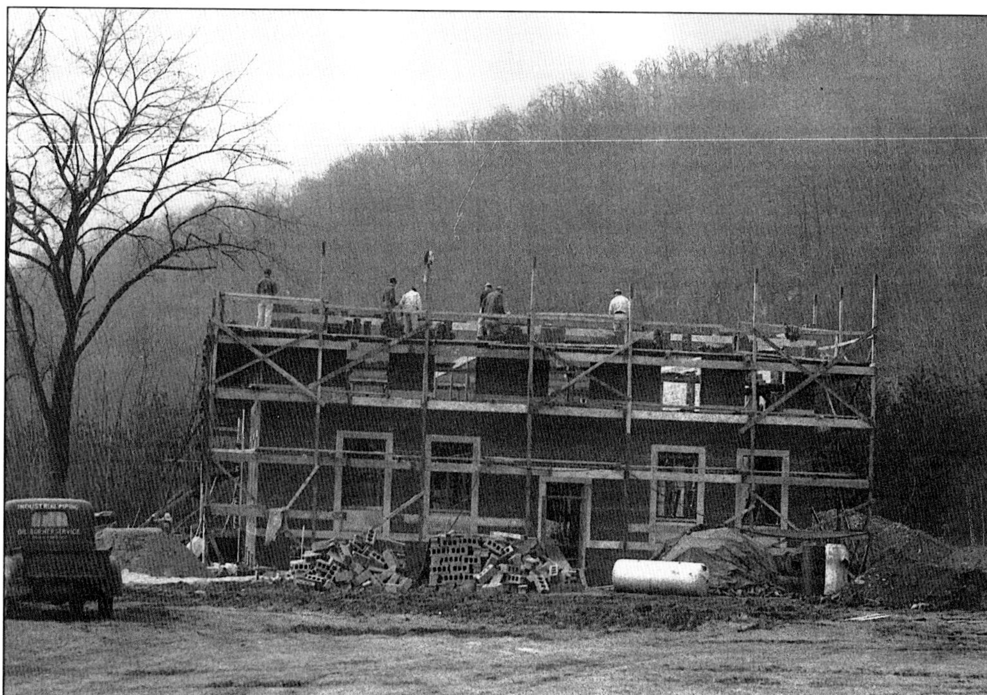

This view of the north side of the new headquarters building was taken on February 6, 1953.

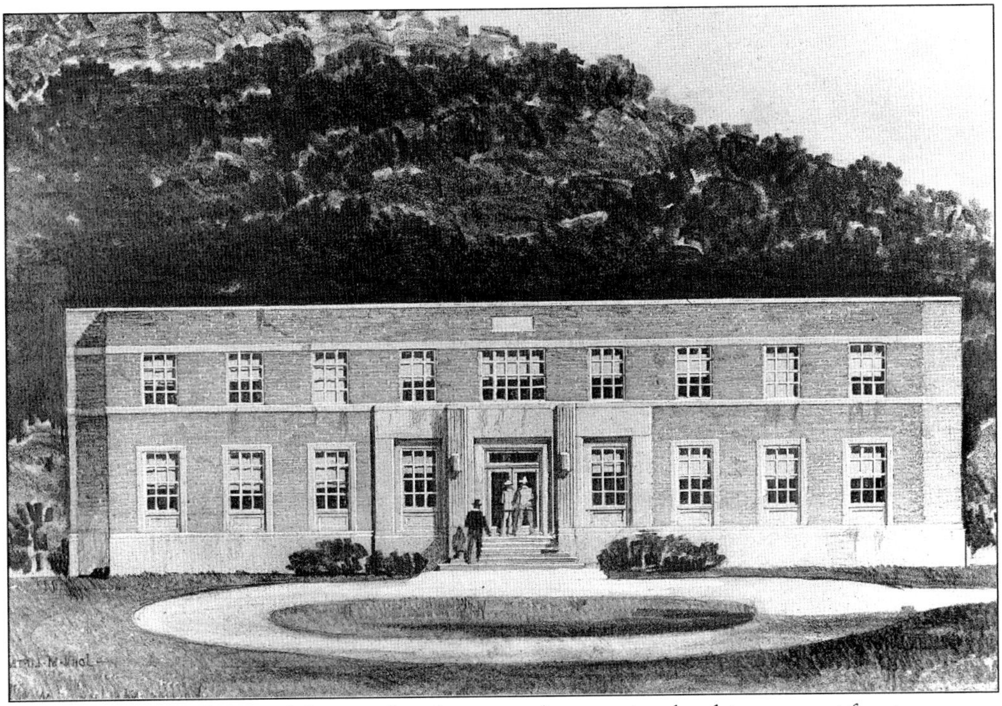

An architect's rendering of the new headquarters shows a circular driveway out front.

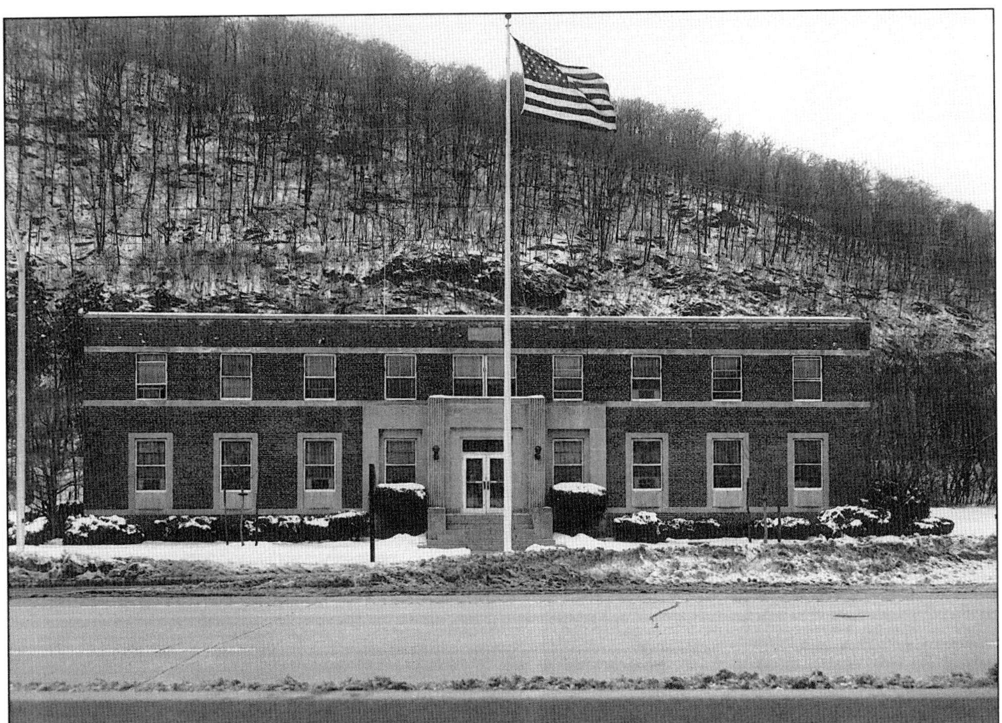

This view of the headquarters building was taken on January 15, 1974. The building was enlarged with an addition in 1987.

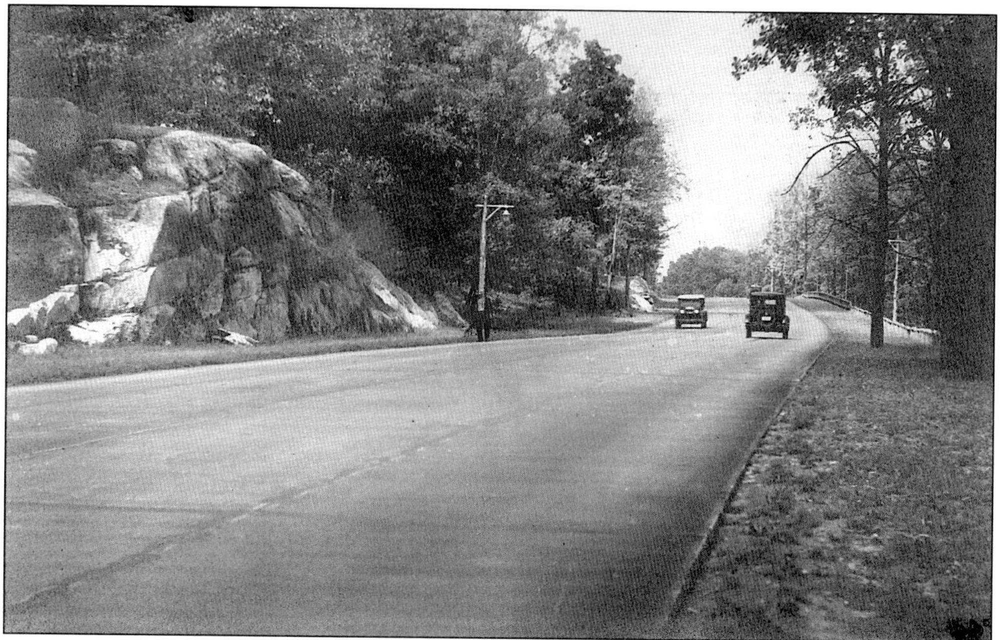

This photograph and several that follow show some of the improvements made in highway construction since the first parkway was opened in Westchester. This is a view of the Hutchinson River Parkway as it passes through the California Park section of Eastchester *c*. 1929. At this stage, there were no barriers between opposing lanes of traffic.

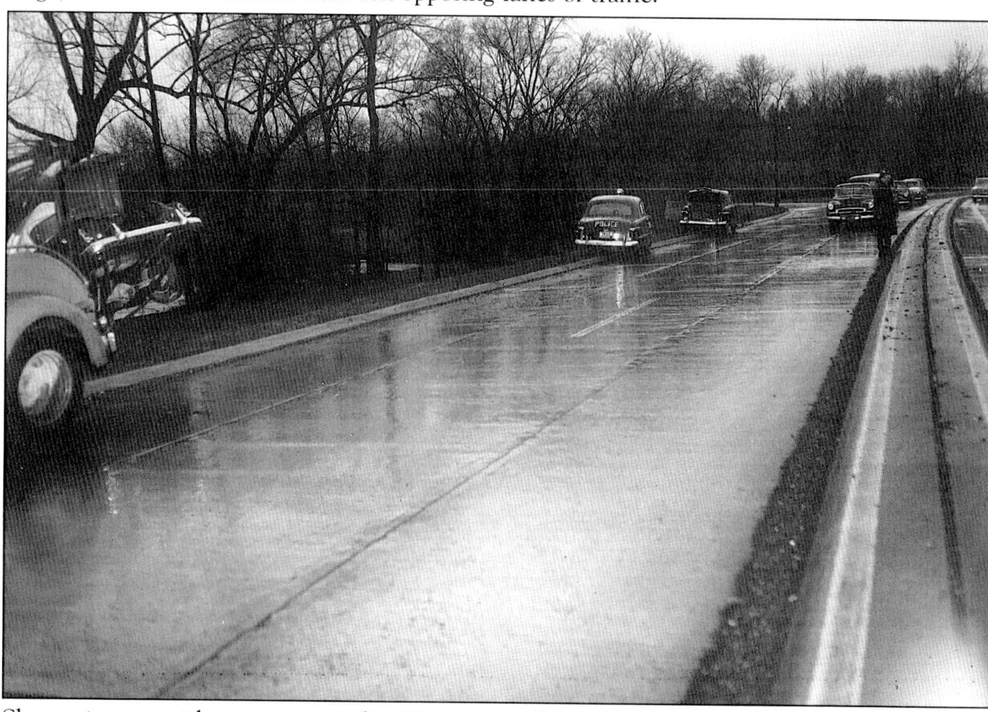

Shown is an accident scene on the Hutchinson River Parkway southbound in the area of Westchester Avenue on March 11, 1952. At the time, the only barrier between opposing lanes of traffic was a low curb. A parkway police patrol car and officer are visible in the background.

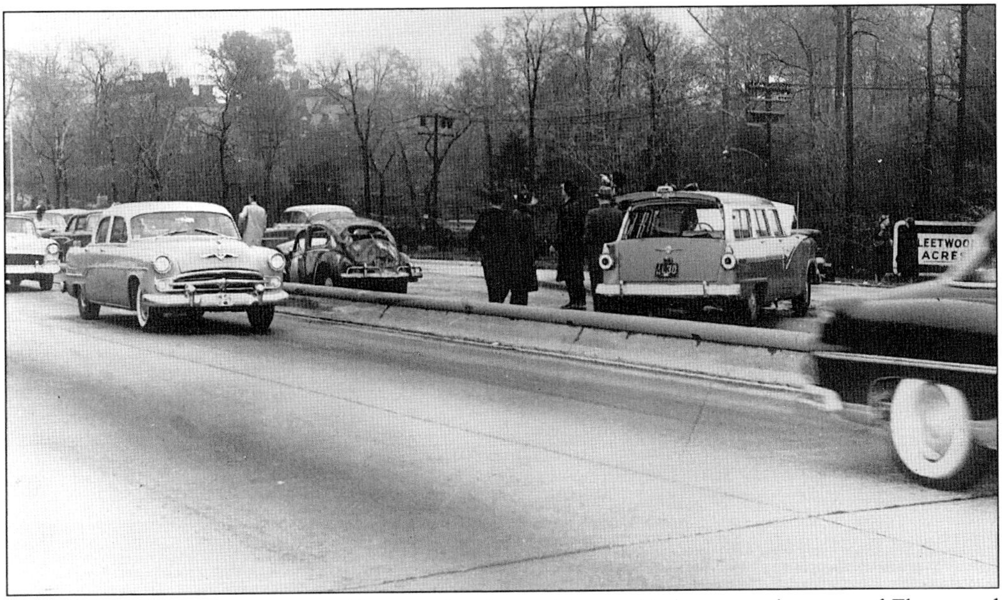

This accident scene from c. 1955 is on the Cross County Parkway in the area of Fleetwood Acres. Pipe has been installed along the top of the curb in an effort to create a more effective barrier to vehicles crossing over the center divider. This improvement did not have the desired effect.

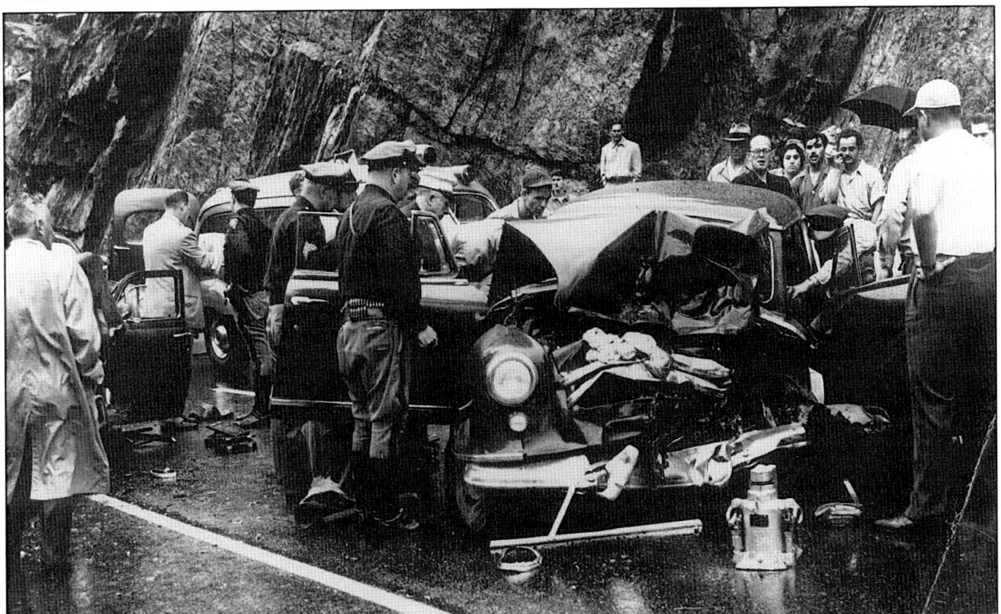

Westchester County Parkway Police officers work at an accident scene with a bottle jack and crowbars to remove a victim from a damaged vehicle. Extricating accident victims from vehicles was a difficult process before the advent of modern tools, such as hydraulic spreaders and portable saws. Any delay in transporting seriously injured persons to appropriate medical care negatively impacts their chances of survival. An ambulance can be seen in the background waiting to transport the victim to the hospital. This accident occurred in 1951 on the Hutchinson River Parkway in the area of Red Oak Lane.

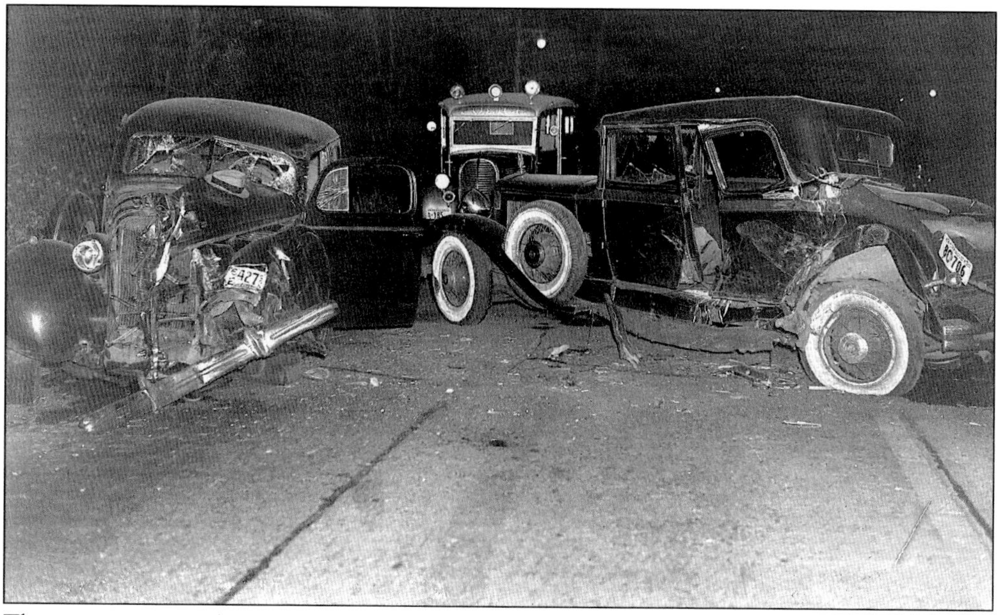

The investigation of motor vehicle accidents was a common occurrence for members of the parkway police. The damage to these two vehicles *c.* 1939 demonstrates what happens when unrestrained passengers impact with the windshield. The vehicle on the right bears a 1939 New York Worlds Fair license plate. The Westchester County Parkway Police emergency truck is visible in the background.

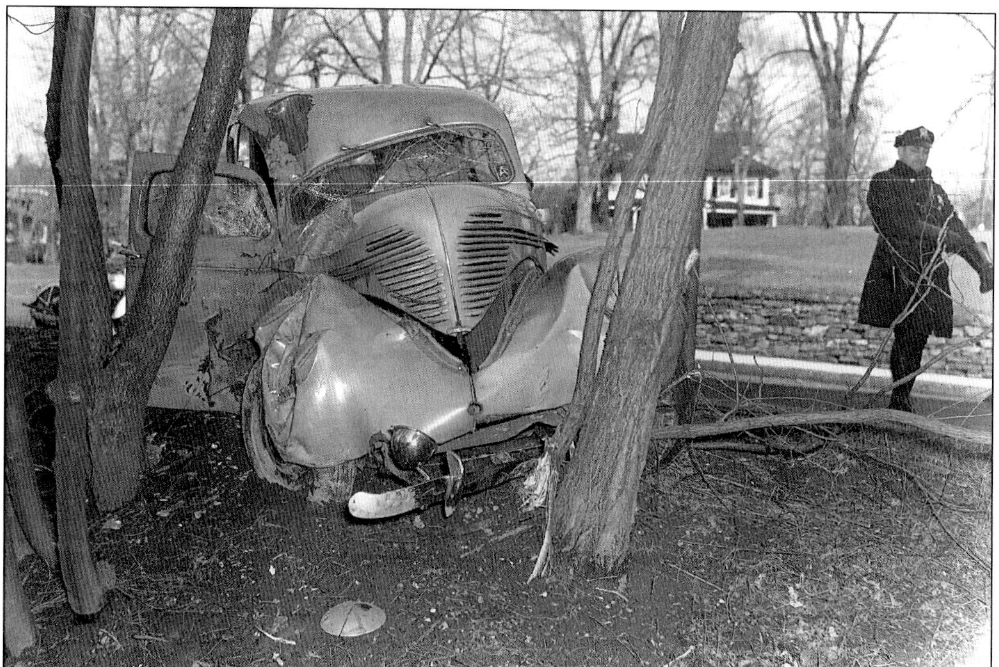

A parkway police officer investigates a motor vehicle accident along the Bronx River Parkway south of Scarsdale Road *c.* 1945. A gas ration sticker is visible in the windshield of the vehicle involved in the accident.

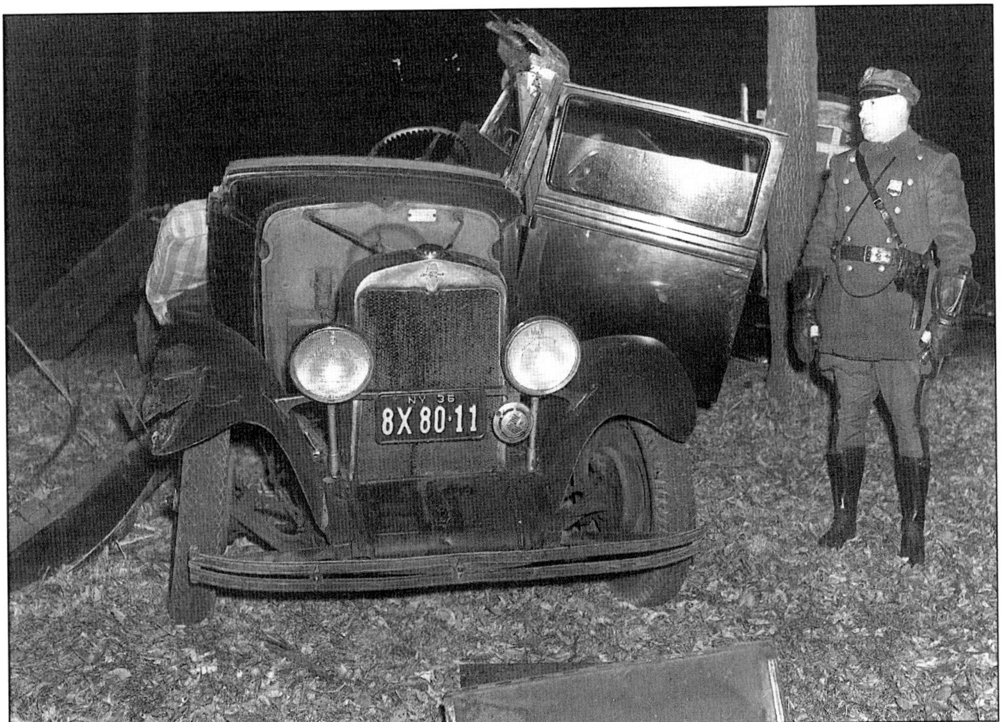

Ptl. Carlos Bishop investigates an accident c. 1936. Bishop was president of the Westchester County Parkway Patrolmen's Benevolent Association from 1944 to 1945. On July 7, 1947, he was killed in a motorcycle accident.

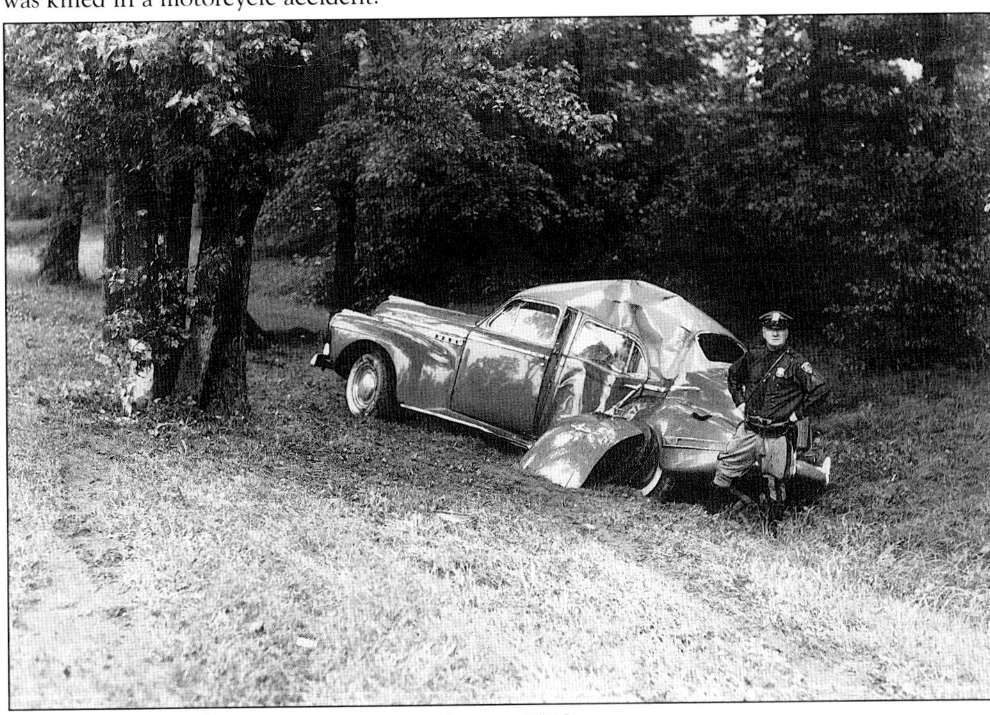

Ptl. Walter Donnelly investigates an accident c. 1948.

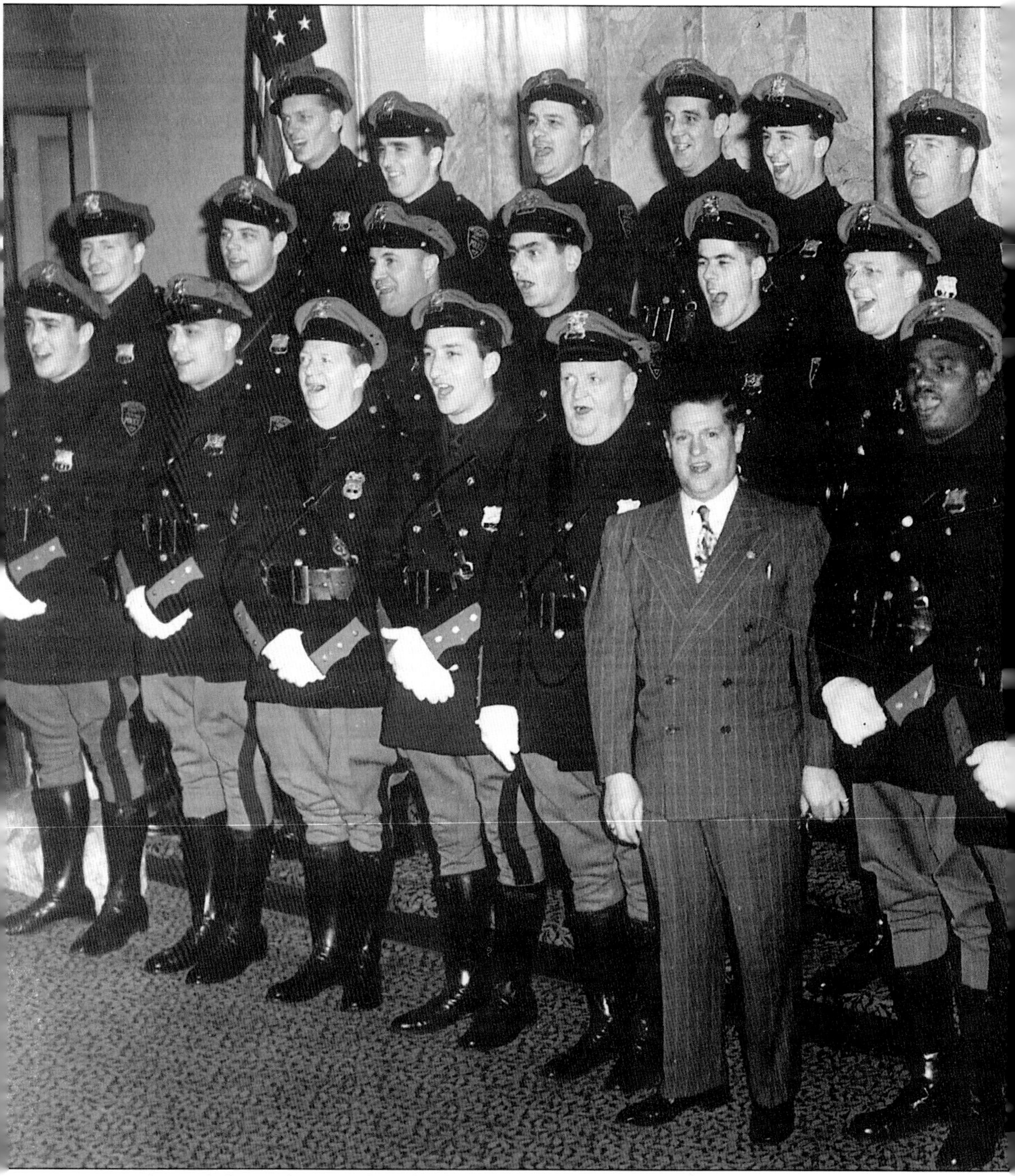

Members of the parkway police displayed great camaraderie as evidenced by large number of officers who participated in the Westchester County Parkway Police Glee Club. Here the glee club performs at the Masonic Temple on Prospect Avenue in Mount Vernon on February 16, 1950. Officers, from left to right, are as follows: (front row) Patrick Lifrieri, William Waterhouse, James Clarke, Carlo Fulgenzi, Thomas Delahanty, director Emil Fanning, ? Strayhorne, John Paton, Edward Boland, Sgt. Raymond Rouse, and Sgt. Raymond Foster;

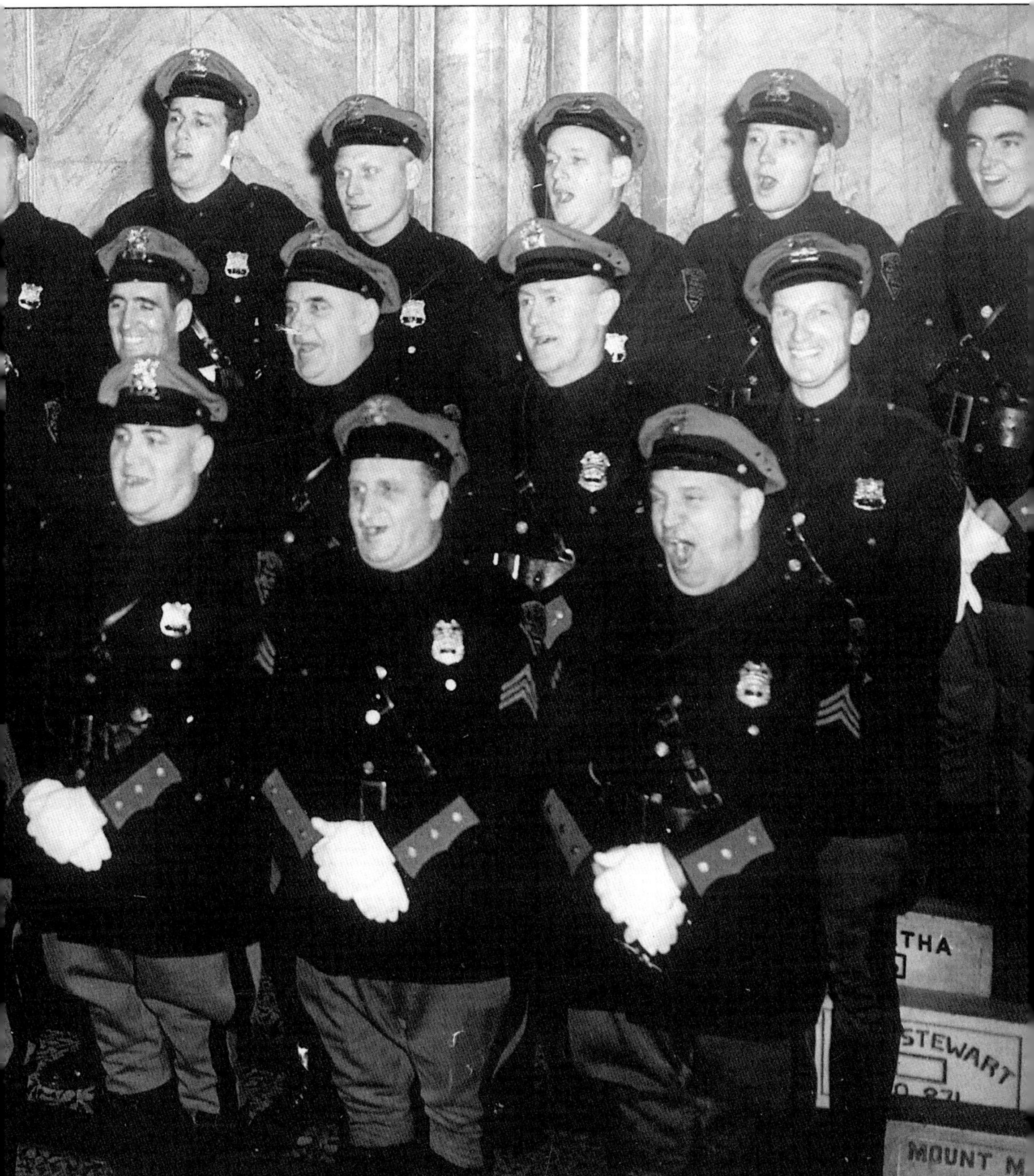

(middle row) Timothy English, Edward Meltz, Daniel Carriero, Cortland "Babe" Swift, Walter Nugent, Alexander McKechnie, Nicholas Maniscalco, Frank Harte, William Lloyd, Robert Stankey, and Marvin Ericson; (back row) I. Ericson, Chester Rodesky, unidentified, John McMahon, Alfred Pardy, Francis Clarke, John McKeon, Charles Hunter, John Puchir, Gasper Harris, James McGovern, and Raymond Buckley.

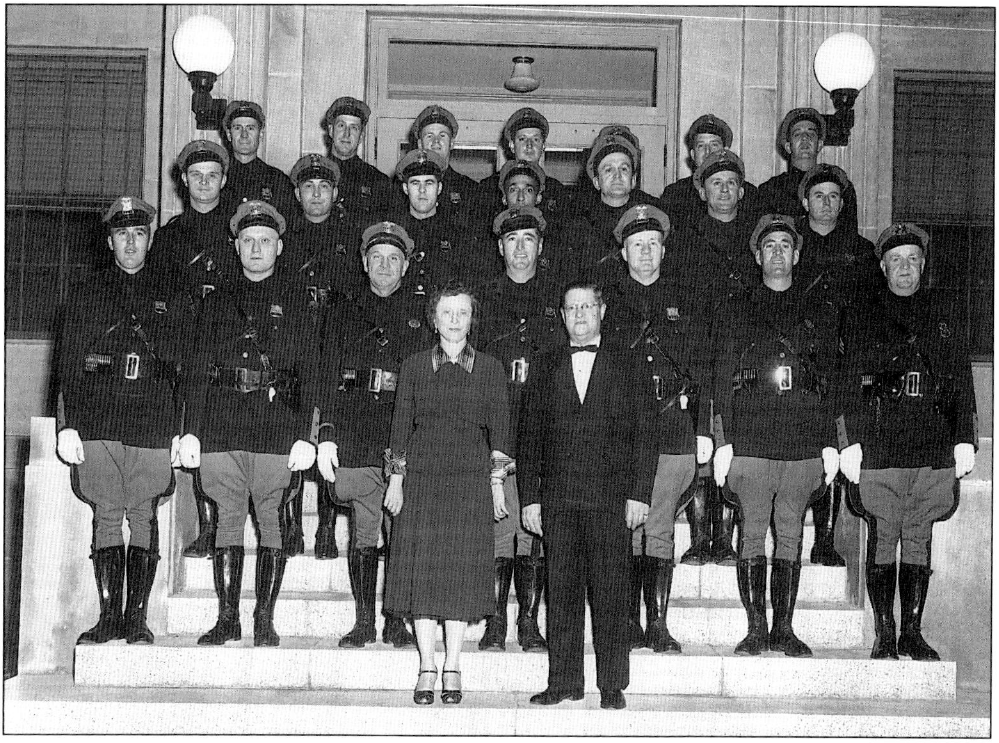

This photograph of the members of the Westchester County Parkway Police Glee Club was taken outside headquarters in November 1953. In front are Helen Gulan, the accompanist, and Emil Fanning, the director.

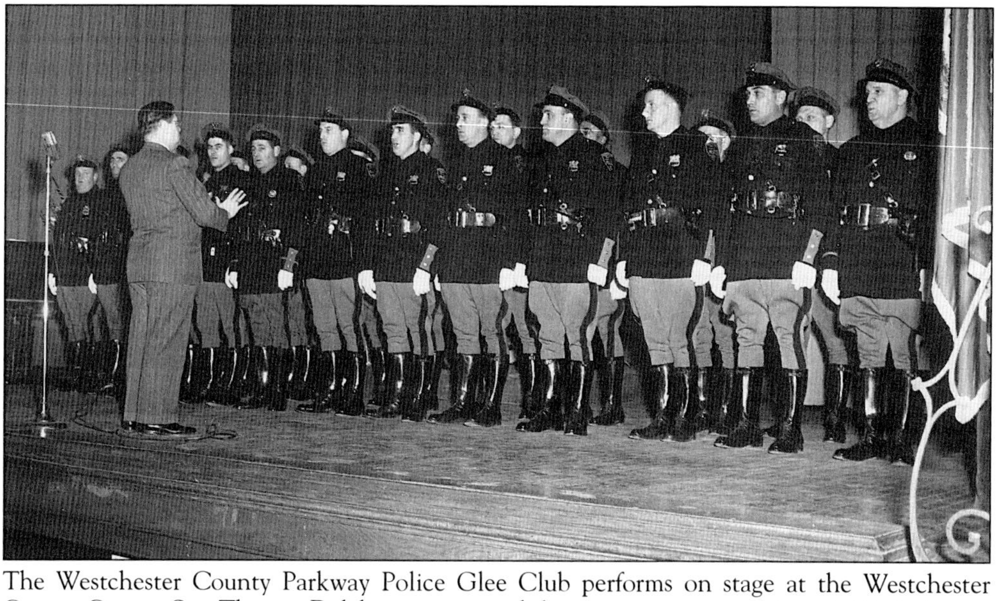

The Westchester County Parkway Police Glee Club performs on stage at the Westchester County Center. Sgt. Thomas Delahanty organized the singing group on May 12, 1948. At one point, 43 of the 118 members of the Westchester County Parkway Police were active in the glee club. They performed at numerous events and appeared on the Ted Mack Amateur Hour. The group remained active through 1956.

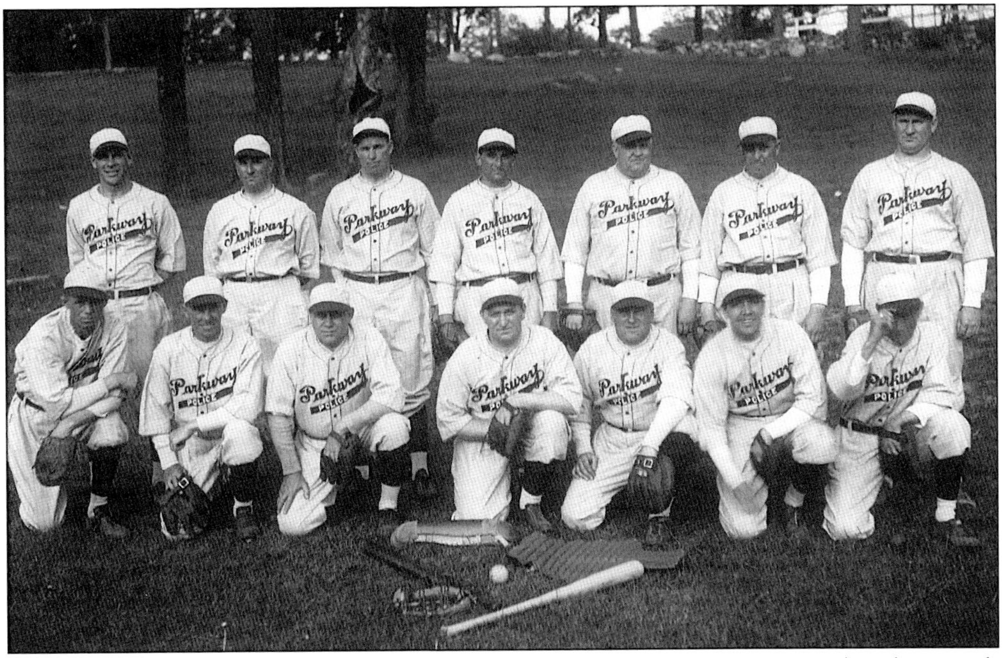

Members of the parkway police were also active in a baseball team, as seen in this photograph taken c. 1936 at California Field in the Chester Heights area of Mount Vernon. Capt. Frank J. McCabe (front center) organized the baseball team on May 1, 1933. Among the players is Frederick Trimpe (front, second from right.)

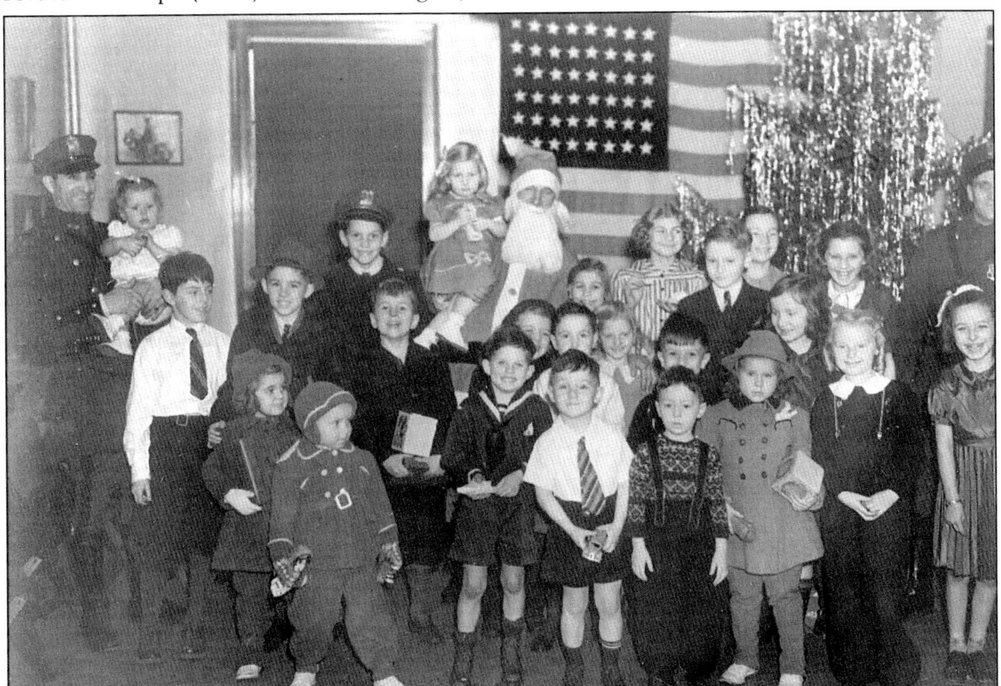

A Christmas party is held for the children of the Westchester County Parkway Patrolmen's Benevolent Association membership at the parkway police headquarters in Bronxville c. 1945.

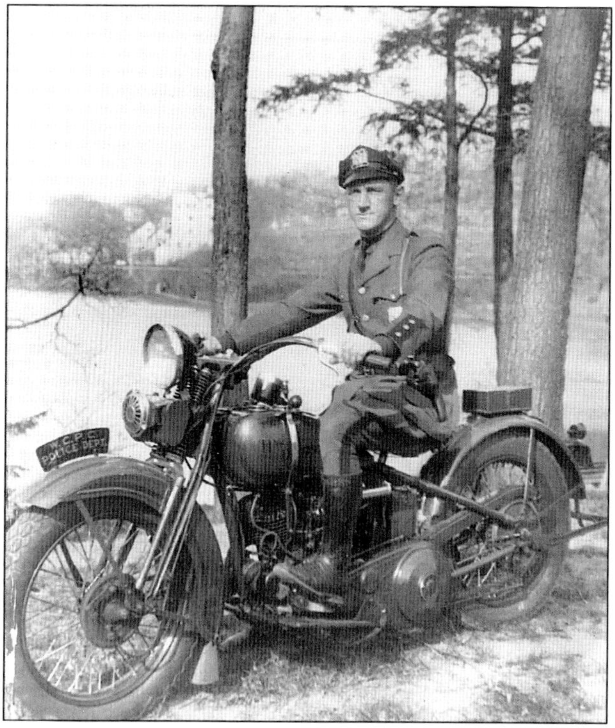

Ptl. John J. Rosko Sr. is pictured on a Harley Davidson motorcycle in the area of Bronxville lakes on the Bronx River Parkway *c.* 1935. He was appointed to the Westchester County Park Commission Police Department on May 1, 1931.

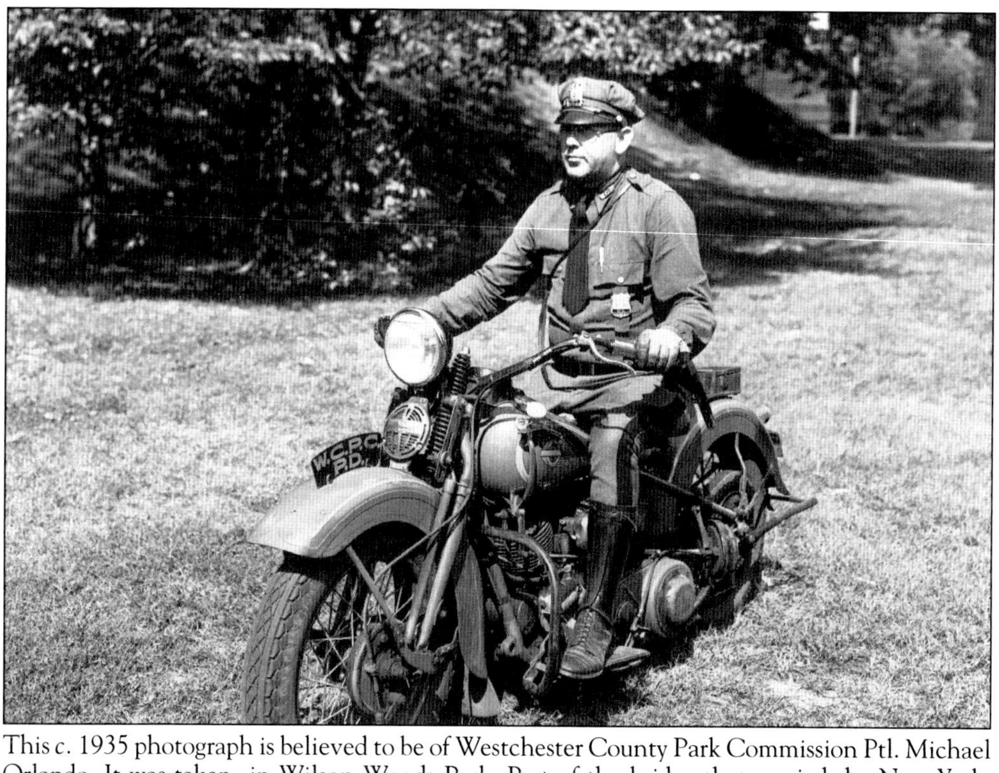

This *c.* 1935 photograph is believed to be of Westchester County Park Commission Ptl. Michael Orlando. It was taken in Wilson Woods Park. Part of the bridge that carried the New York, Westchester & Boston Railroad through Wilson Woods Park is visible in the background.

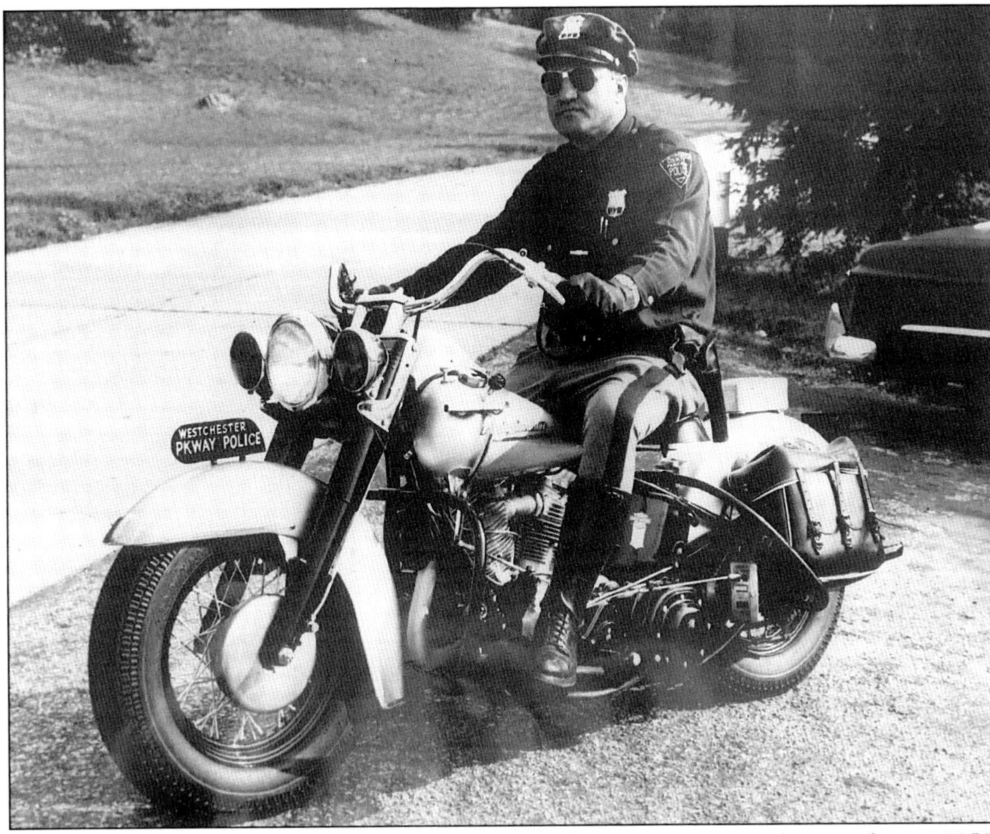

This photograph of Ptl. Daniel Carriero on a Harley Davidson motorcycle was taken c. 1950. Carriero was appointed to the Westchester County Parkway Police on April 16, 1945.

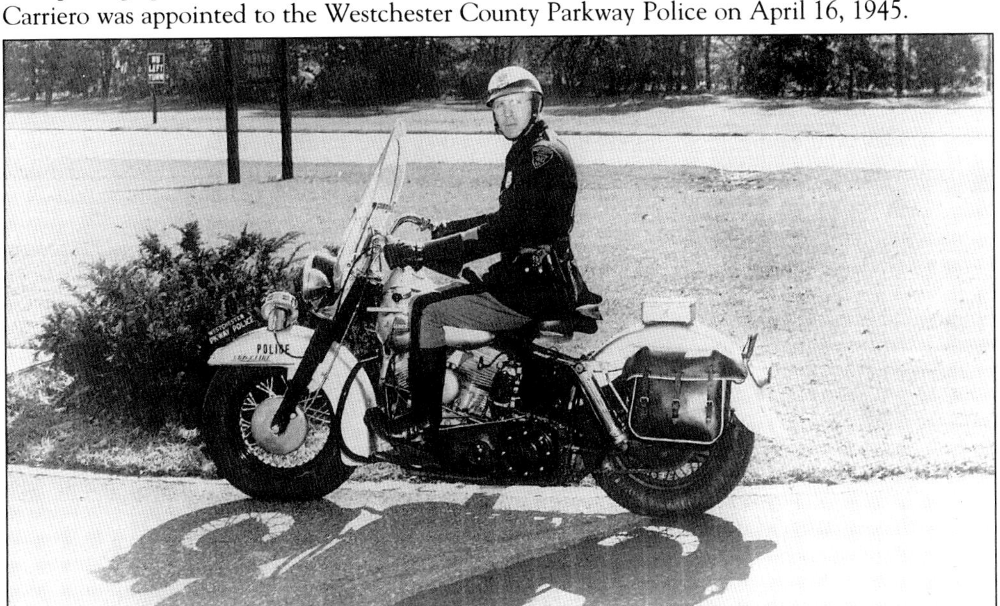

Ptl. Richard Crawford pauses in front of the parkway police headquarters in Hawthorne c. 1960. Crawford was appointed to the Westchester County Parkway Police on January 1, 1953.

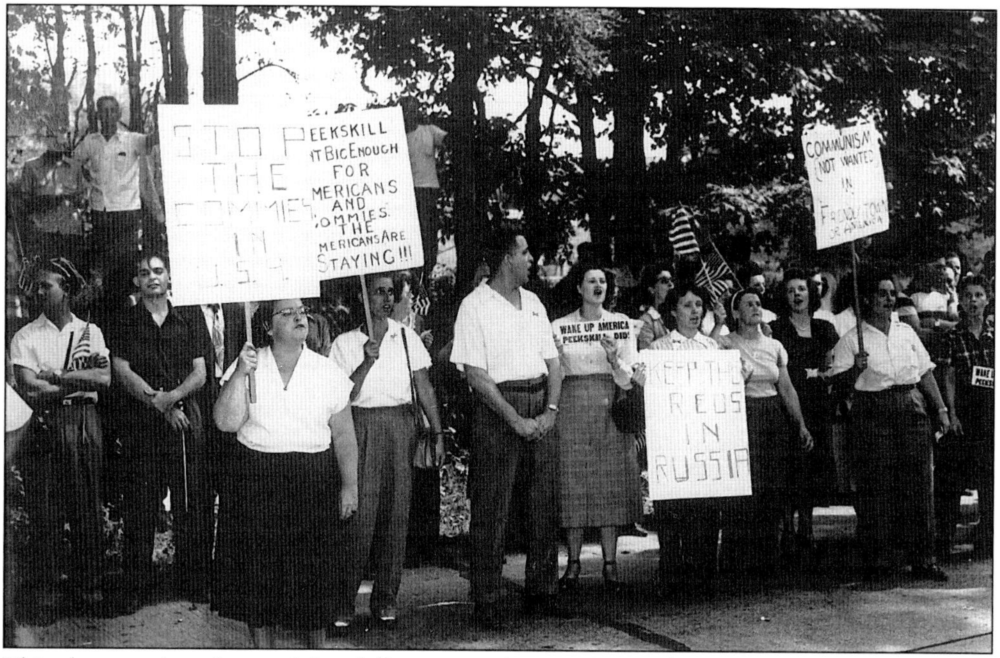

This photograph and several that follow were taken on September 4, 1949, in the area around the Hollow Brook Country Club in Cortlandt Manor, New York. They document the disorder that accompanied the appearance of singer and social activist Paul Robeson, whose support for communism made him unpopular with some local residents.

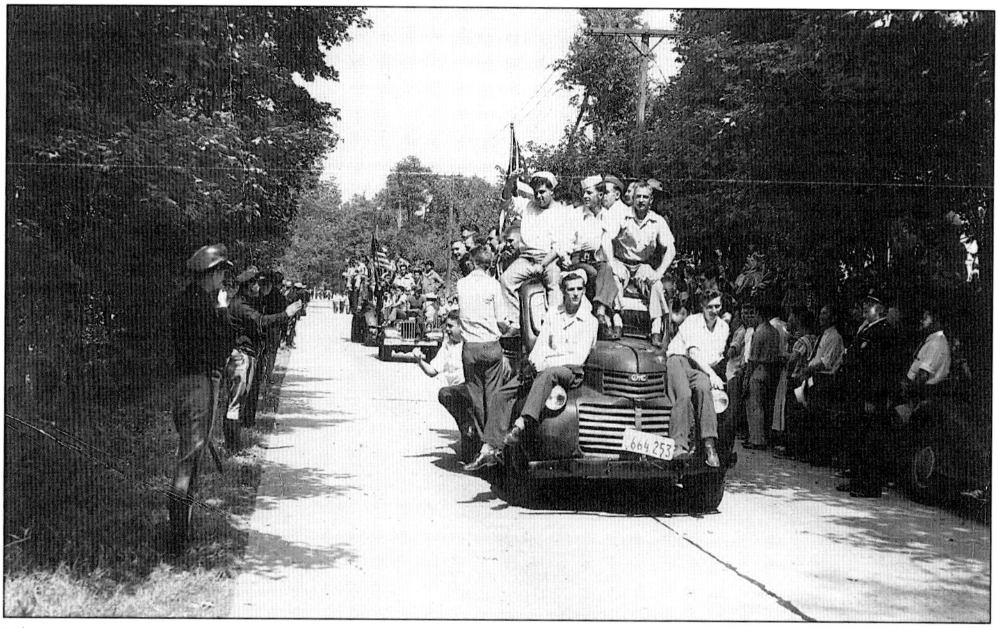

The unrest occurred first on August 27, 1949, at the Lakeland Acres picnic grounds in Cortlandt Manor and again on September 4, 1949, at the Hollow Brook Country Club, also in Cortlandt Manor. The scheduled appearance of Paul Robeson on August 27, 1949, upset some local residents, who fought with the singer's supporters. As a result. Robeson was unable to appear on that date.

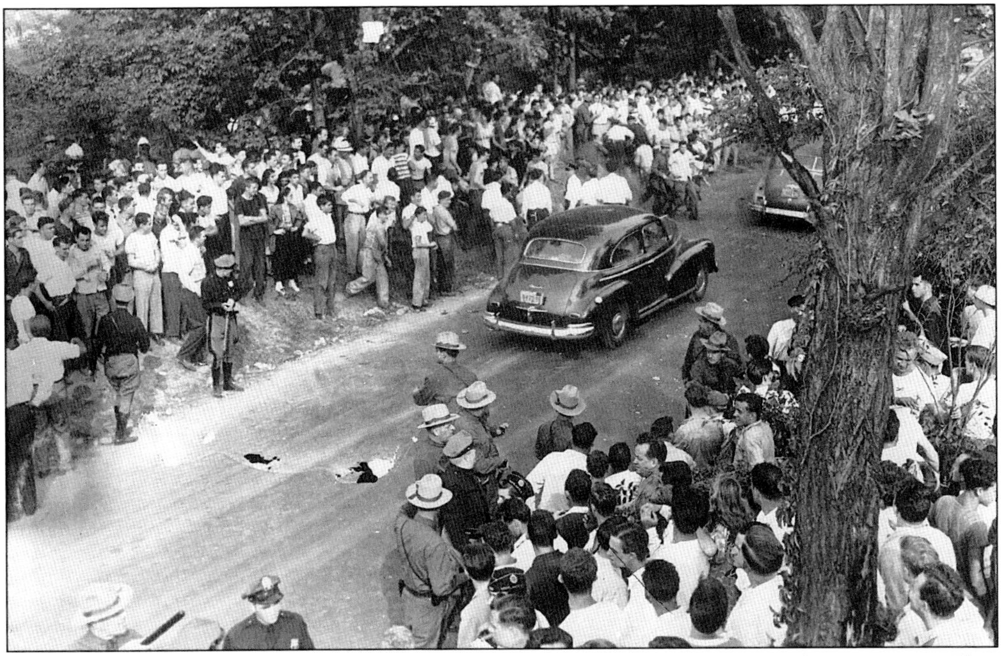

Supporters of singer Paul Robeson arranged another concert for September 4, 1949. That attracted thousands of people both for and against the ideals that Paul Robeson supported.

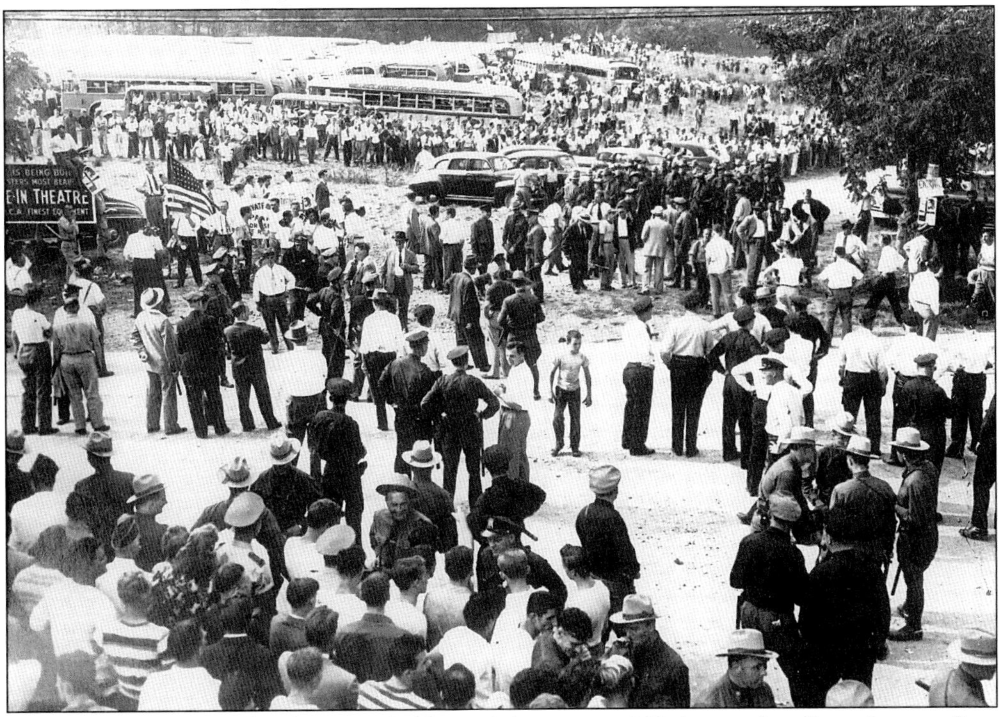

Westchester County officials responded by mobilizing over 900 deputy sheriffs, parkway police, state police, and local police. Violence was widespread on September 4, 1949, but Paul Robeson was able to appear, and the assembled officers prevented the situation from escalating out of control.

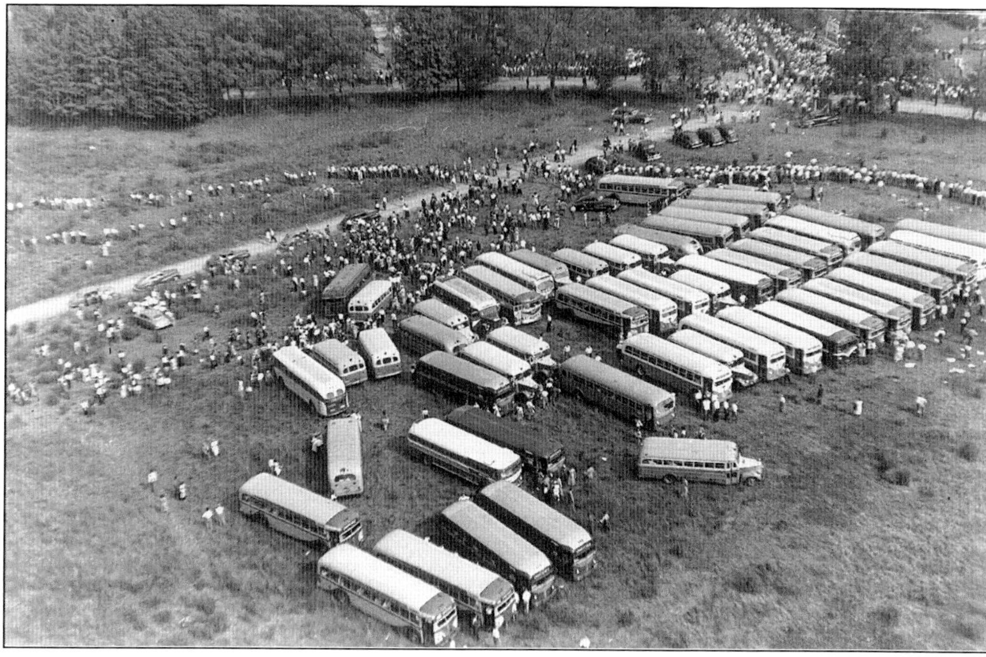

This aerial view of the grounds of the Hollow Brook Country Club was taken at 4:10 p.m. on September 4, 1949.

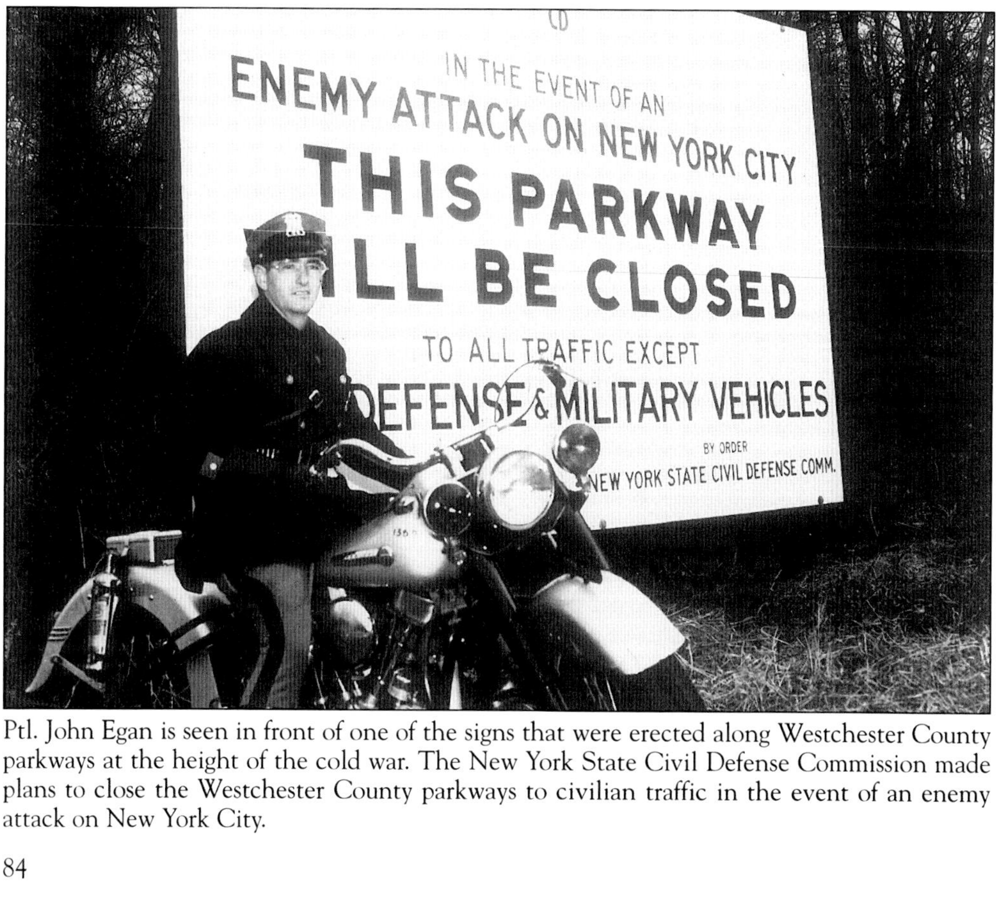

Ptl. John Egan is seen in front of one of the signs that were erected along Westchester County parkways at the height of the cold war. The New York State Civil Defense Commission made plans to close the Westchester County parkways to civilian traffic in the event of an enemy attack on New York City.

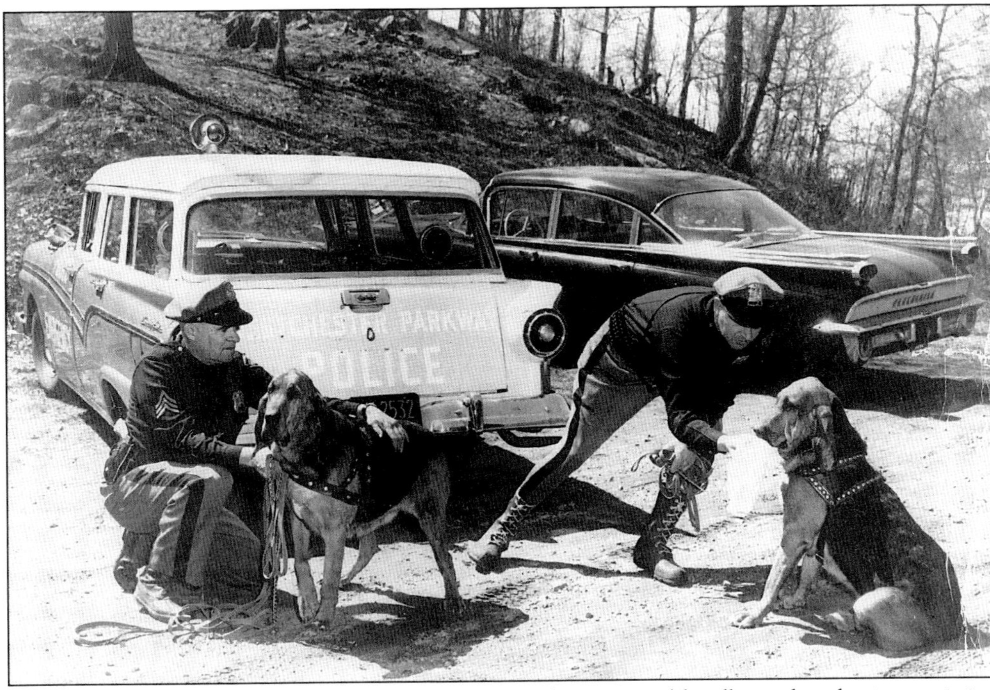

Sgt. James Jack and Ptl. William DeBrocky prepare department bloodhounds to begin a training search for a lost boy.

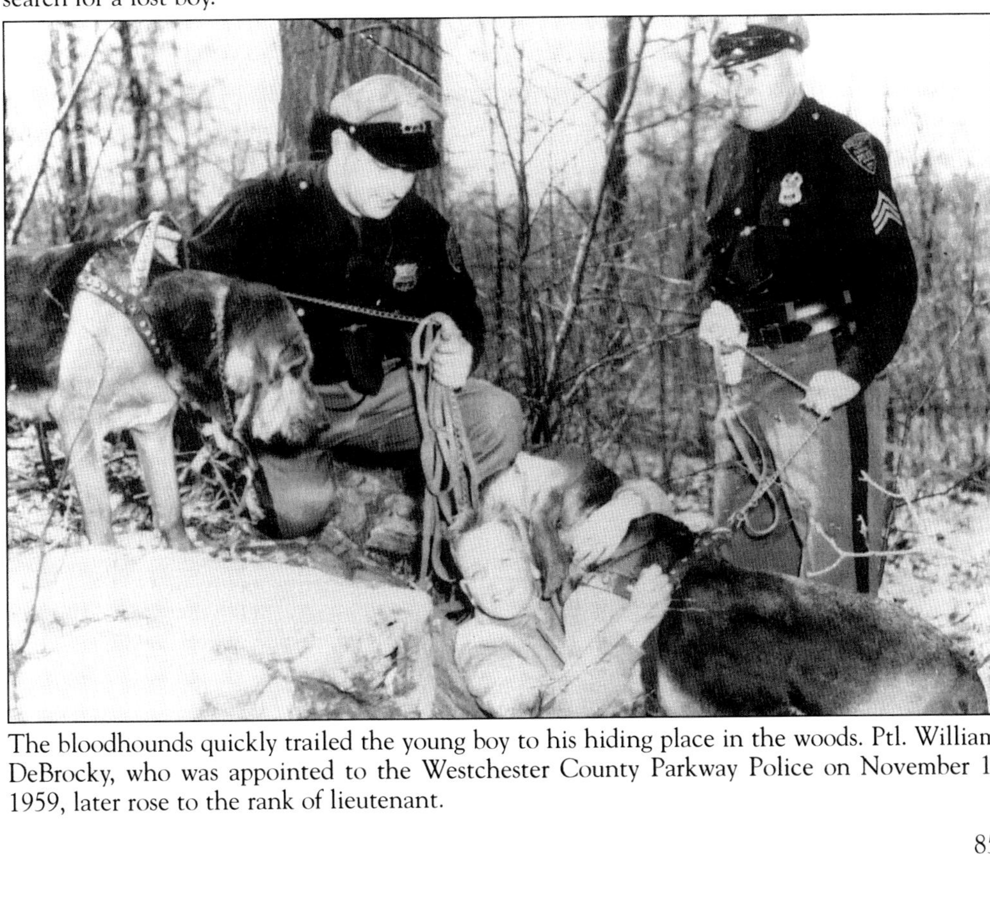

The bloodhounds quickly trailed the young boy to his hiding place in the woods. Ptl. William DeBrocky, who was appointed to the Westchester County Parkway Police on November 1, 1959, later rose to the rank of lieutenant.

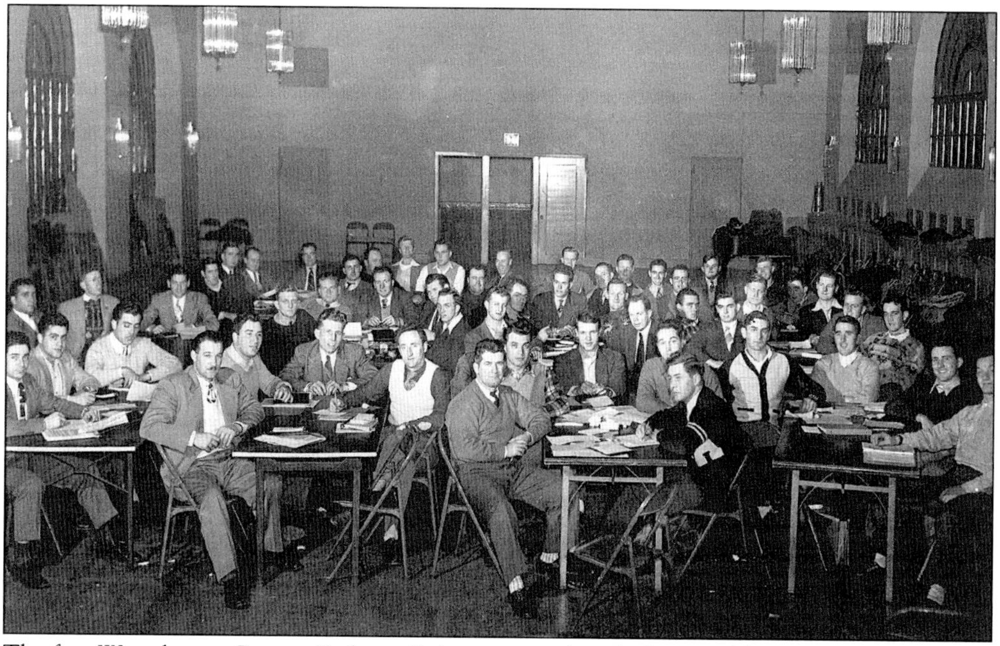

The first Westchester County Parkway Police recruits hired after World War II were appointed on December 8, 1947. Part of their initial training was conducted at Iona College in New Rochelle. Ptl. Cortland "Babe" Swift sits at the table in the right foreground, wearing a cardigan sweater. After this class was hired, the workweek was reduced from 48 to 40 hours.

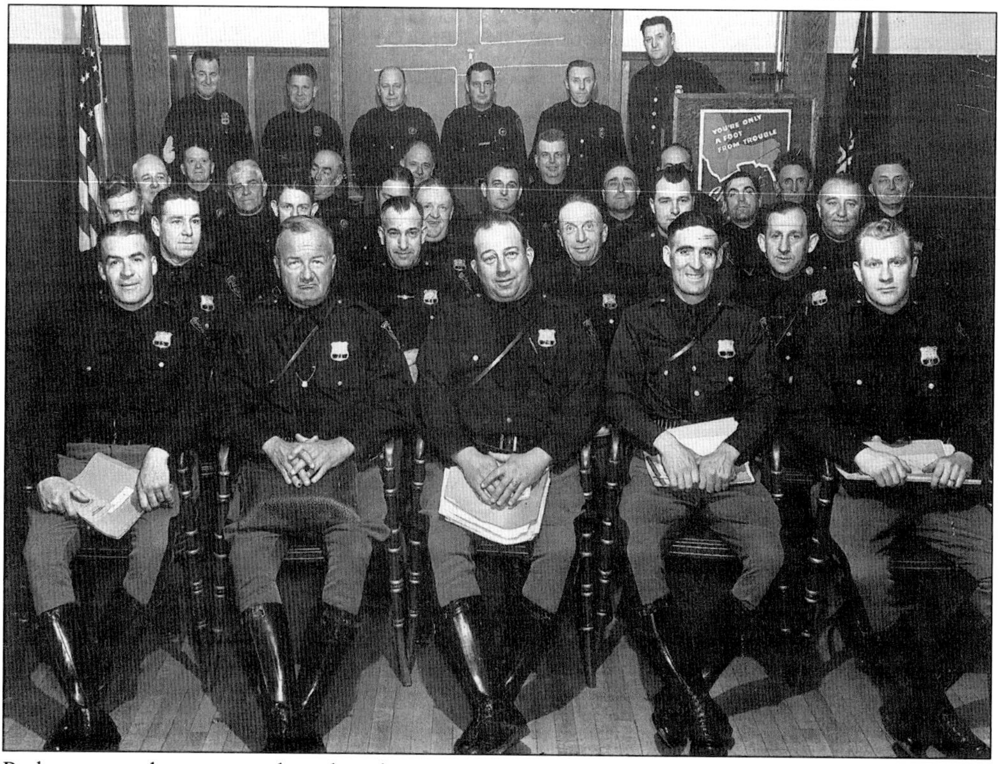

Parkway patrolmen are gathered at the Bronxville headquarters for in-service training c. 1945.

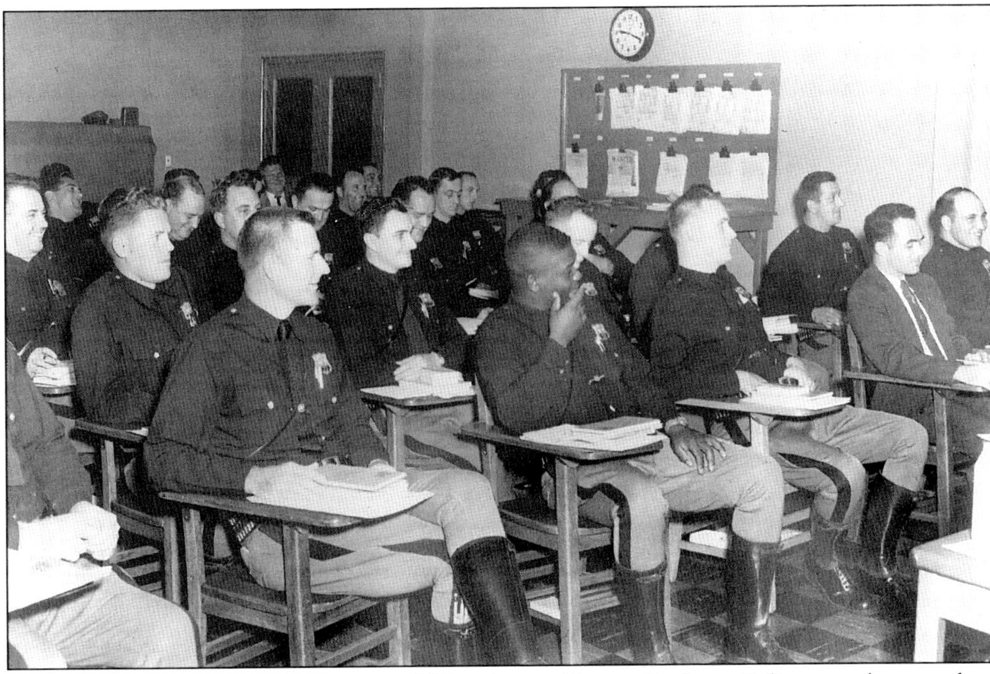

In later years, *c.* 1955, another group of Westchester County Parkway Police patrolmen gathers for training at the Hawthorne headquarters.

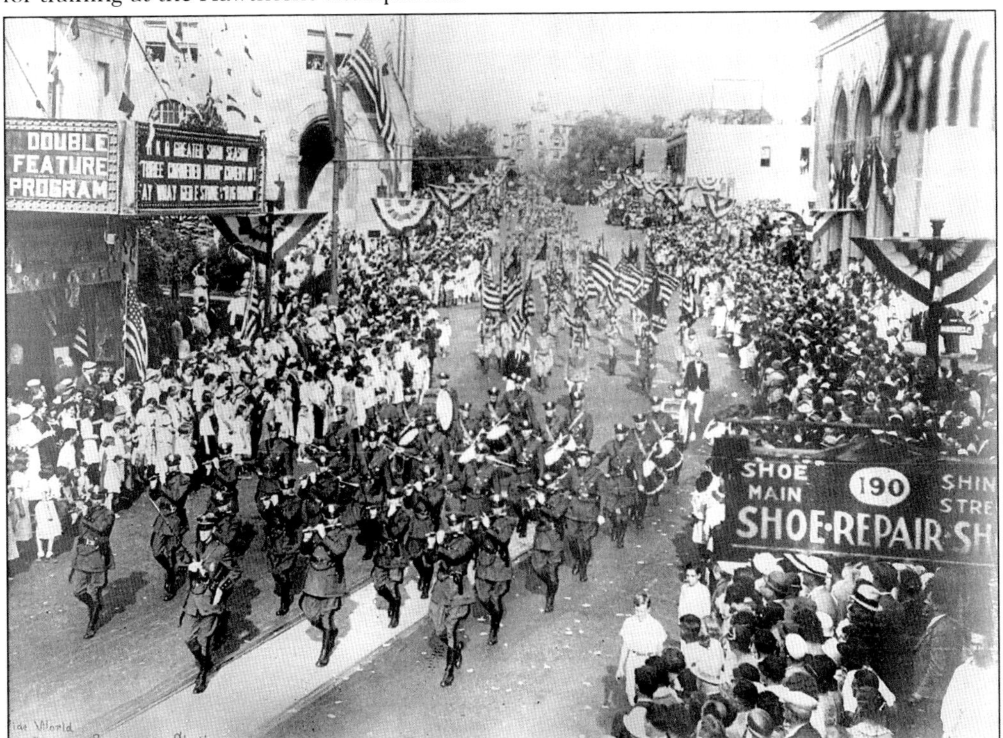

The Westchester County Parkway Police Fife and Drum Corps marches along Main Street at Mamaroneck Avenue in White Plains *c.* 1935.

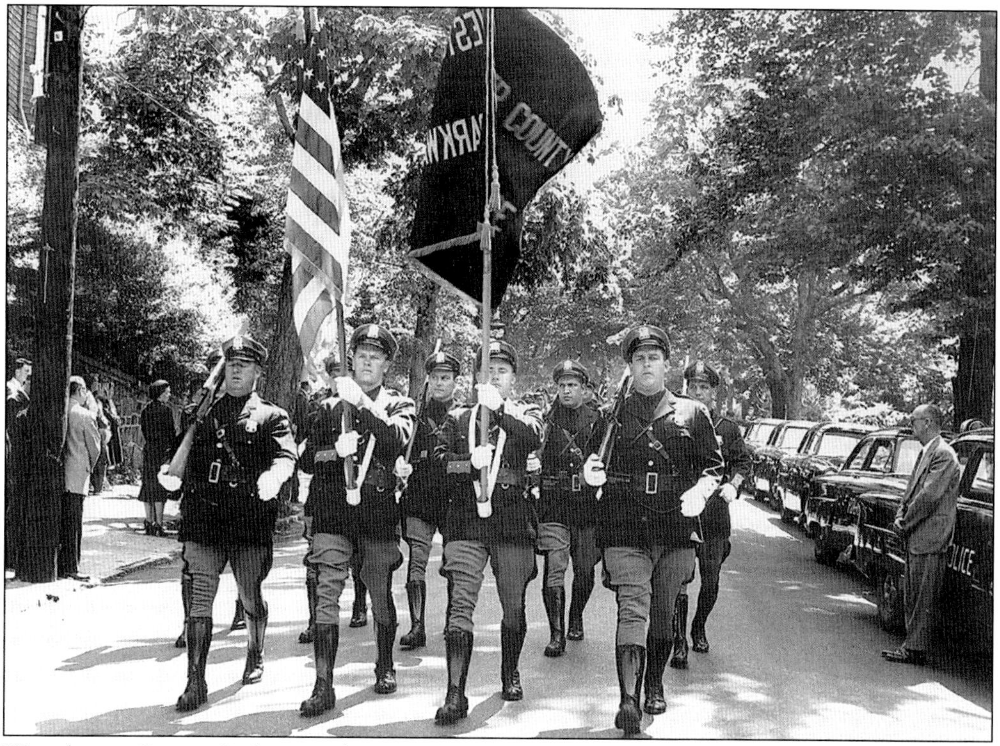

Westchester County Parkway Police patrolmen participate in a parade *c.* 1954. Members of the color guard are, from left to right, Charles "Moose" Clark, Edward Hatzman, Albert "Buzzie" Reynolds, and Charles Hunter.

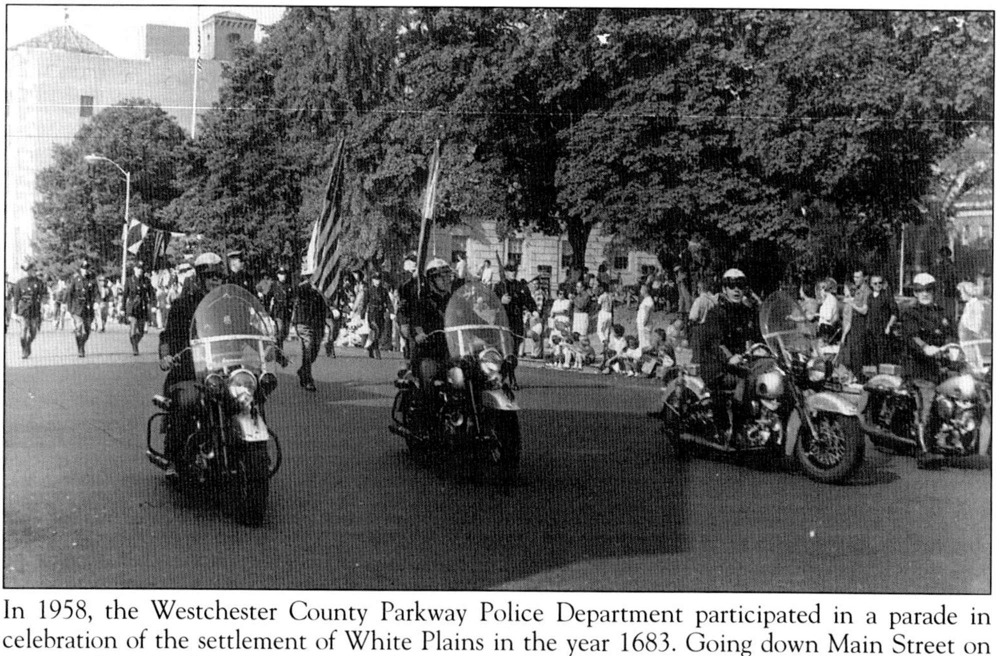

In 1958, the Westchester County Parkway Police Department participated in a parade in celebration of the settlement of White Plains in the year 1683. Going down Main Street on motorcycles are, from left to right, Patrolmen Samuel McBride, William Conkling, George Donnelly, and Frank Harte.

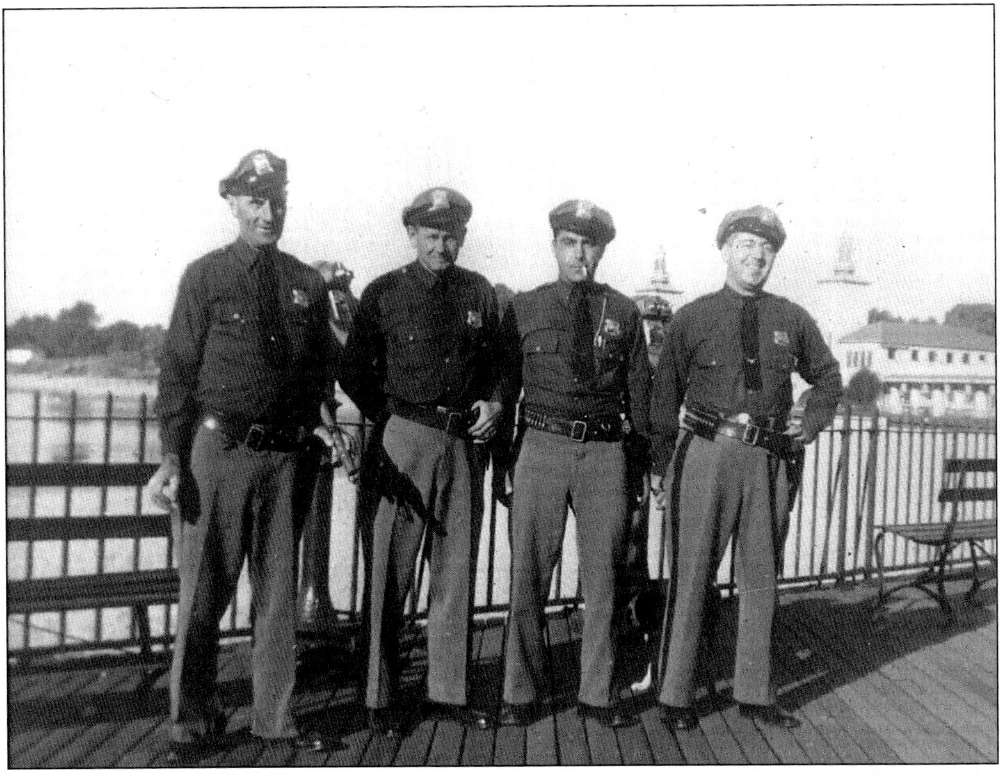

Westchester County Parkway Police patrolmen pause to have their picture taken on the boardwalk at Playland in Rye *c.* 1933.

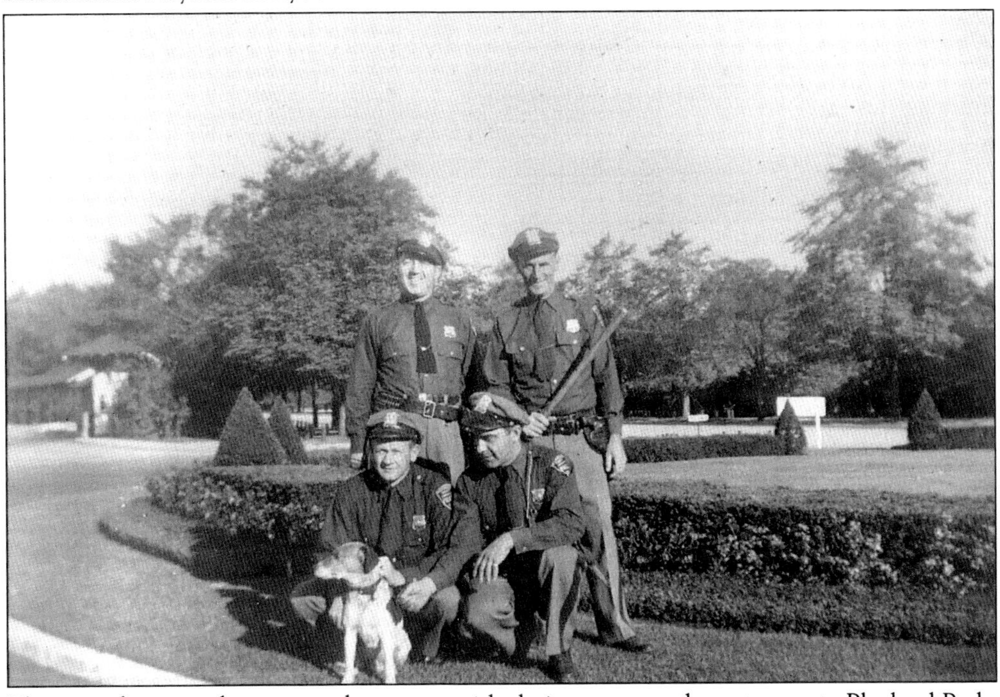

The same four patrolmen seen above pose with their mascot at the entrance to Playland Park.

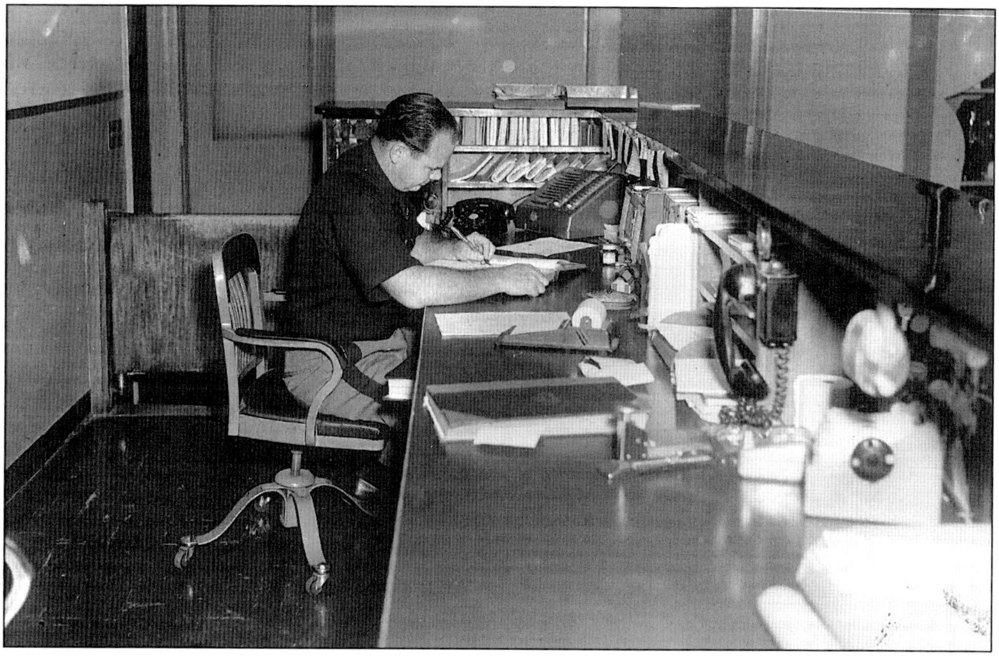

Lt. William Nelson works at the desk area in the Westchester County Parkway Police headquarters at Hawthorne *c.* 1965. Nelson was appointed to the parkway police on December 8, 1947, and retired at the rank of chief.

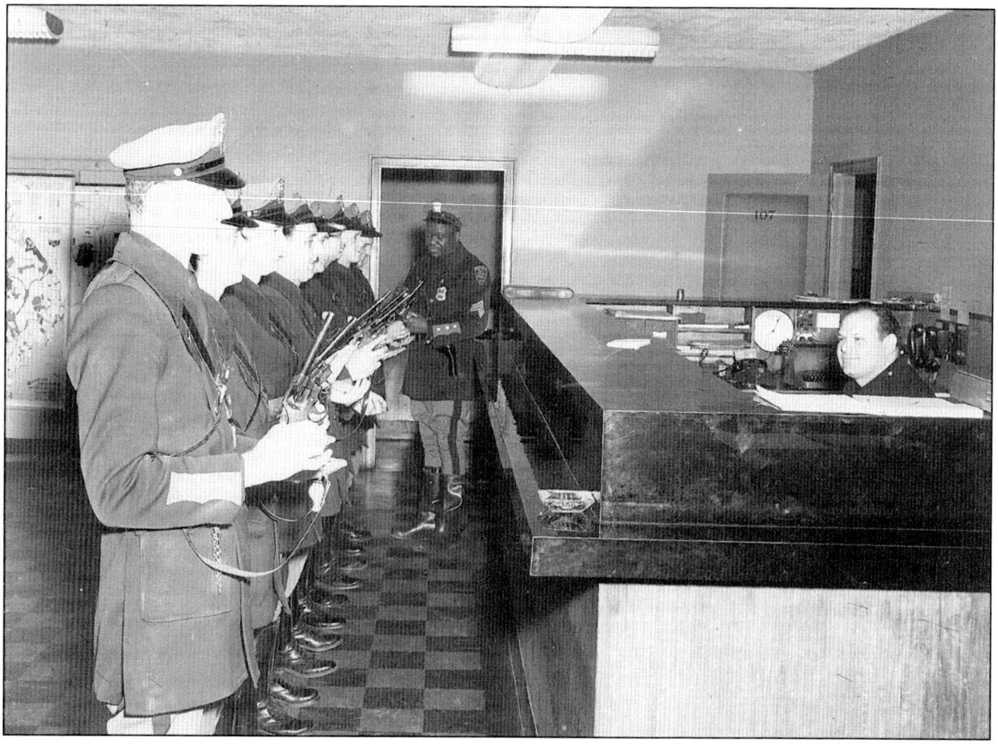

Lt. William Nelson (right) oversees the roll call at the beginning of a tour of duty. Sgt. James Brooks (center) inspects the assembled officers.

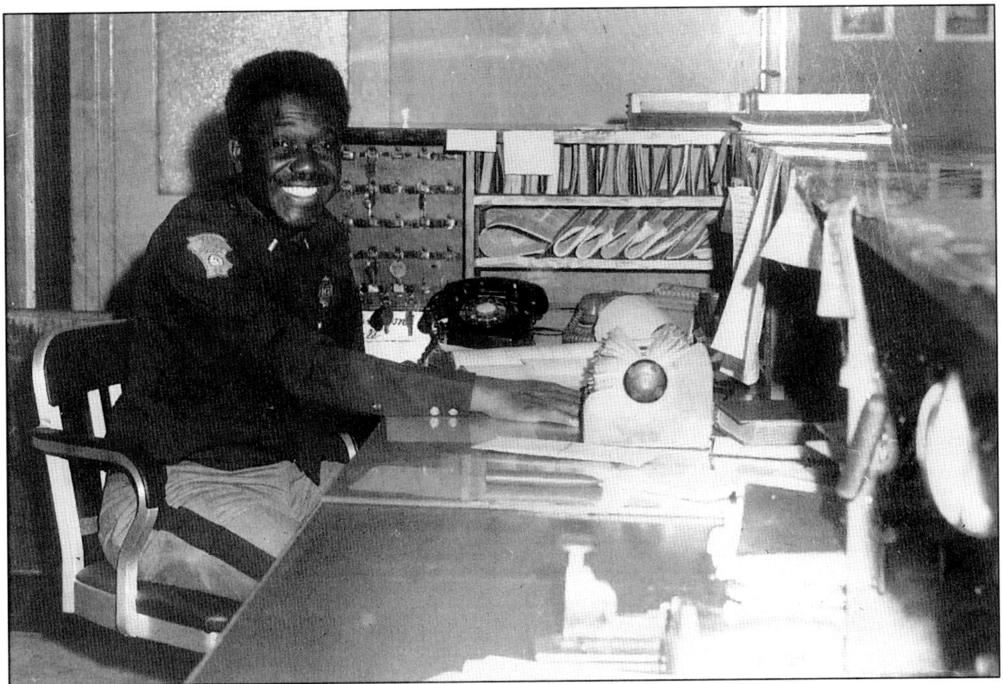

Lt. James Brooks is seated at the desk area of the Hawthorne headquarters c. 1975. Brooks was appointed to the Westchester County Parkway Police on March 1, 1952.

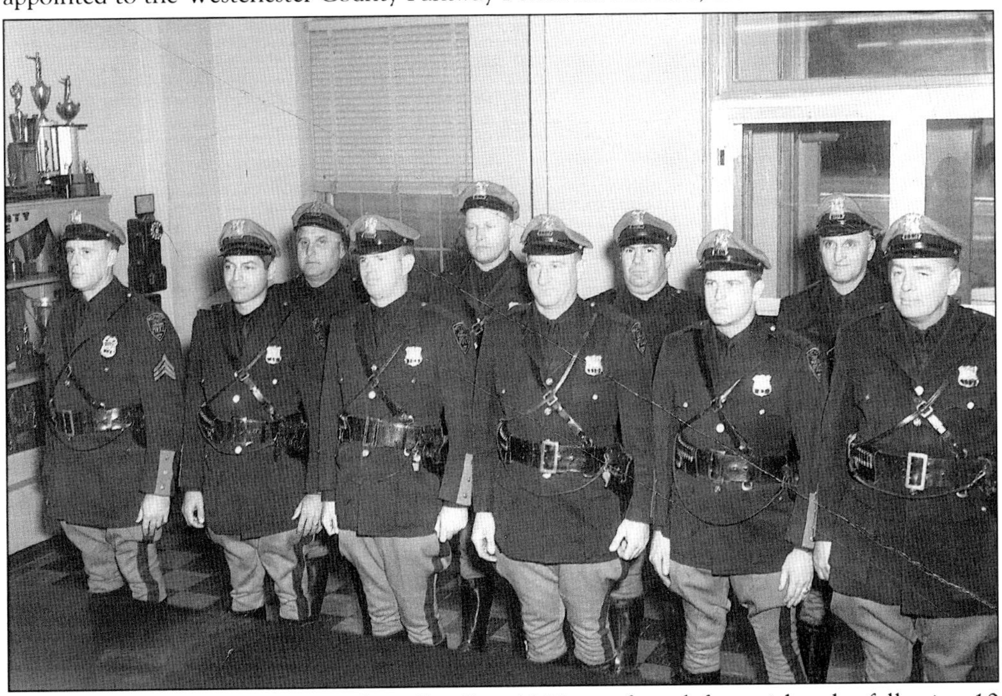

Assembled before the desk area for roll call c. 1968 are, from left to right, the following 10 men: (front row) Sgt. Robert Kmetz, and Patrolmen Leonard Salerno, Thomas Doyle, Dominic Locatelli, George Kane, and Albert Bolwell; (back row) Patrolmen Stephen Wasylenko, Edwin Cermak, Frederick Vosatka Jr., and John Gonda.

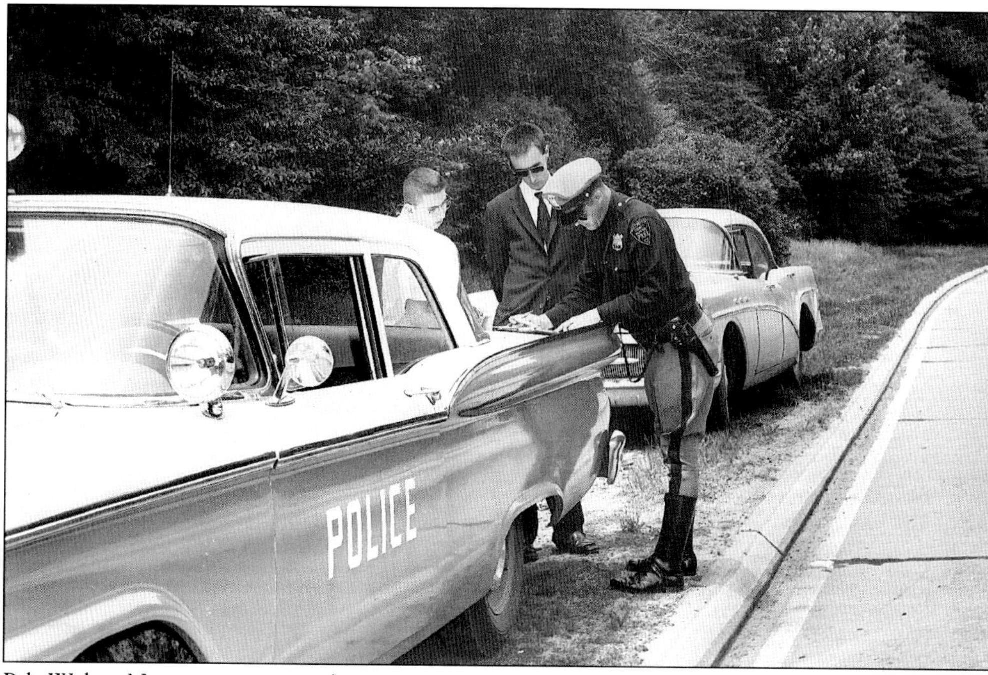

Ptl. Walter Nugent issues a ticket to a motorist on the Hutchinson River Parkway in 1957. At that time the Westchester County Parkway Police uniform still included puttees and cross-draw holsters.

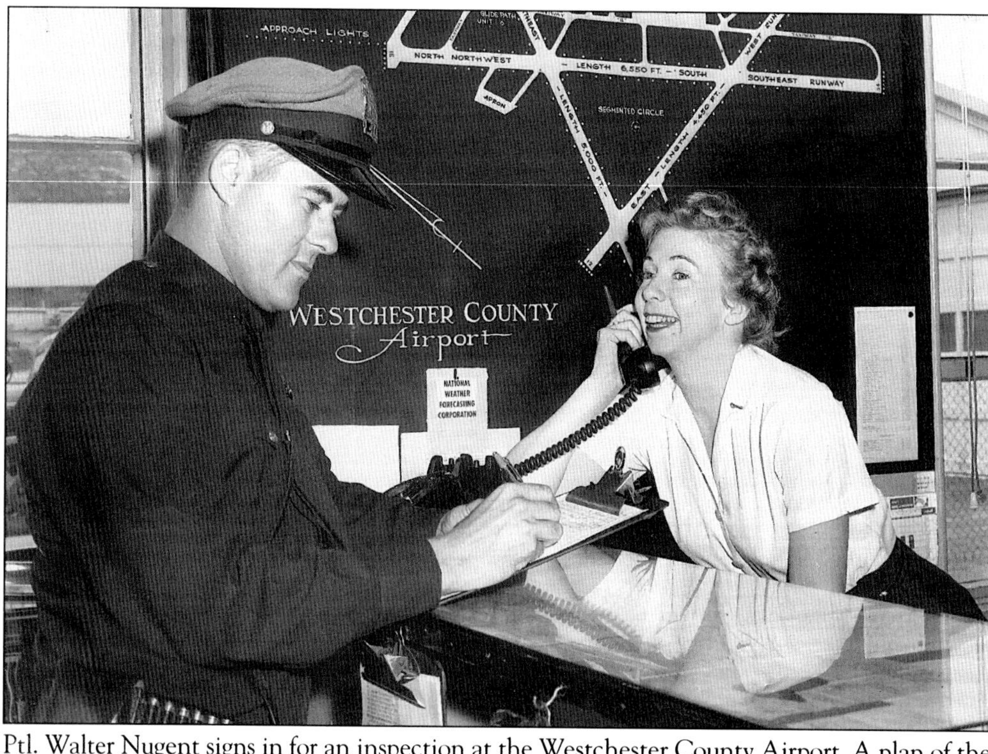

Ptl. Walter Nugent signs in for an inspection at the Westchester County Airport. A plan of the airport is visible behind him.

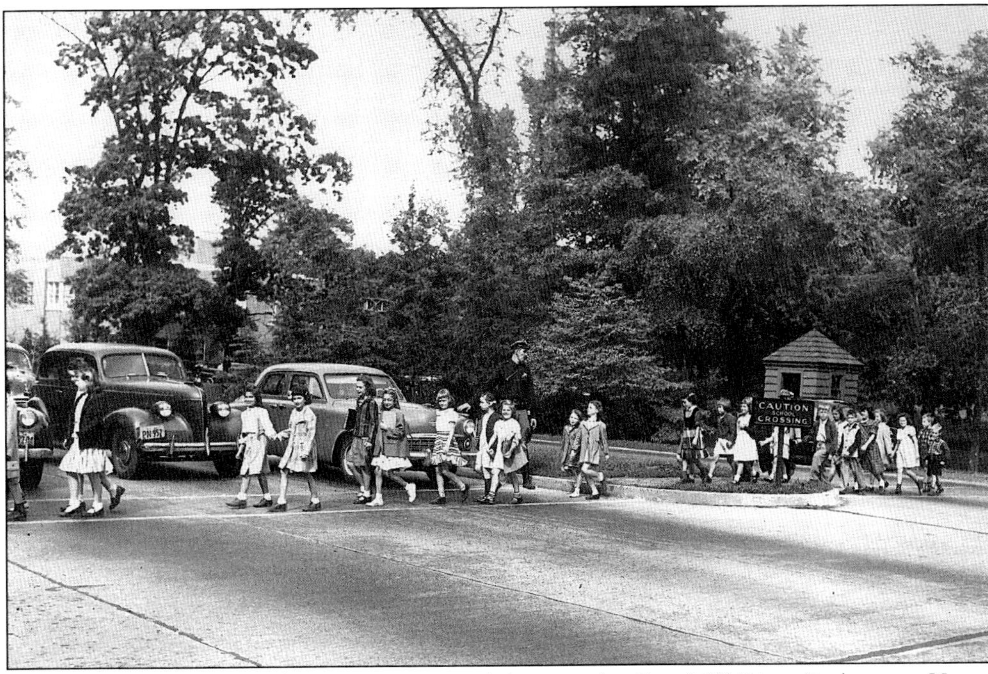

Ptl. Howard MacNeil performs crossing-guard duty on the Saw Mill River Parkway at Hearst Street in Yonkers c. 1949. The booth visible on the right is for the officer assigned to the crossing-guard detail.

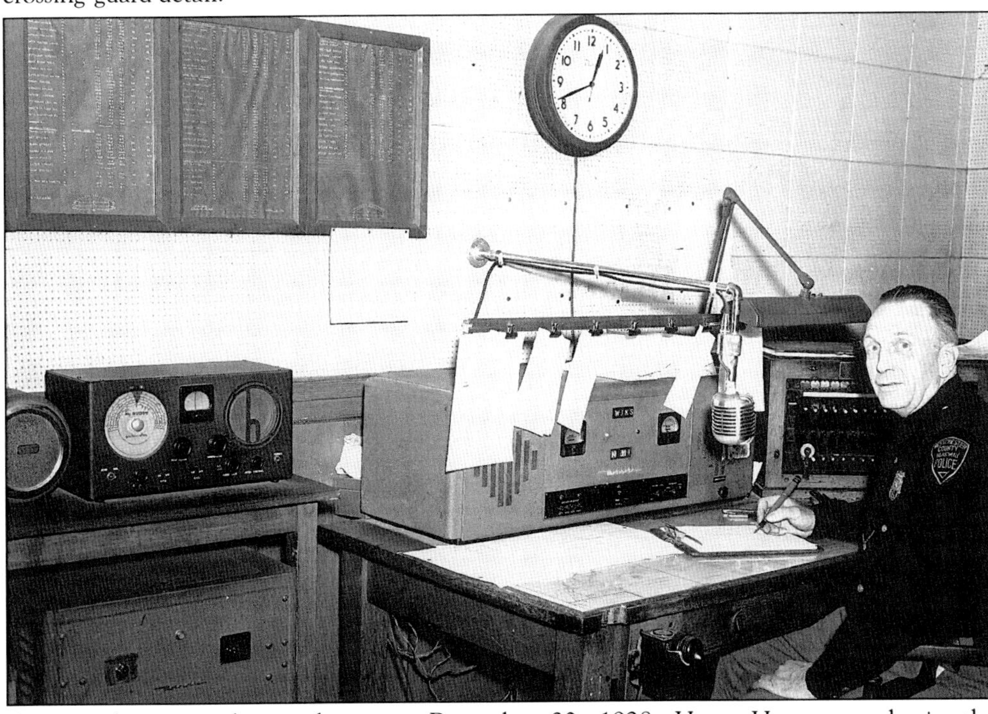

Appointed as a park patrolman on December 20, 1928, Harry Hopper, works in the communications area of the Westchester County Parkway Police headquarters in Bronxville c. 1950.

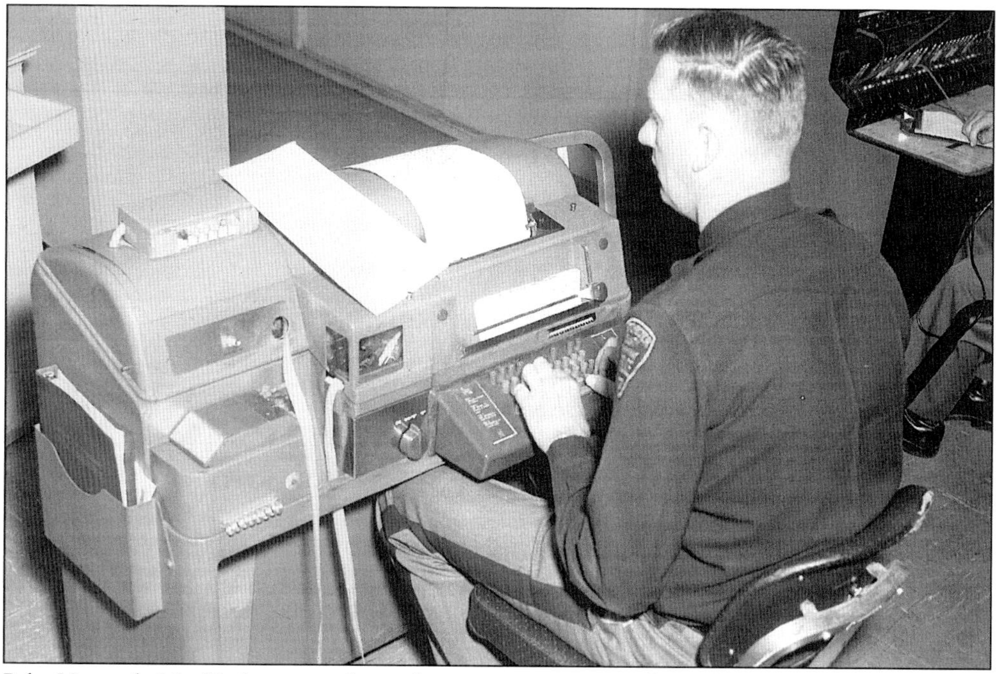

Ptl. Howard MacNeil mans the teletype position in this photograph taken in the communications area at the Westchester County Parkway Police headquarters in Hawthorne c. 1960. The switchboard position is visible on the right.

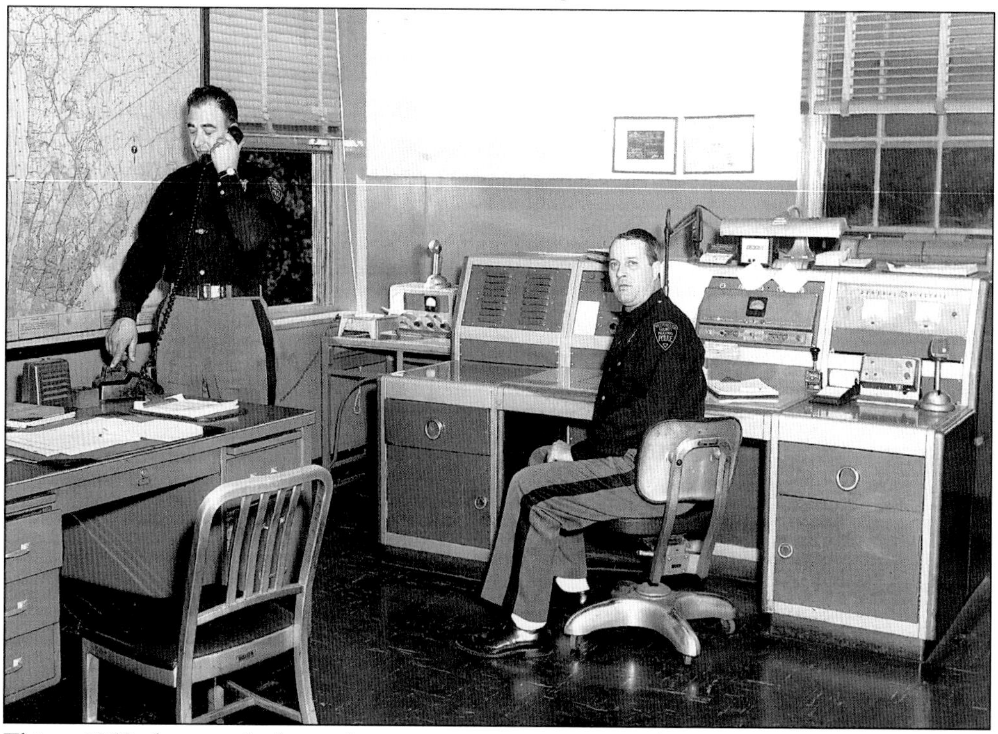

This c. 1953 photograph shows the communications area, with Ptl. Joseph Manganello (left) on the telephone.

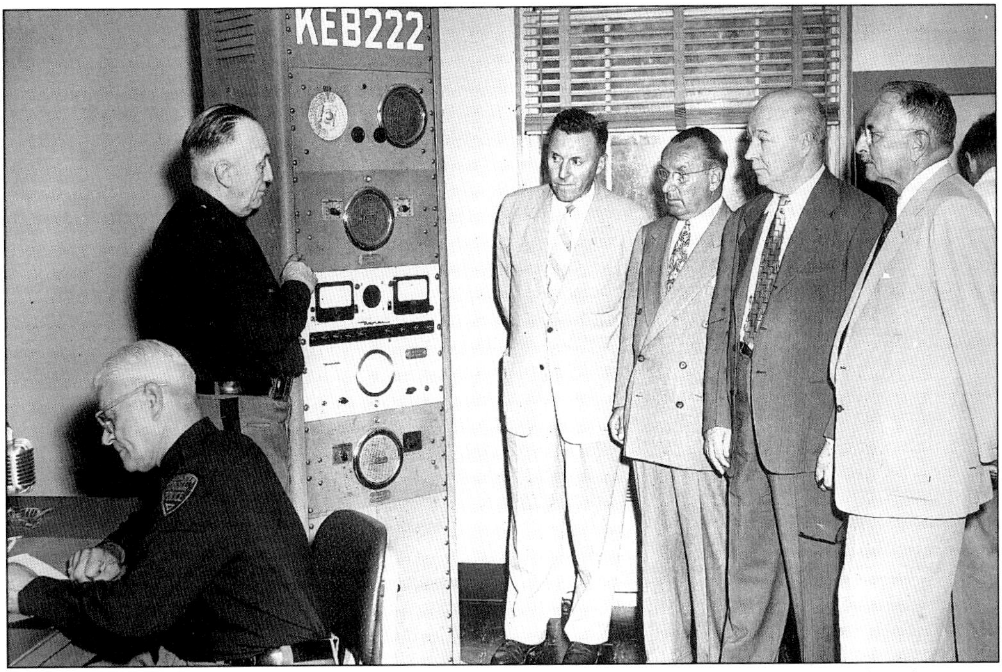

County officials inspect new communications equipment at the just opened headquarters building in Hawthorne on July 20, 1953. Pictured, from left to right, are Patrolmen Charles Fischer and Harry Hopper; William Slater, director; Edward Ganter, finance commissioner; Orrie Kelly, police commissioner; and Herbert Gerlach, county executive.

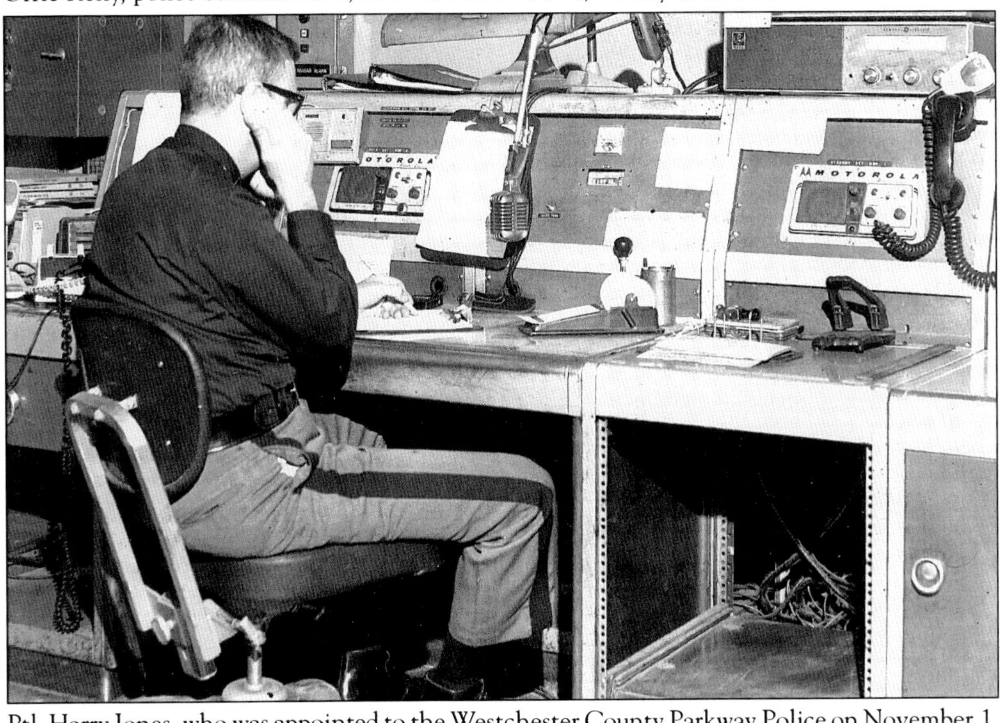

Ptl. Harry Jones, who was appointed to the Westchester County Parkway Police on November 1, 1956, takes a call at the dispatcher station c. 1960.

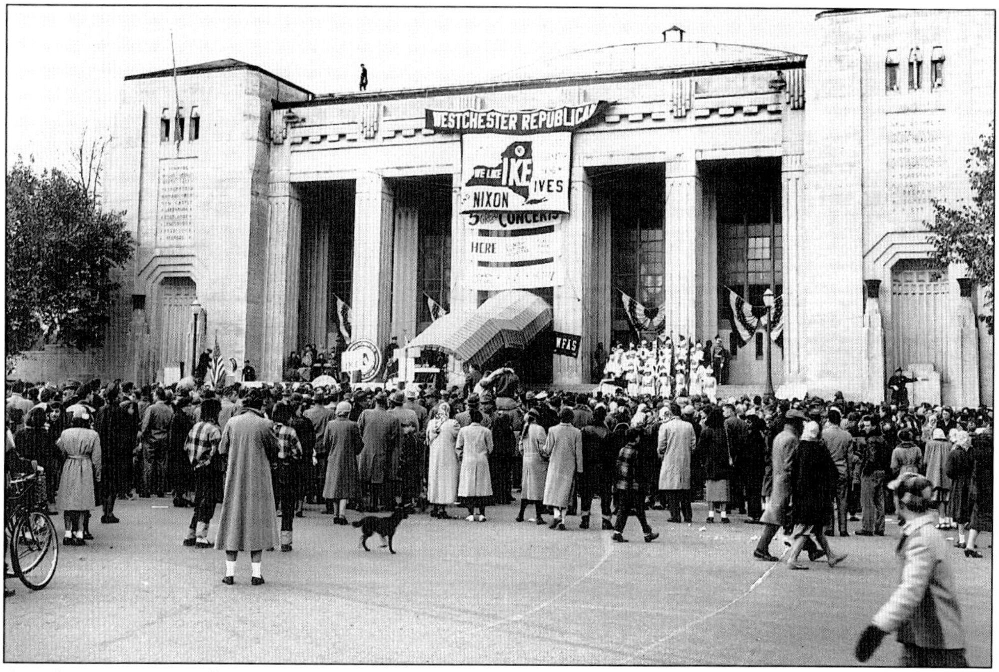

An election-year rally for Dwight D. Eisenhower was held at the Westchester County Center in White Plains in 1952. An officer of the Westchester County Parkway Police is visible on the roof of the county center building.

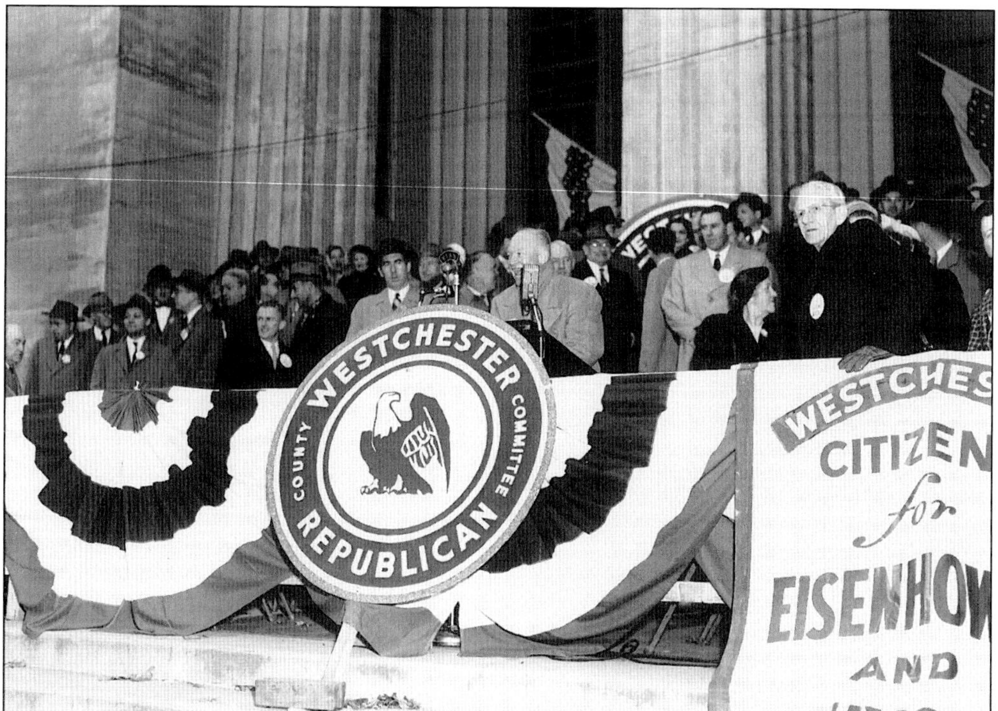

Dwight D. Eisenhower is at the podium in this photograph taken in front of the Westchester County Center.

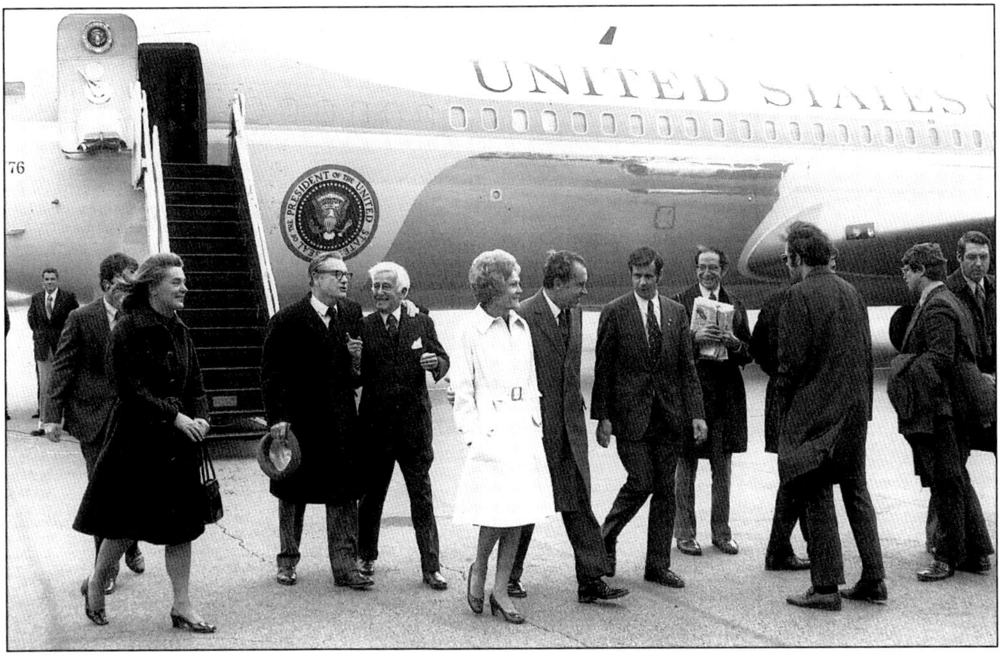

Pres. and Mrs. Richard Nixon (center) arrive at the Westchester County Airport on October 20, 1972, along with Gov. and Mrs. Nelson Rockefeller. Members of the Westchester County Parkway Police were frequently assigned to provide security for dignitaries visiting or passing through Westchester County.

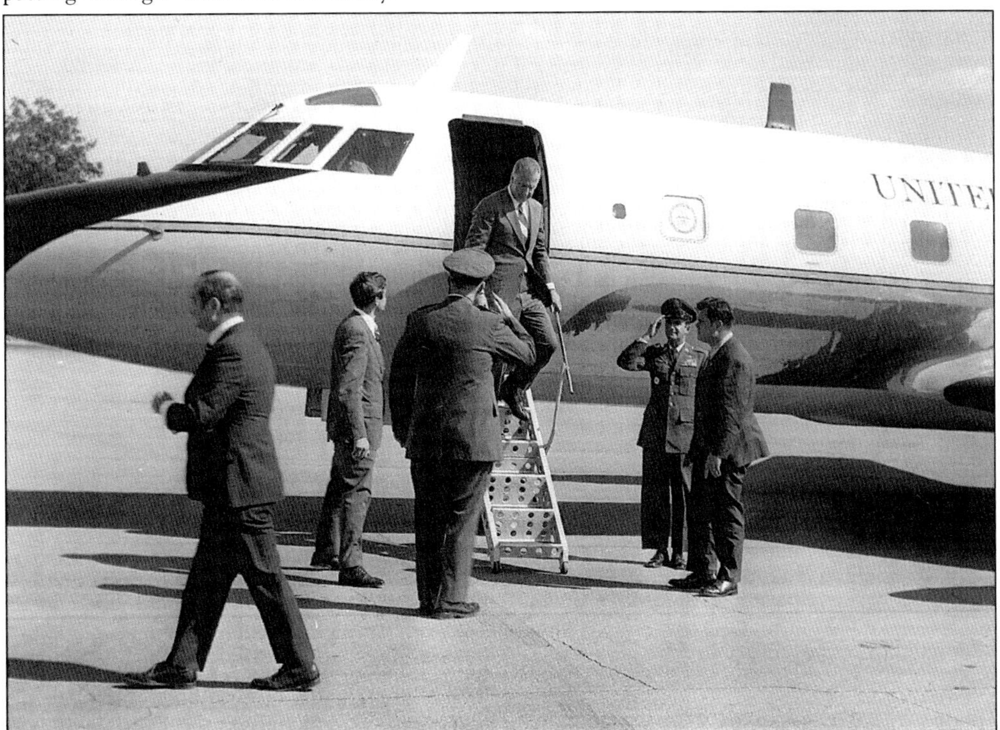

Vice Pres. Spiro Agnew arrives at the Westchester County Airport on October 8, 1971.

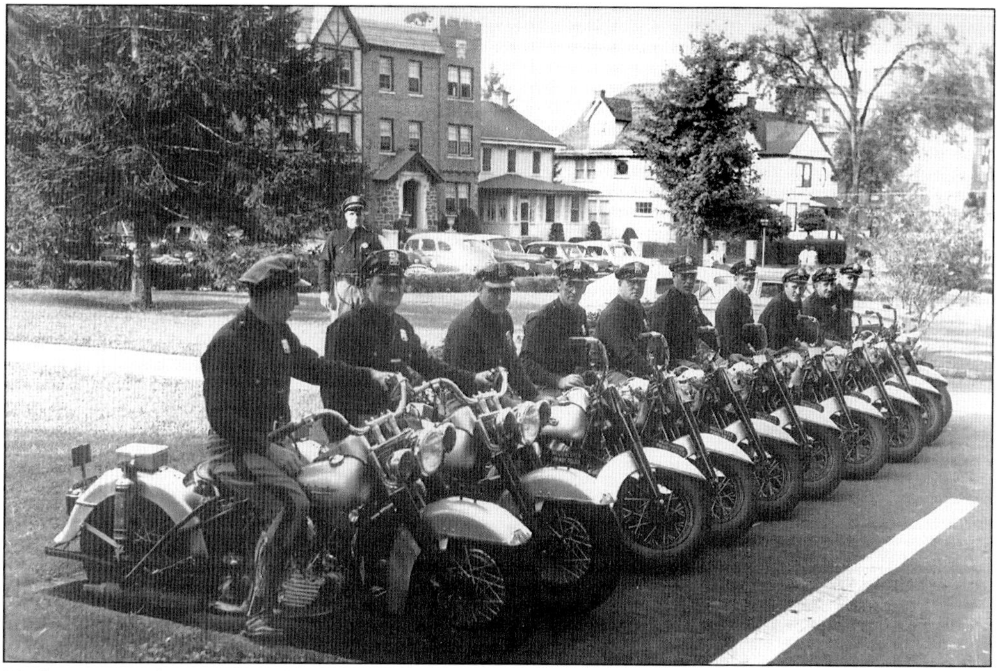

Highway patrol was one of the main missions of the Westchester County Parkway Police in 1926, and it remains an important mission for the Westchester County Department of Public Safety. Motorcycles were used extensively to perform patrols from 1926 until the early 1960s. Officers assembled for a special detail c. 1950 are, from left to right, Edward Colville, John McKeon, Louis Mackey, Frank Harte, Francis "Moose" Clarke, Frank "Turk" Mueller, George Ruthven, Albert Swanson, Harry Rubin, and Daniel Carriero. Standing in the background is Lt. Raymond Rouse.

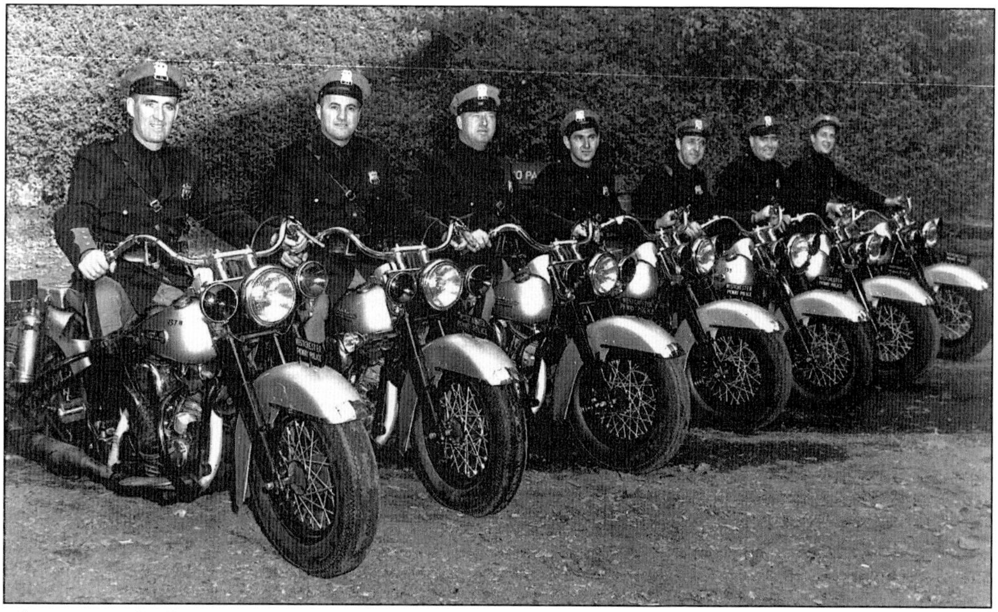

This group of officers includes, from left to right, Frank Harte, Daniel Carriero, Francis Clarke, Cortland "Babe" Swift, Edward Berletic, Louis Mackey, and William DeBrocky.

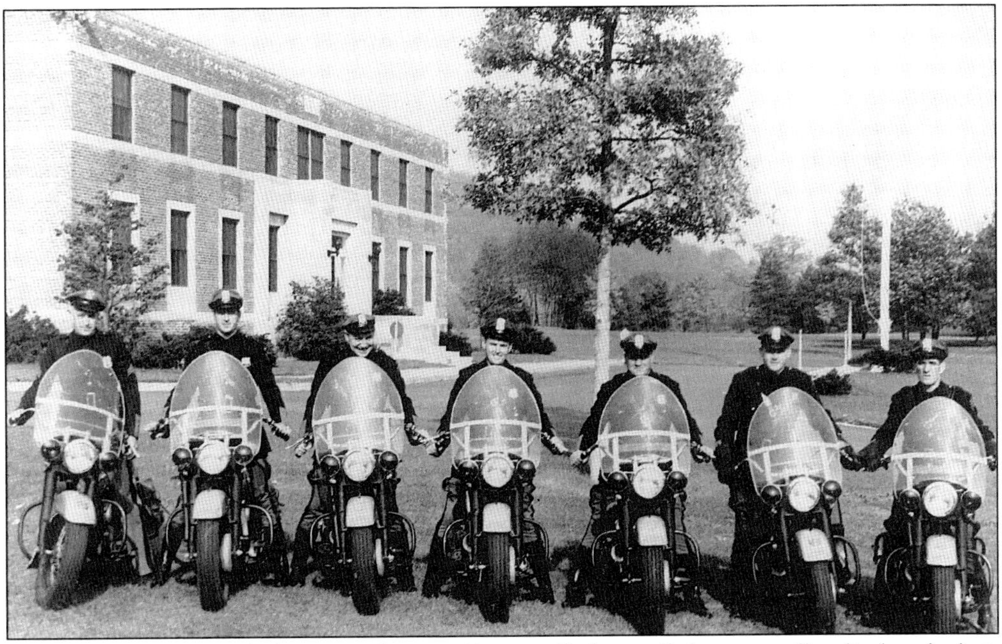

In 1955, members of the Westchester County Parkway Police proudly displayed their motorcycles with newly installed windshields. They are, from left to right, Sgt. Carl Taylor, William DeBrocky, William Waterhouse, Robert Trimpe, Daniel Carreiro, Albert Reynolds, and Frank Harte. The headquarters building at Hawthorne is visible in the background.

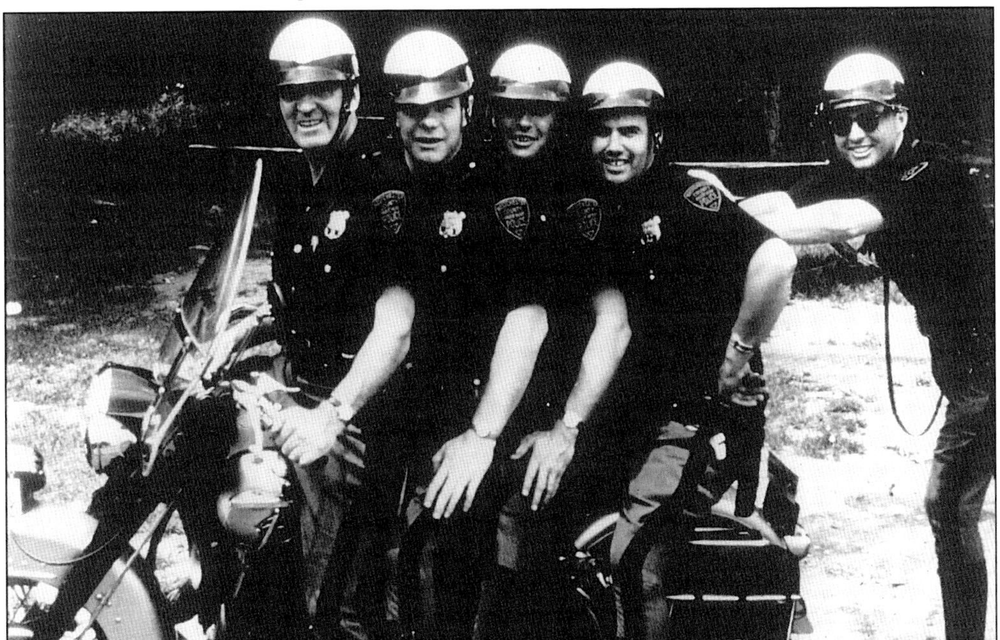

The camaraderie felt among the members of the Westchester County Parkway Police is evident in this c. 1960 photograph of a lighthearted moment showing, from left to right, Frank Harte, Samuel McBride, Thomas Ryan, Aldolph Tripoli, and Robert Trimpe. Parkway patrolmen were equipped with helmets around this time.

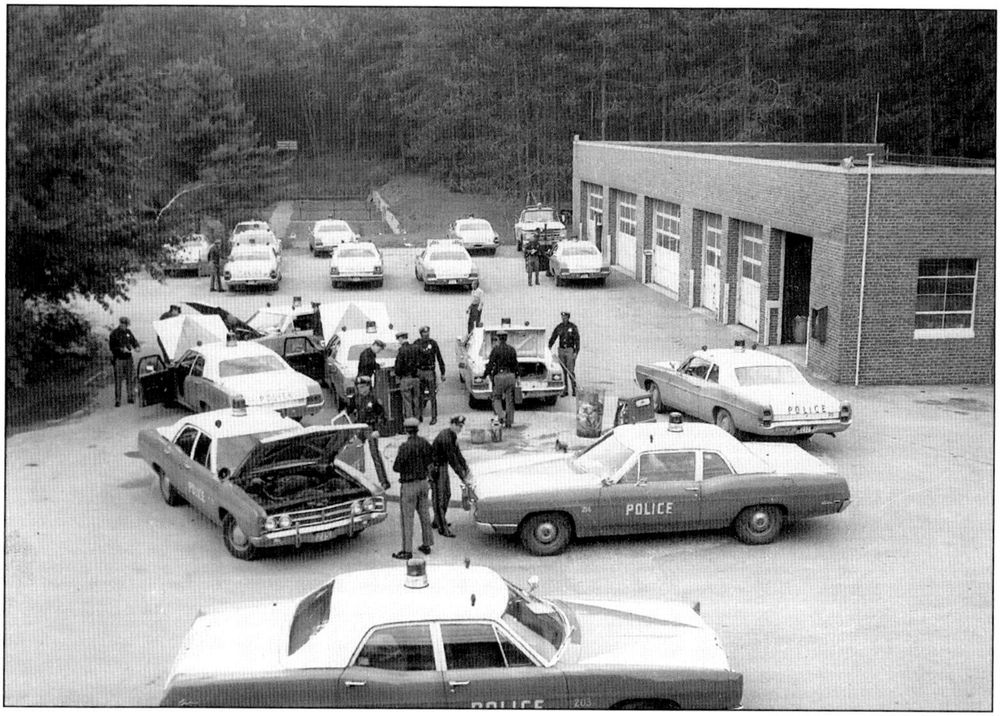

This view of the south side of the headquarters building in Hawthorne, taken in 1969, shows the former pistol range and the gas pumps mounted on a circular traffic island.

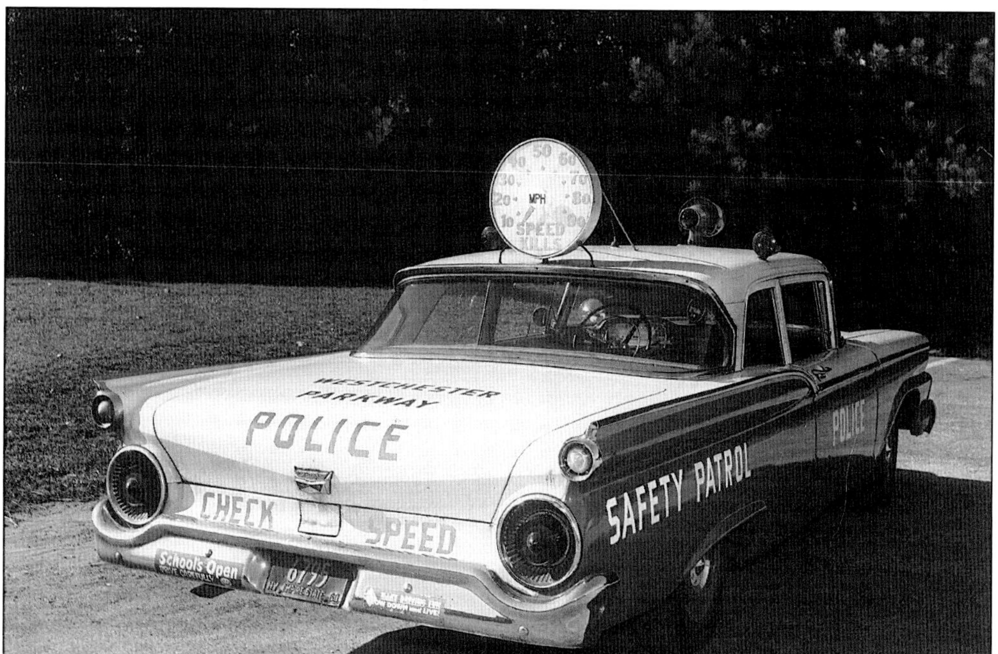

This 1959 Ford was equipped with a large exterior speedometer in an effort to make motorists more aware of their own speed. It was deployed in response to a motor vehicle accident that occurred on a Memorial Day weekend and resulted in deaths of seven people.

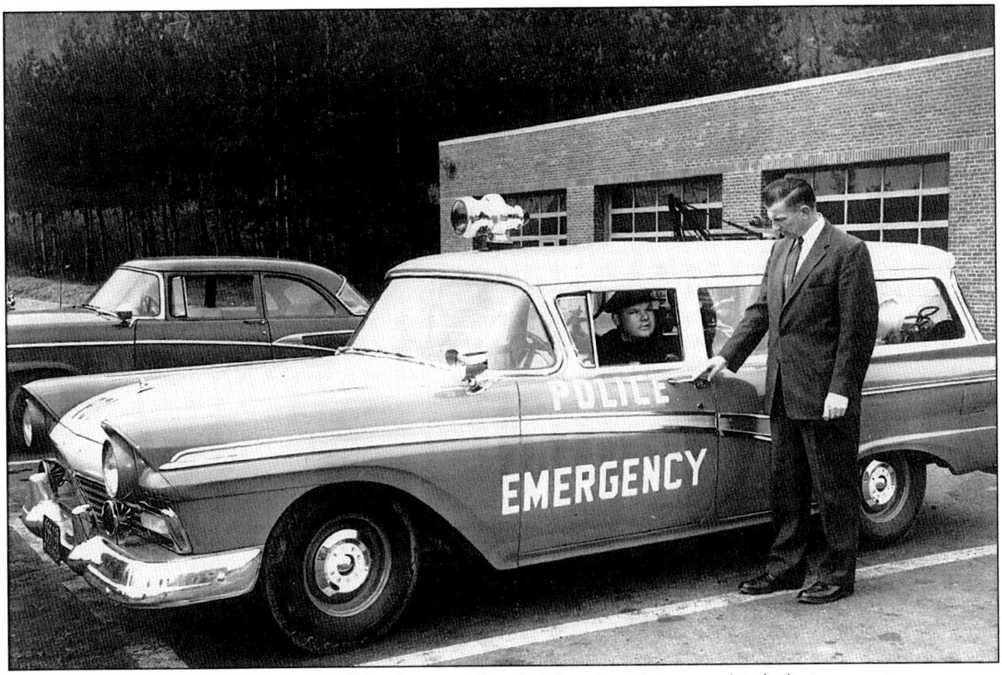

This photograph, taken *c.* 1957, shows Chief Marvin Ericson (right) inspecting a new emergency response vehicle. William Nelson (left) later became chief of the Westchester County Parkway Police.

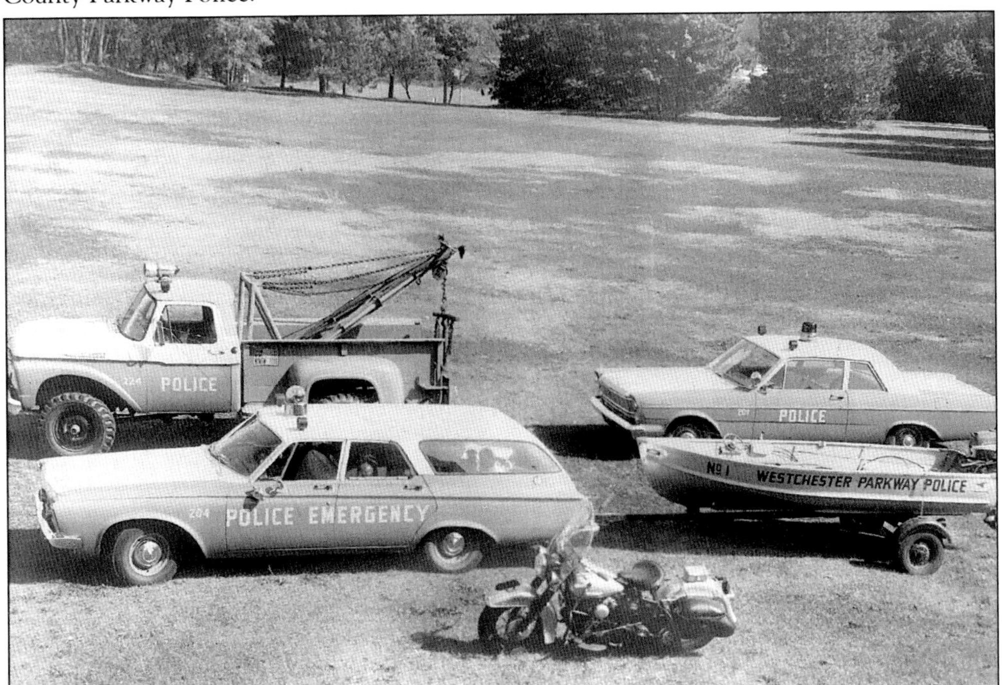

Some of the equipment used by the Westchester County Parkway Police is on display in this *c.* 1964 photograph. By this time, the department, due to the number of officers either killed or injured while operating motorcycles, had phased out motorcycle patrols.

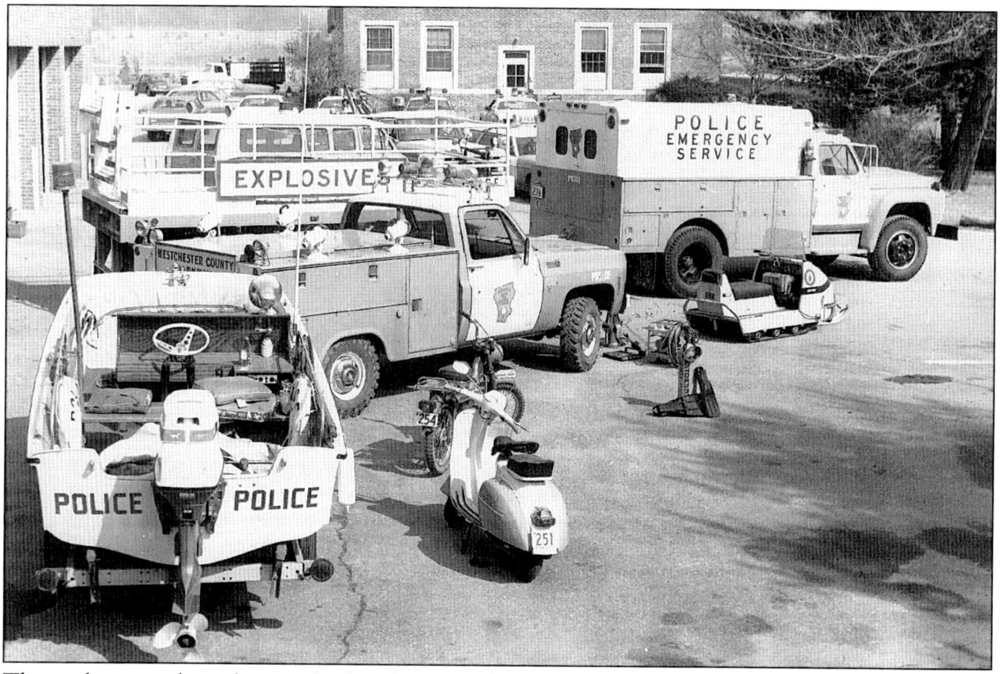

These photographs, taken at the headquarters building in Hawthorne in April 1978, show the wide variety of equipment in use by the department. The emergency service unit vehicles and bomb squad truck frequently responded to assist other jurisdictions.

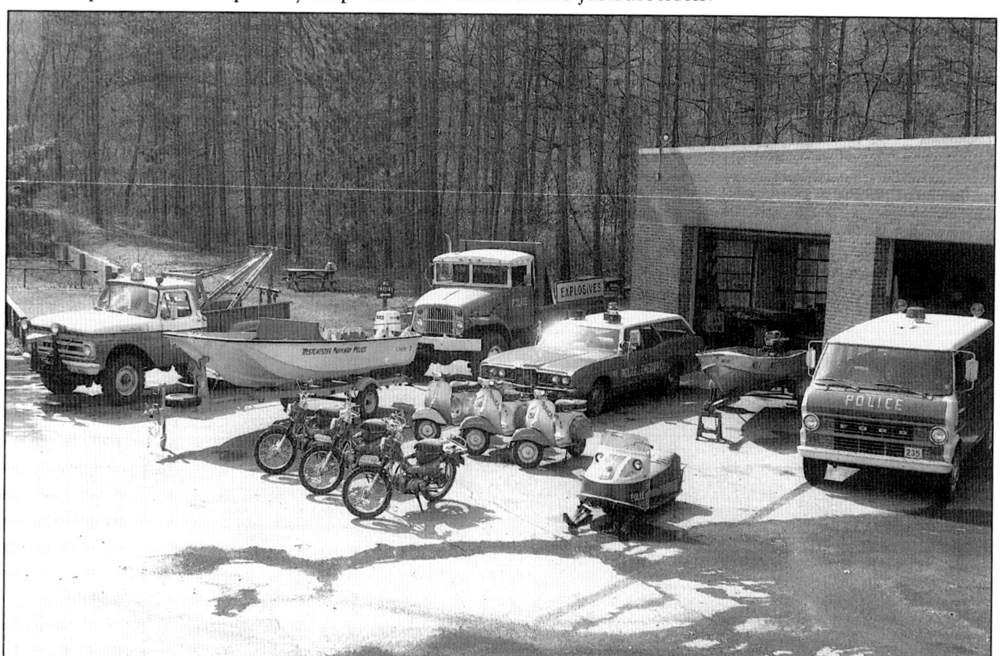

The emergency service vehicles were well equipped with modern extrication tools and well-trained officers, at a time when such equipment was not readily available in many areas of Westchester County.

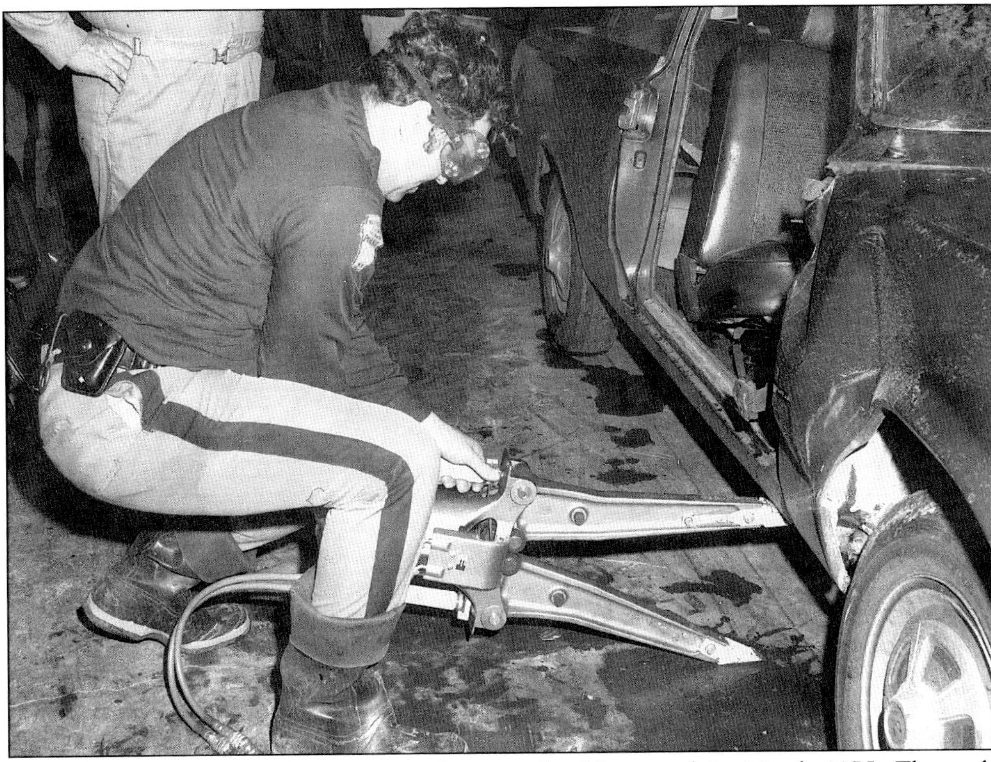

Officer George Graham demonstrates the use of a Hurst tool in March 1975. The early commitment that the Westchester County Parkway Police made in deploying such equipment on the county parkways saved numerous lives.

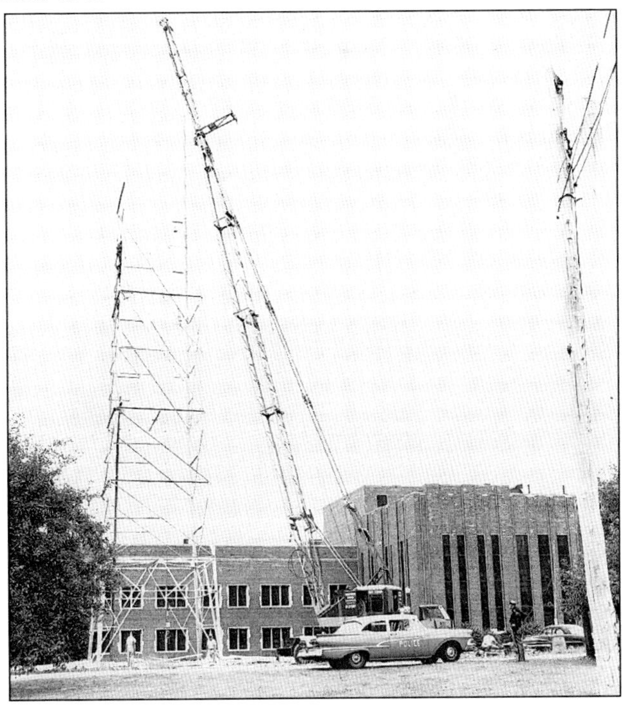

A radio tower was erected on the Grasslands Reservation adjacent to the county jail in order to improve radio communications in Westchester County. A parkway police officer observes the work in progress c. 1960.

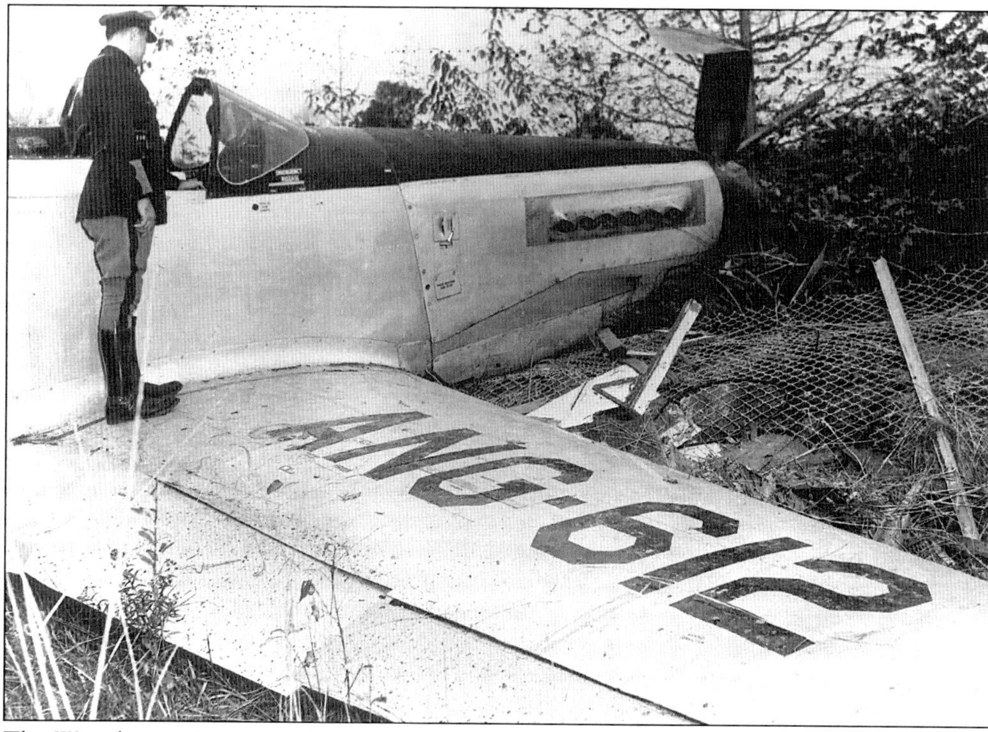

The Westchester County Parkway Police were called upon to respond to a number of aircraft accidents over the years. This accident involves a military aircraft that crashed at the Westchester County Airport on October 21, 1951.

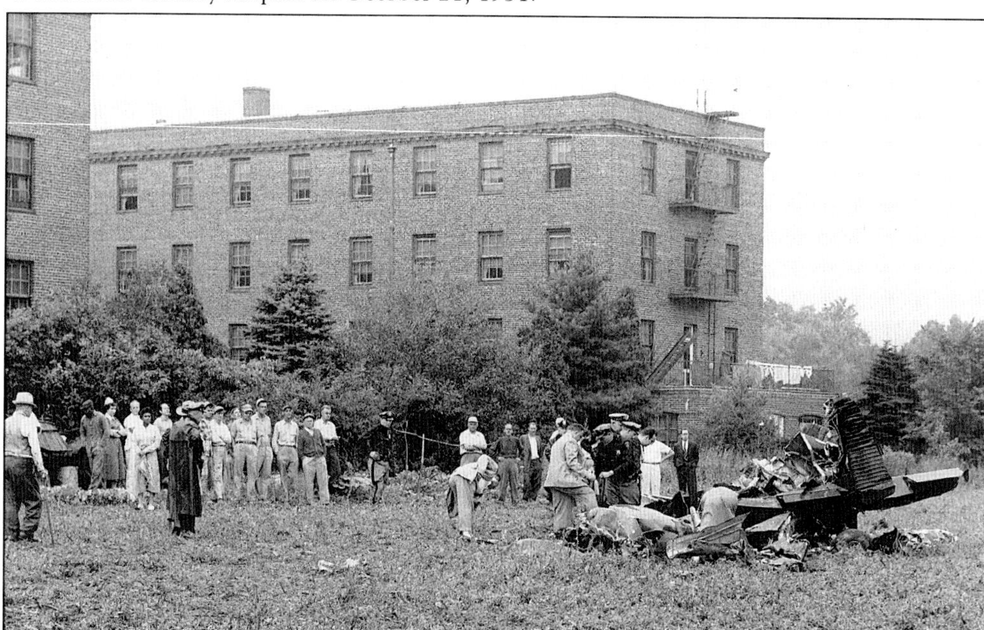

A later aircraft accident involved a Navion that crashed on the grounds of the Westchester County Medical Center on August 30, 1954. Westchester Hall, which was recently demolished to make room for the new children's hospital, is visible in the background.

Commissioner Orrie Kelly is seen examining new prisoner cells at the Westchester County Parkway Police headquarters in Hawthorne c. 1958. During the late 1950s and early 1960s, the commissioner of the parkway police maintained his office in the county office building in White Plains and the chief of the Westchester County Parkway Police managed the day-to-day affairs of the department from headquarters.

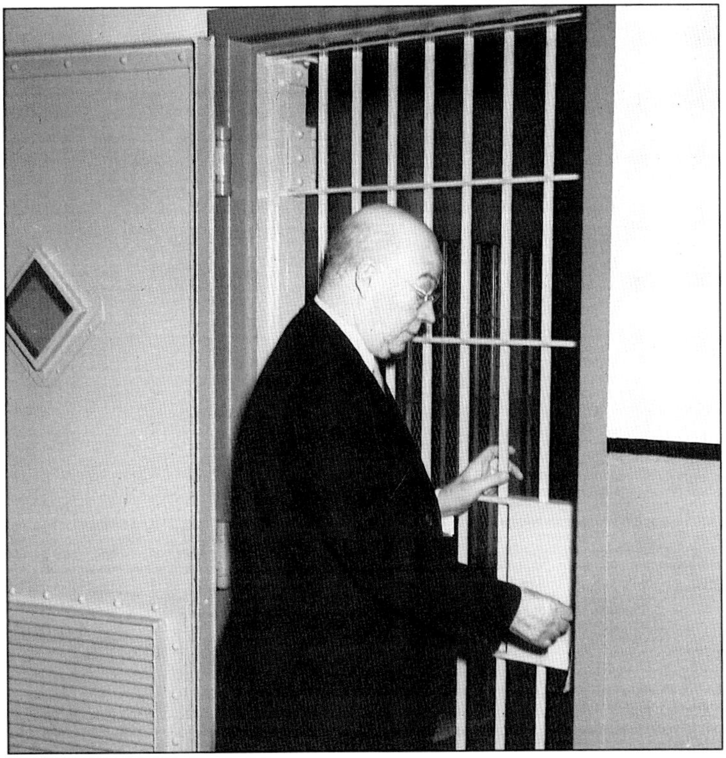

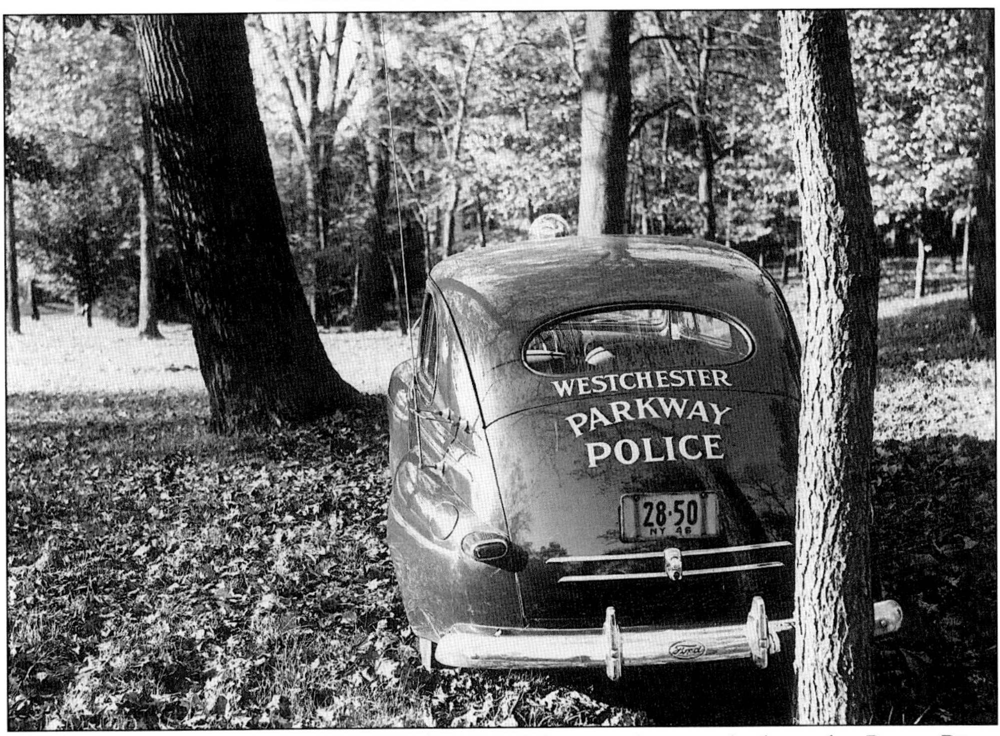

This Westchester Parkway Police Ford automobile was photographed on the Bronx River Parkway on October 21, 1946.

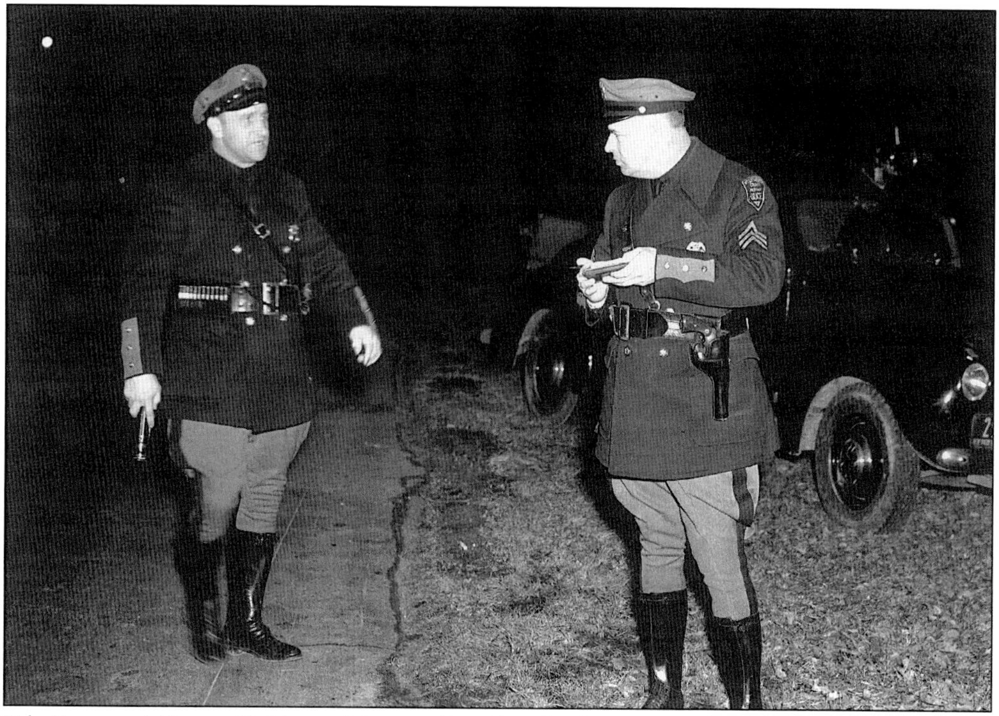

Ptl. Raymond Rouse (left) speaking to Sgt. Orville Perry *c.* 1930s photograph. Perry was appointed a park patrolman on May 9, 1927, and retired as commissioner of the parkway police in 1958.

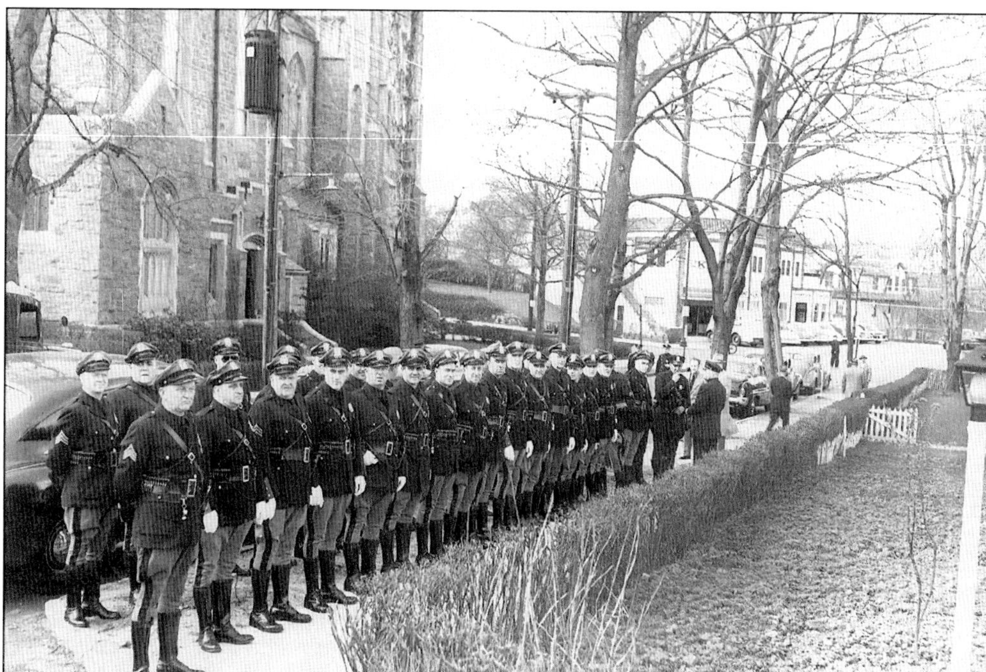

This group of Westchester County Parkway Police patrolmen was photographed in front of St. Joseph's Church on Kraft Avenue in Bronxville *c.*1950.

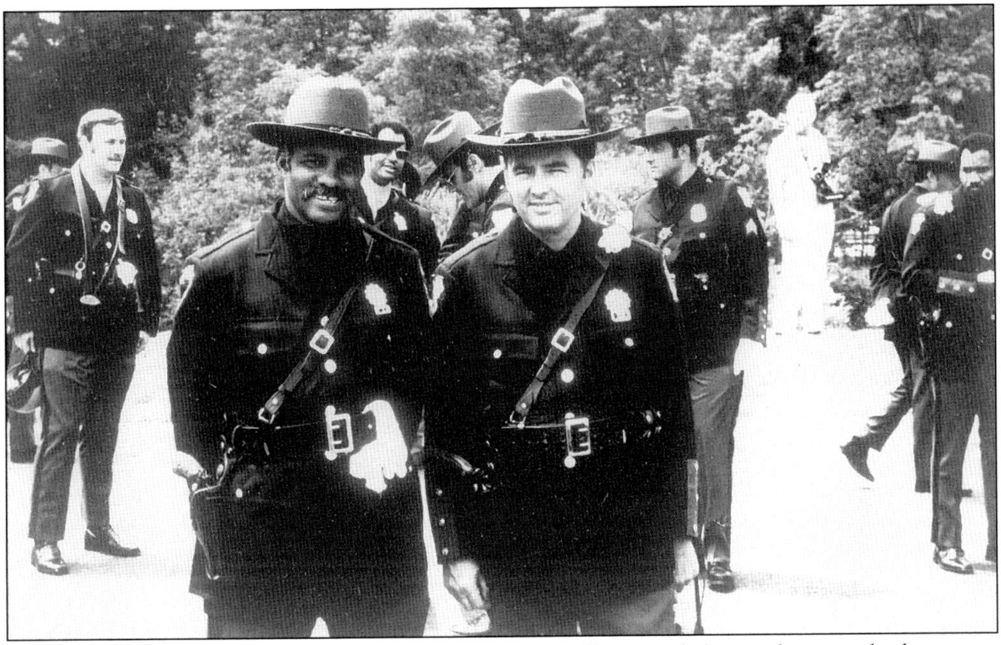

Dets. Clarence Holst (front left) and Robert Trimpe (front right) are photographed wearing Stetson hats.

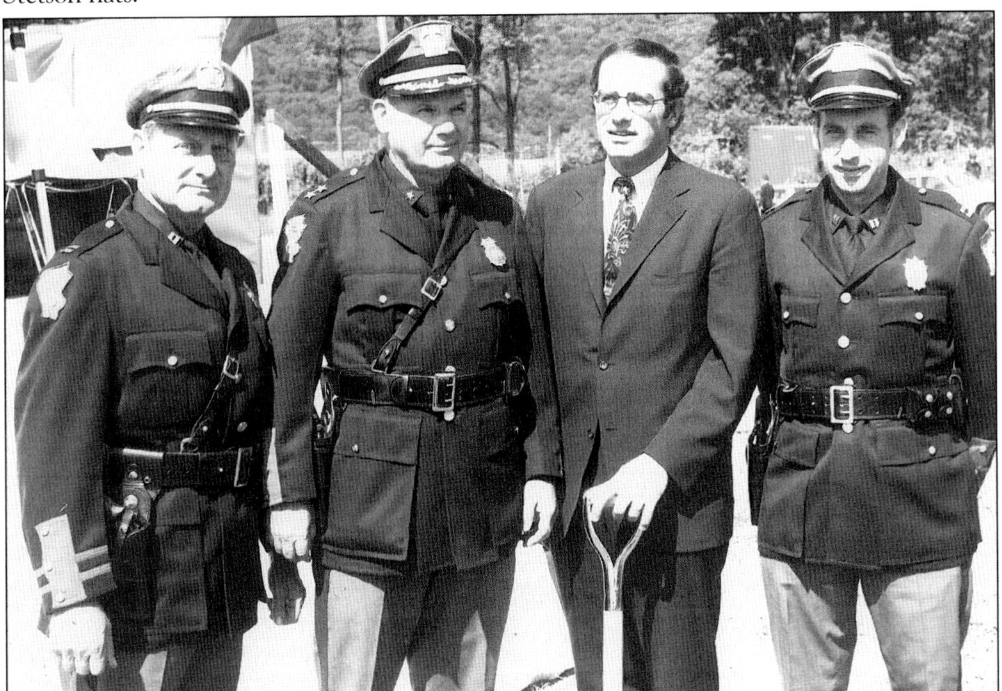

A groundbreaking ceremony for the Westchester County Police Academy at the Grasslands Reservation was held on September 16, 1975. Present at the groundbreaking ceremony are, from left to right, Capt. John Puchir; Chief William Nelson; Alfred DelBello, county executive; and Capt. Robert Wilson. The Westchester County Department of Public Safety continues to administer the Westchester County Police Academy.

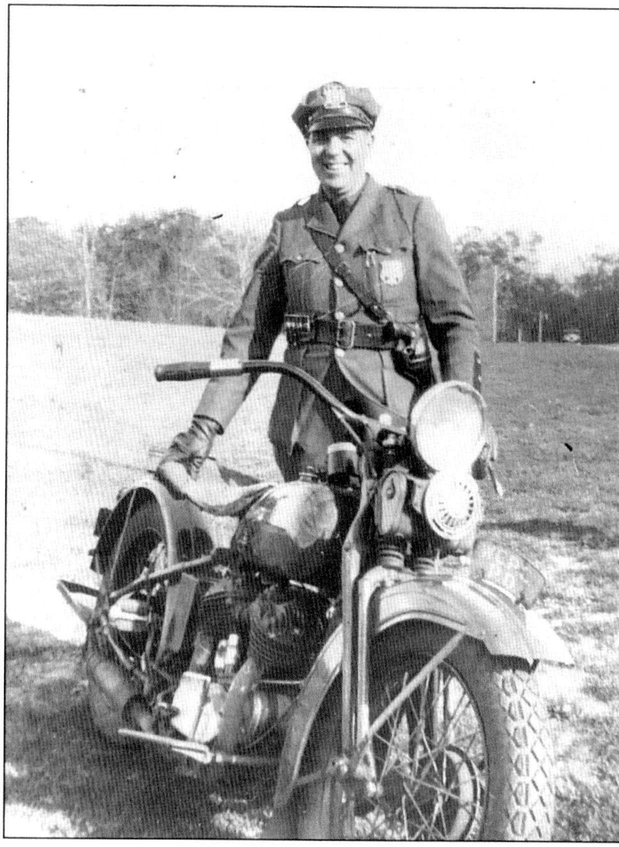

Manuel Borgos was 31 years old when he was appointed as a park patrolman on July 15, 1929. On June 23, 1938, he was seriously injured in a motor vehicle accident on Mill Road at Oakridge Place in Eastchester. He was taken to Lawrence Hospital, where he died, leaving behind a wife and child.

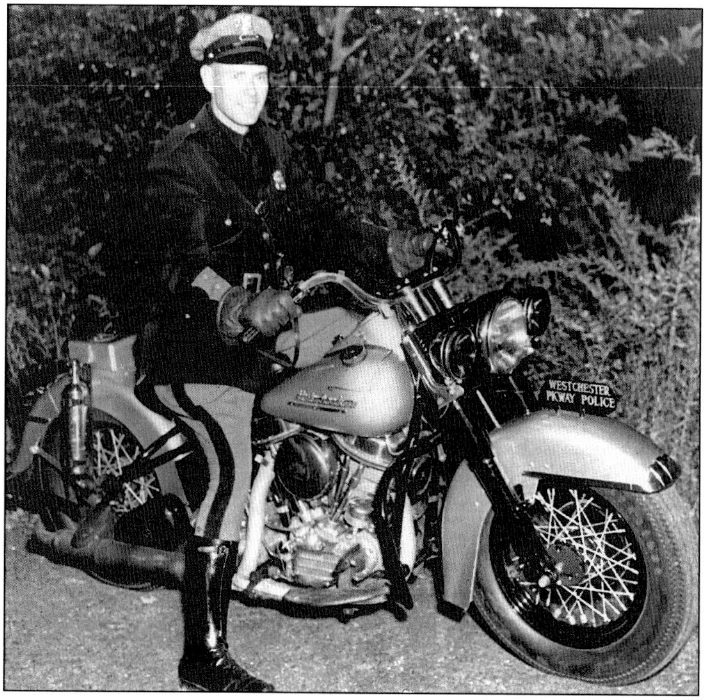

George Ruthven was appointed to the Westchester County Parkway Police on December 7, 1947. He had served as a pilot in the U.S. Army Air Force during World War II. He was 35 years old and a patrolman when he was killed in a motor vehicle accident on Westchester Avenue at Wards Lane in White Plains. He left behind a wife and two daughters, aged eight and four.

Three

The Westchester County Department of Public Safety: 1979–Present

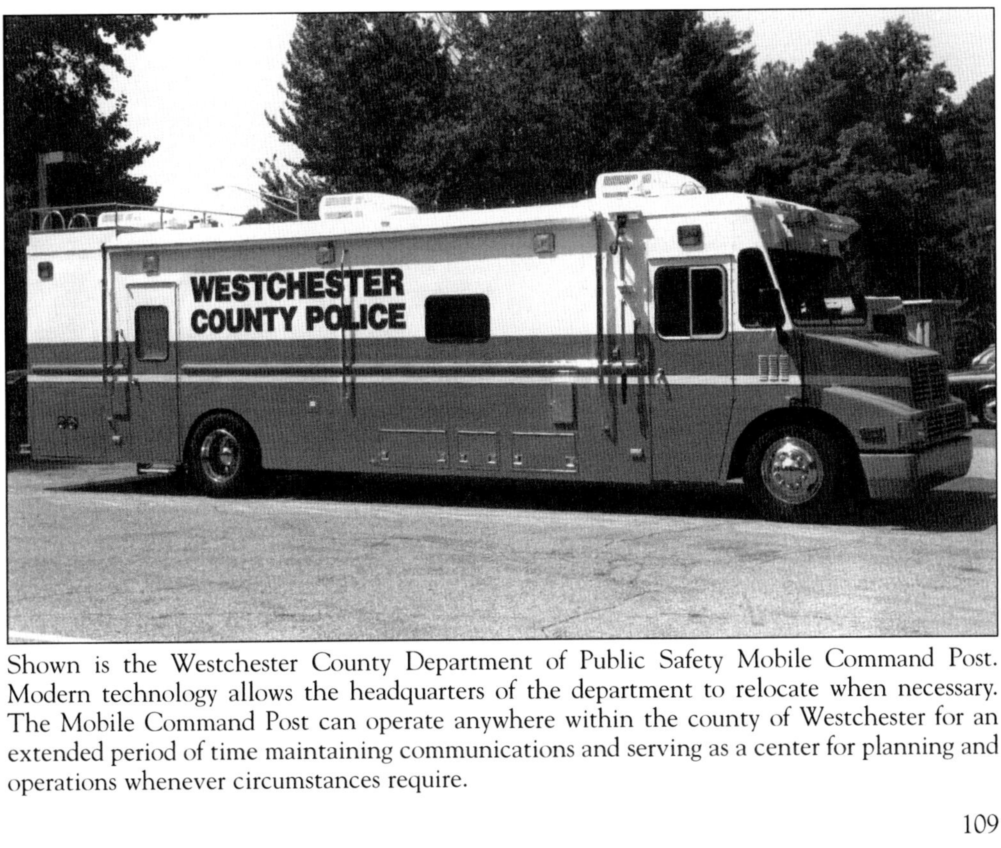

Shown is the Westchester County Department of Public Safety Mobile Command Post. Modern technology allows the headquarters of the department to relocate when necessary. The Mobile Command Post can operate anywhere within the county of Westchester for an extended period of time maintaining communications and serving as a center for planning and operations whenever circumstances require.

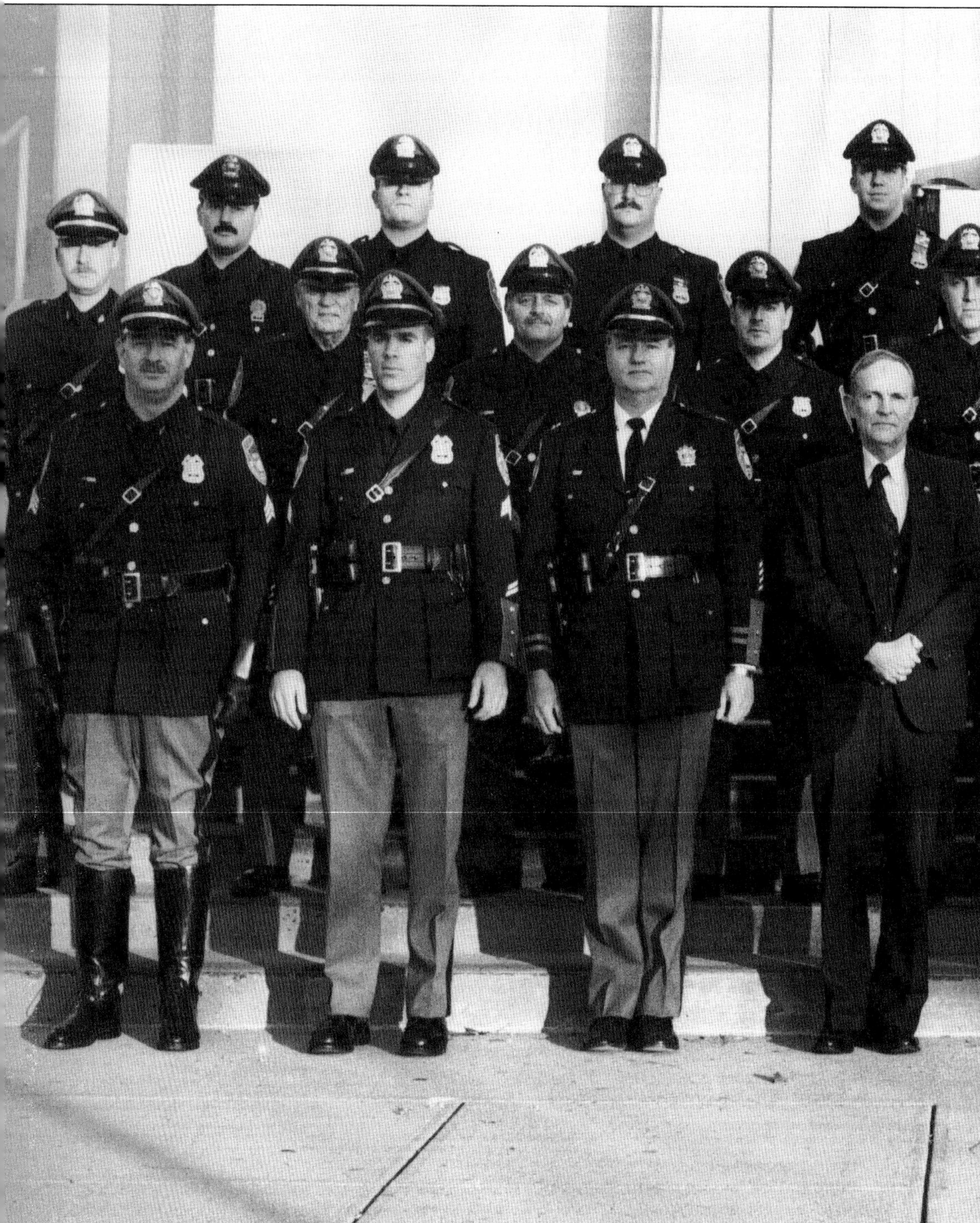

This portrait was taken in front of the Westchester County Center in White Plains in December 1998. Shown, from left to right, are the following: (front row) Sgt. Matthew Seman, Sgt. Frank J. Donovan, Capt. Martin McGlynn, Liam Murphy, Commissioner Louis S. D'Aliso, John Scamarzuo, Raymond Albanese, Sgt. Ralph Angeletta, and Det. Gary McGrath; (middle

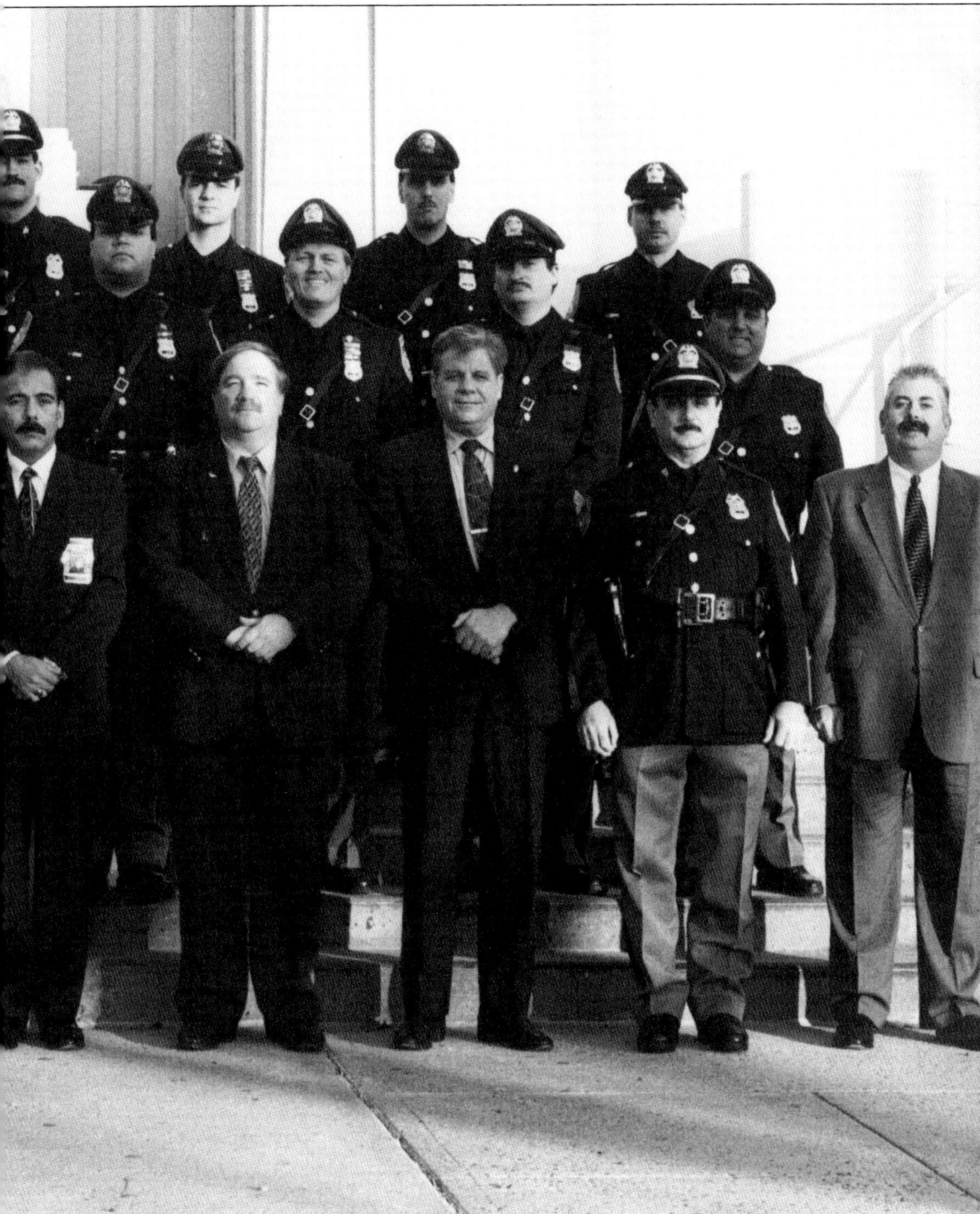

row) officer Dennis D'Alessio, Sgt. Joseph Reich, Det. Dolph Tutoni, and officers Michael Grossi, William Johnson, Eric Facey, Robert Brown, John Lodge, and Carl Eberle; (back row) Det. Roger Piccirilli, officers Edward Reich, Peter Farrell, and Steven Koehler, Sgt. Michael Lavin, officers Charles Geraci and Frank Tirri, and Det. Thaddeus Polant.

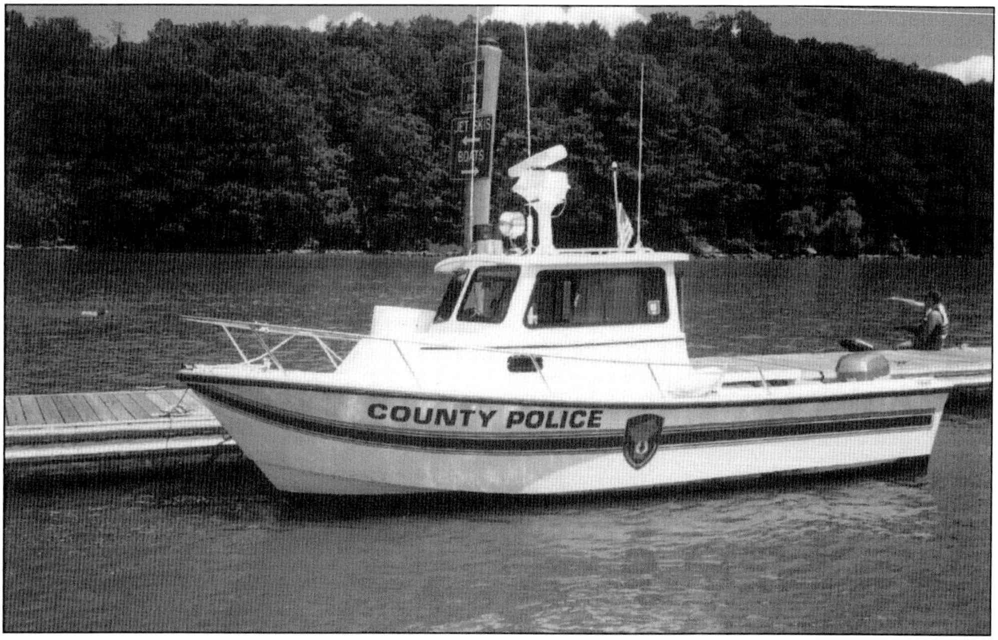

The Westchester County Department of Public Safety maintains a large number of specialized units to respond to incidents for which the department is primarily responsible and to assist other jurisdictions within and adjacent to Westchester County. The Westchester County Department of Public Safety Marine Patrol actively patrols the Hudson River during the boating season.

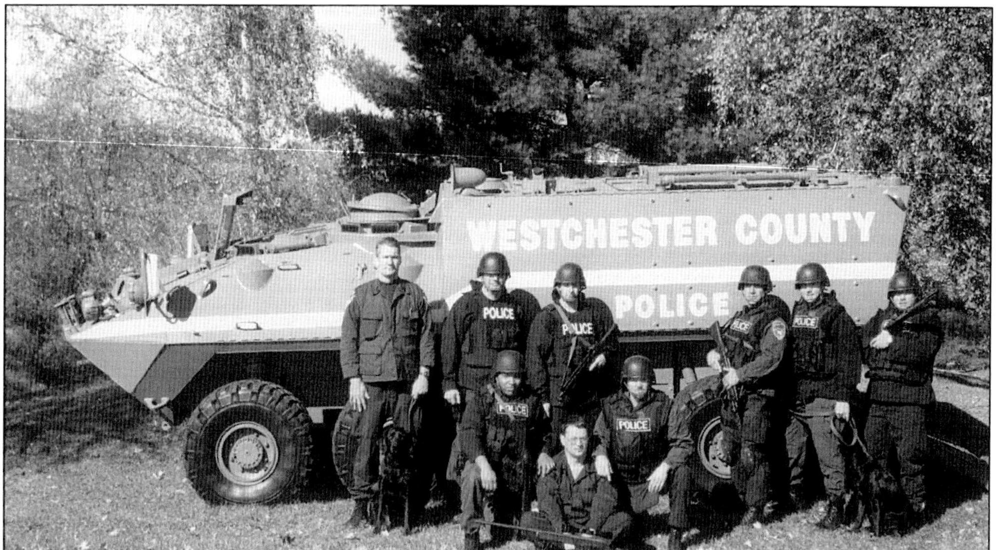

The Westchester County Department of Public Safety Special Response Team is equipped with tactical weapons as well as a light-armored vehicle. The light-armored vehicle can be used to protect department members who are engaged in high-risk operations. The officers are, from left to right, Sgt. Richard Daubman with canine Simon, Sgt. Michael Dowd, officer Michael Samuel, Det. Vincent Antonecchia, officer David Hecker, Lt. John Hodges, Sgt. James Luciano, officer Daniel Langford with canine Pretzel, and officer Richard DeMichael.

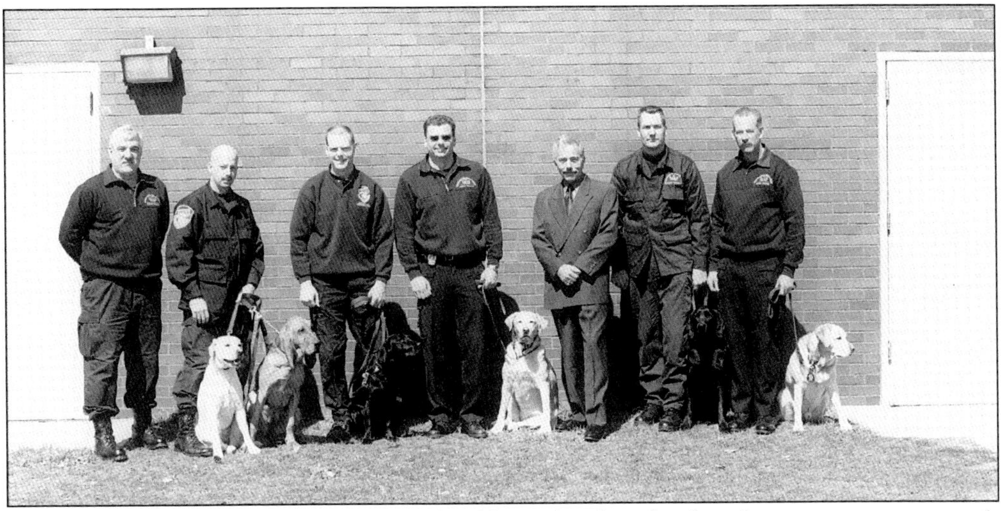

The Westchester County Department of Public Safety has developed a canine program with dogs trained to search for people, explosives, and illicit drugs. The canine units assist patrolmen in the regular course of their duties and they also take part in operations involving facility security and dignitary protection. Like other department resources, the services of the canine units are available to all local and neighboring police jurisdictions. The department members are, from left to right, Capt. Paul Stasaitis, officer Mitchell Serlin with canines Winnie and Gracie, officer Daniel Langford with canine Pretzel, Det. Robert Outhouse with canine Amy, Commissioner Louis S. D'Aliso, Sgt. Richard Daubman with canine Simon, and Det. Donald Gray with canine Brant.

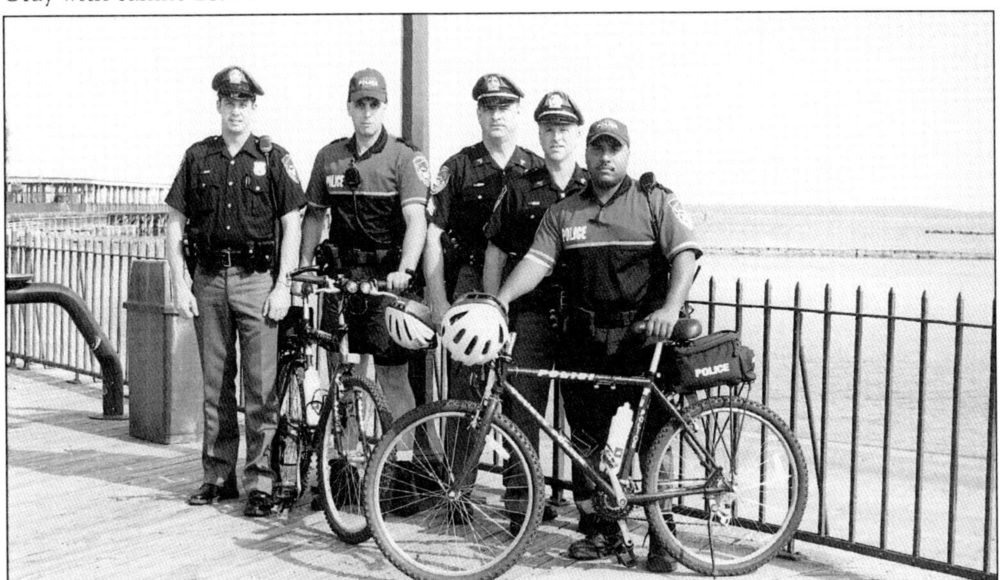

Community-based patrols are conducted throughout the year, but increase dramatically during the summer months, when the Westchester County parks experience peak visitation. The precinct at Playland Park is staffed continually from Memorial Day to Labor Day and at other times as conditions require. Some of the personnel assigned to the Playland precinct during the summer of 2001 are, from left to right, officer Edward Kelch, Det. Frank Tirri, Sgt. Matthew Seman, Sgt. John Krippel, and officer Khalid McClendon.

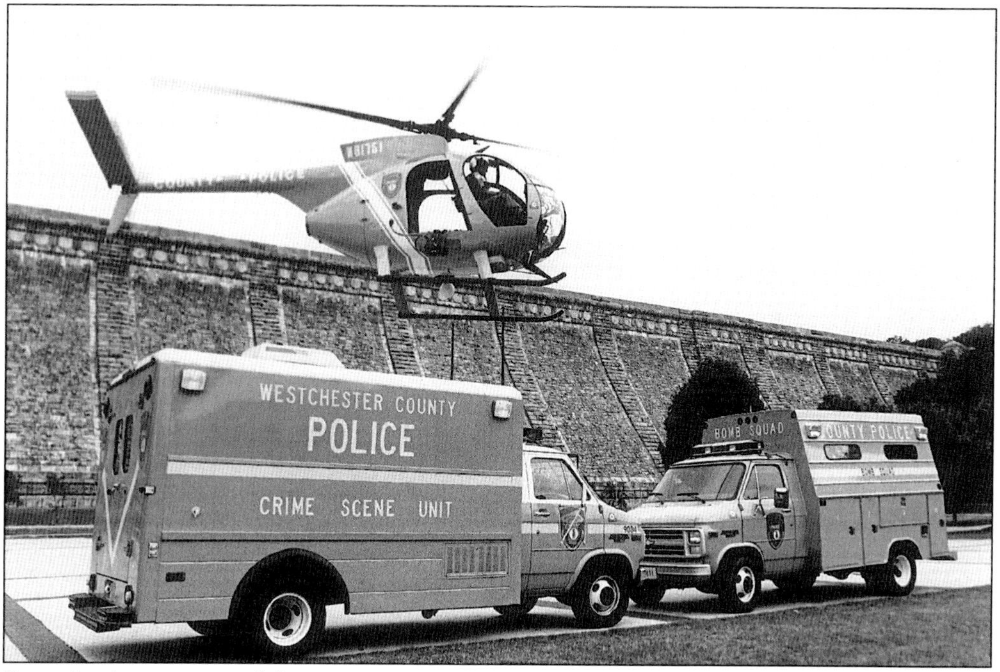

Specialized equipment of the crime scene unit, aviation unit, and bomb squad is photographed on the plaza in front of the Kensico Dam in Valhalla. All of the personnel assigned to these units are well trained and available to respond anywhere within the county on short notice.

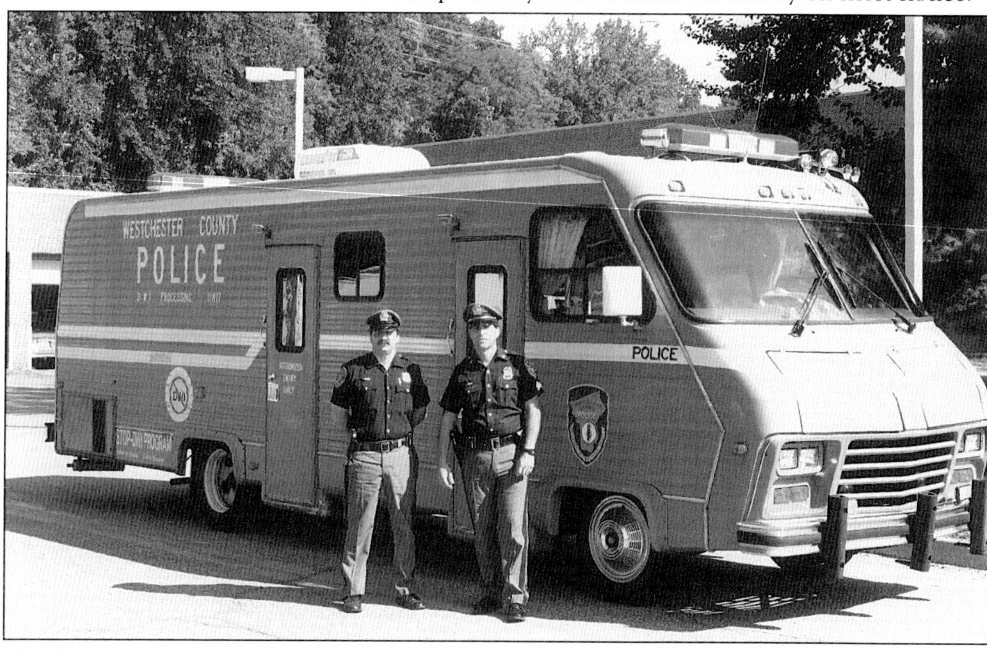

The Westchester County Department of Public Safety has taken part in and supported Stop DWI programs for many years. While some programs focus on education, others focus on enforcement. The mobile DWI (driving while intoxicated) processing vehicle seen here has been used to support DWI roadblocks throughout Westchester County. The officers standing in front of the vehicle are Michael Susi (left) and Sgt. Bruce Bellom.

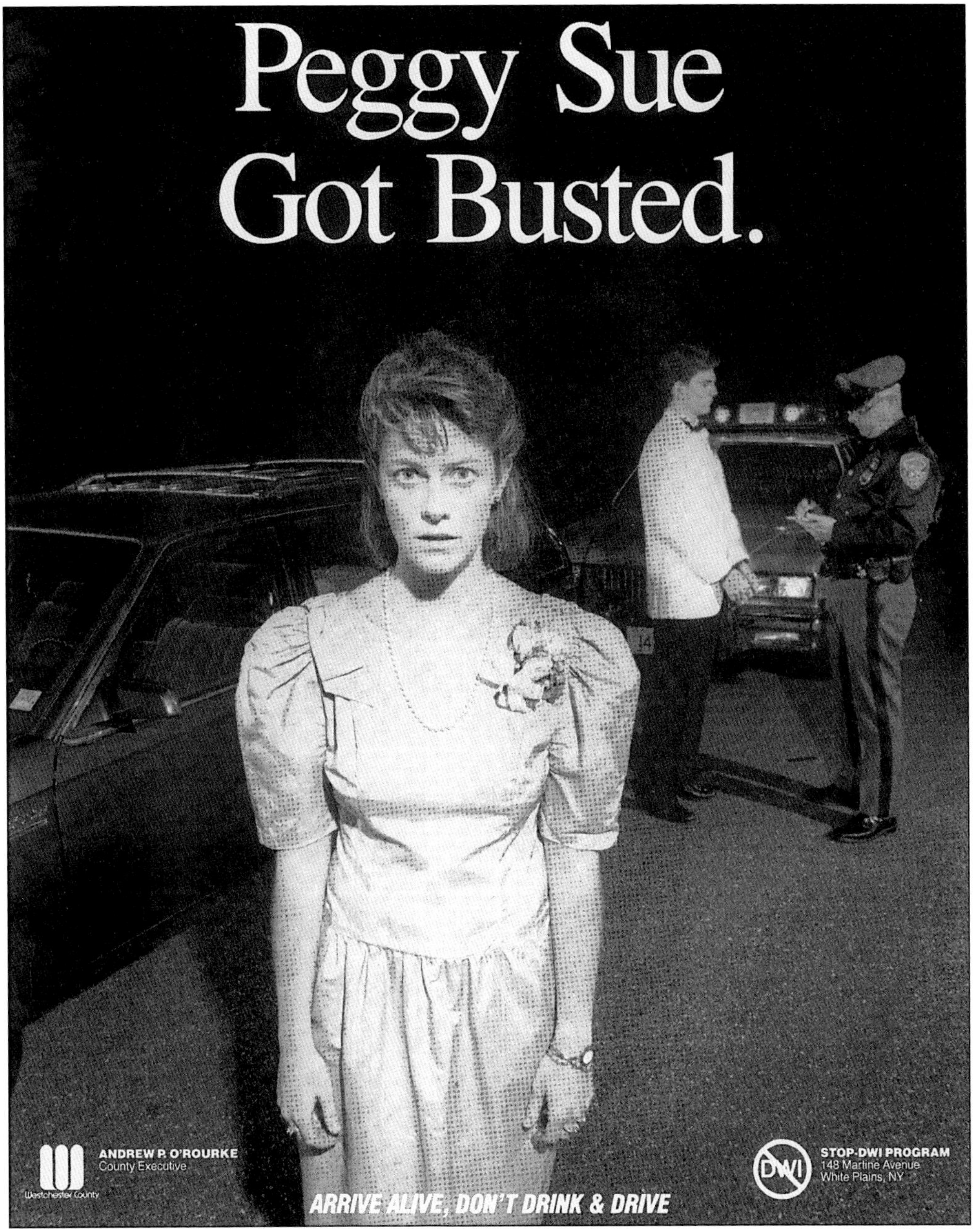

Support for Stop DWI programs has also included the production and distribution of promotional material, such as the poster seen above entitled, "Peggy Sue Got Busted." The models who participated in this project are, from left to right, Meegan Cassidy, Kier DeLeo, and officer Donald McArthur.

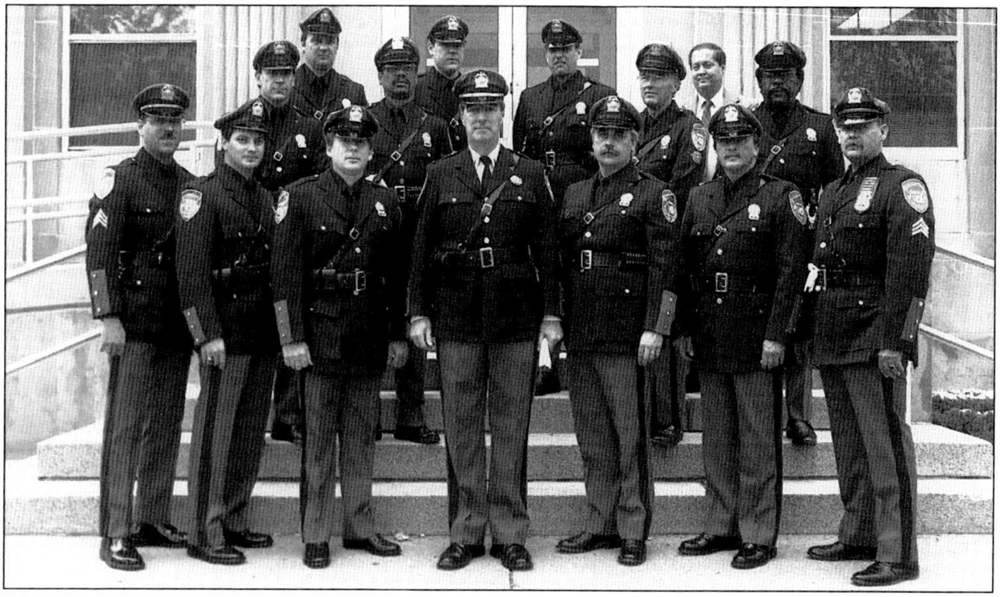

This portrait of the Westchester County Department of Public Safety General Investigations Unit was taken in front of headquarters in May 1987. Shown, from left to right, are the following: (front row) Sgt. Louis Beniamino, Dets. Thomas Gleason and Russell Lowenstein, Lt. John Calvert, Dets. Dennis Zack and Kenneth Cowan, and Sgt. Paul Grutzner; (middle row) Dets. Michael DeRosa, James Parker, Robert Trimpe, and Zion McKenzie; (back row) Dets. Brian Mahelsky, William Rehm, James Bentivenga, and John Gallagher.

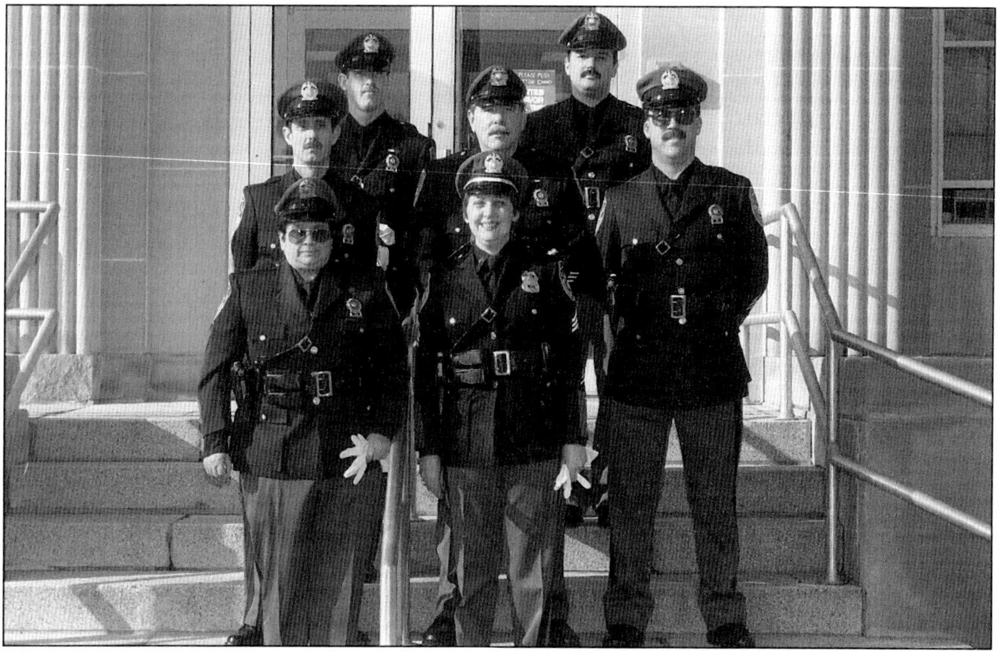

This portrait shows the members of the Westchester County Department of Public Safety Crime Scene and Identification Unit in front of headquarters c. 1987. They are, from left to right, Dets. Gloria Burgess, John Peters, and Patrick Mulligan, Sgt. Lucille DiBullo, and Dets. William Mackey, Roger Piccirilli, and Daniel Rice.

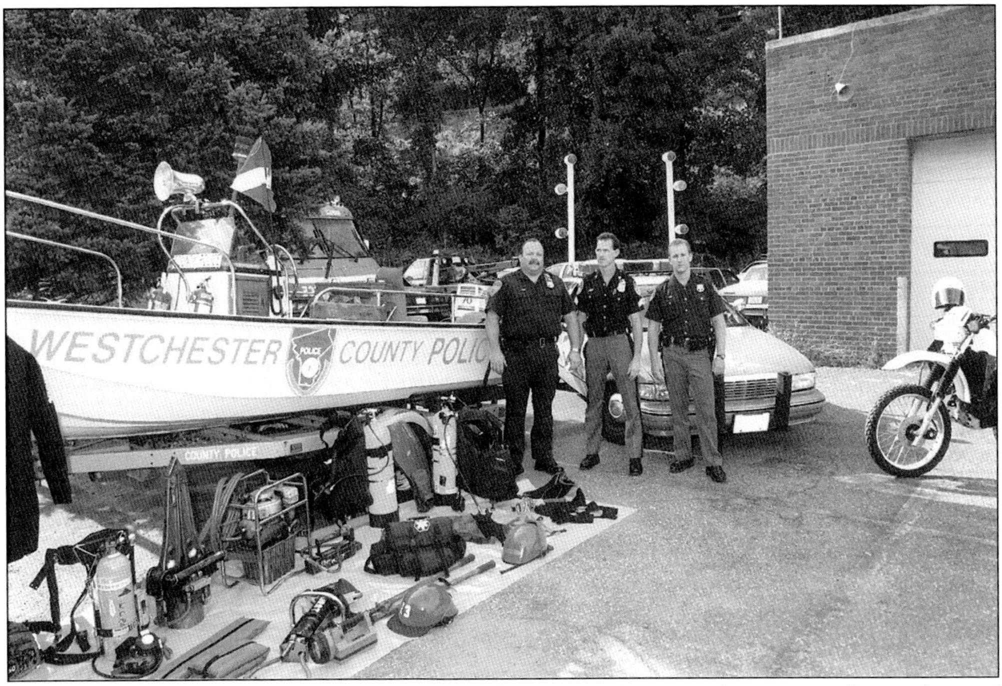

Dennis Suarino, Sgt. Patrick Mulligan, and Vincent Antonnechia were all members of the Westchester County Department of Public Safety Emergency Services Unit when this photograph was taken c. 1991. On display is the unit's rescue and diving equipment.

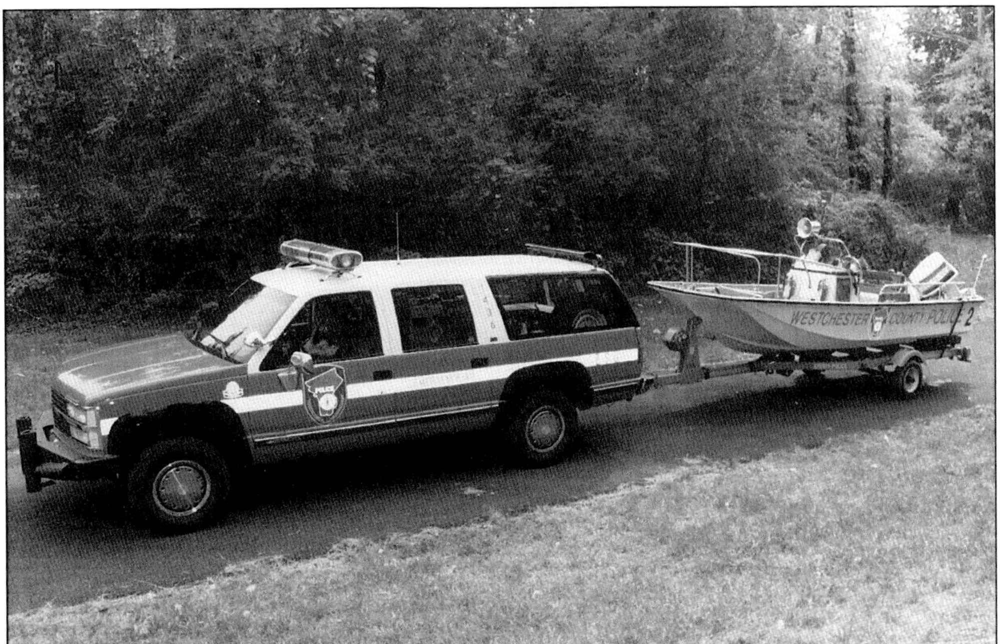

This vehicle with a boat in tow is ready to respond when needed by the Westchester County Department of Public Safety Emergency Services Unit.

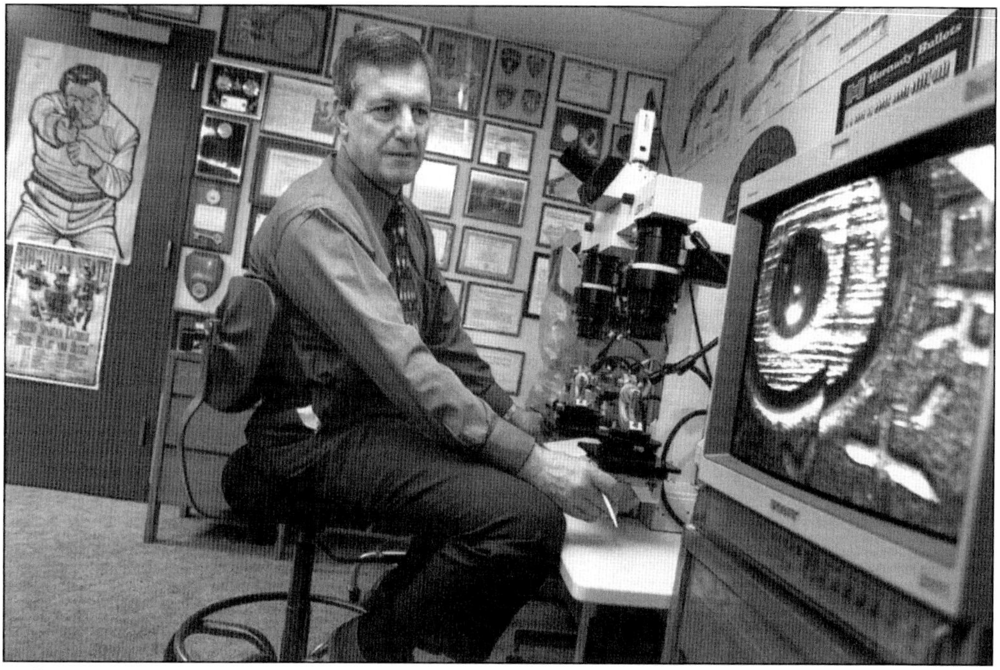

Ballistics examiner Frank Nicolosi uses a comparison microscope to examine two shell casings to determine whether they were fired from the same gun. The department performs ballistics analysis for all of the police agencies within Westchester County.

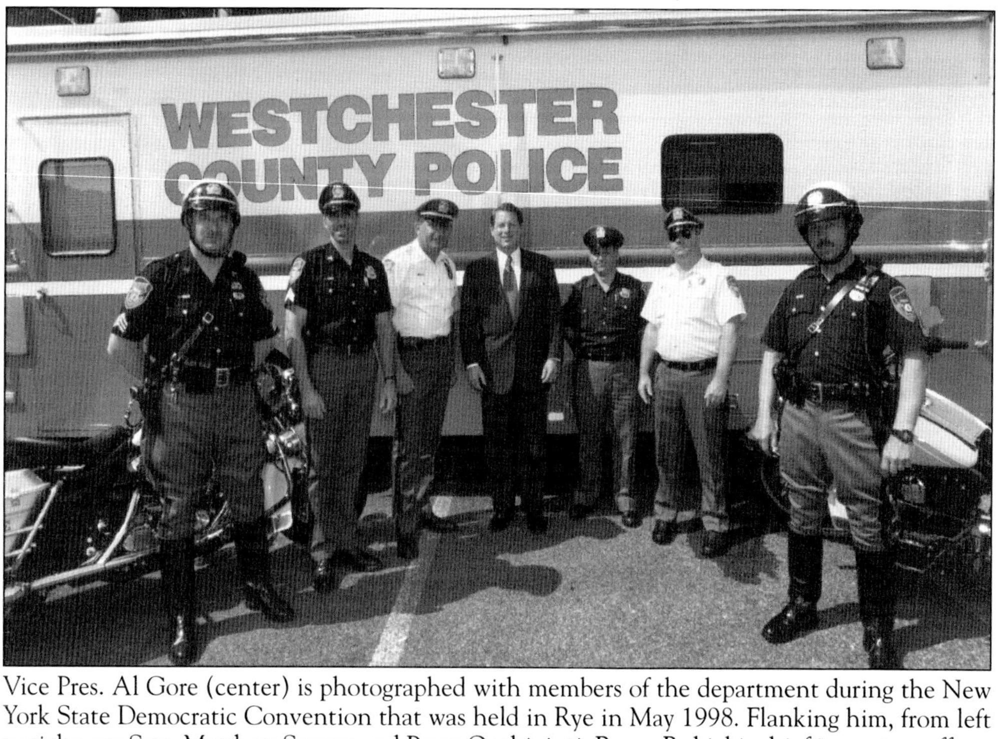

Vice Pres. Al Gore (center) is photographed with members of the department during the New York State Democratic Convention that was held in Rye in May 1998. Flanking him, from left to right, are Sgts. Matthew Seman and Peter Occhipinti; Roger Rokicki, chief inspector; officer Peter Rubeo; Lt. Robert O'Connor; and officer Timothy Joyce.

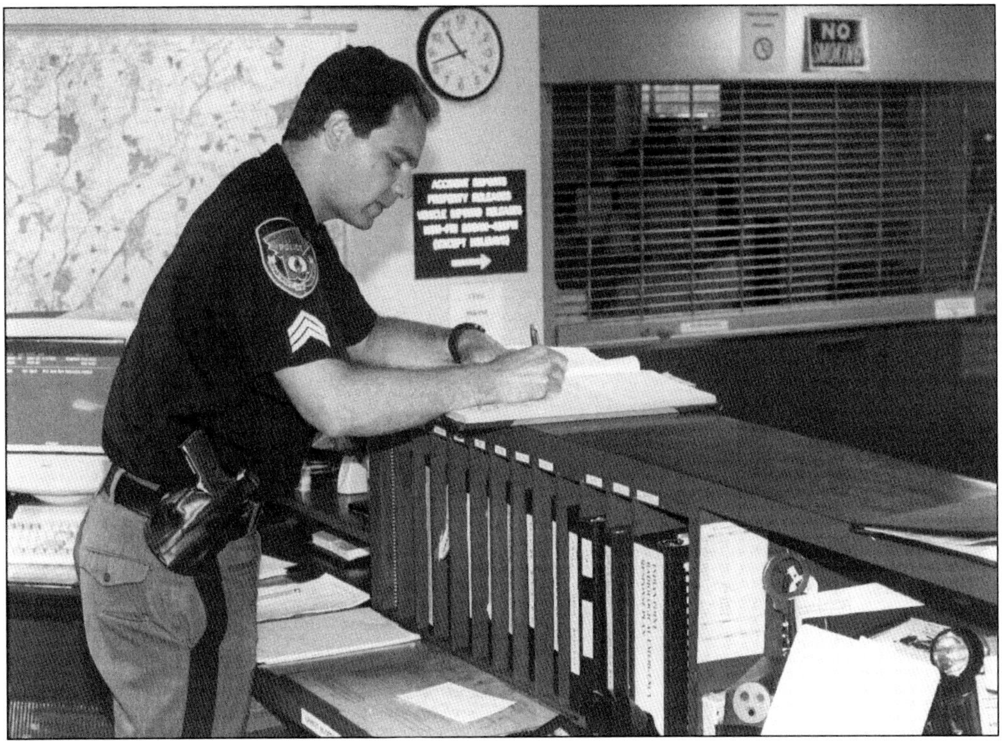

Sgt. Charles Geraci stands at the desk area in headquarters in July 2001. While on duty, the desk officer has overall responsibility for all department activity.

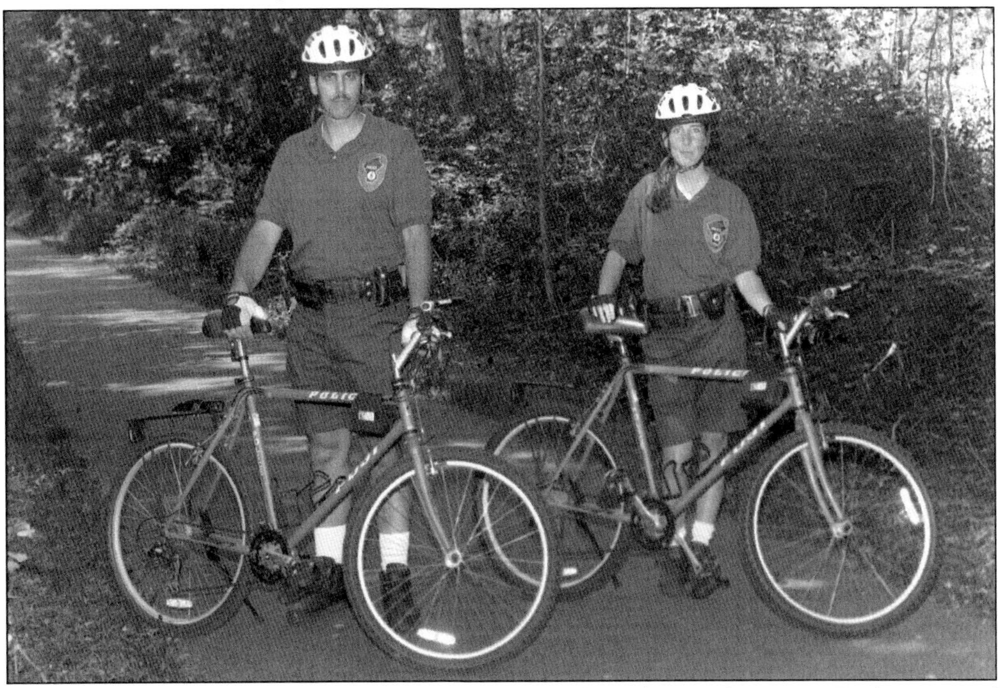

Officers Frank Tirri and Margaret Nardelli are shown along the North County Trailway, one of the many Westchester County trails, in May 1997.

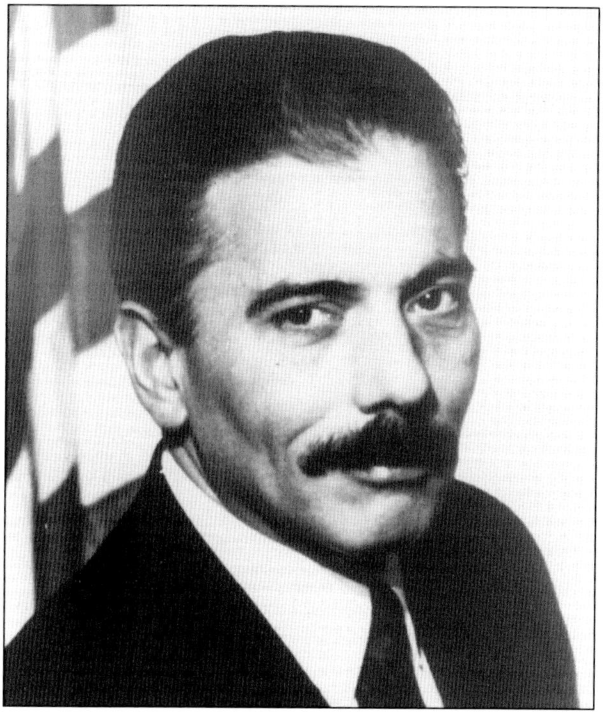

Louis S. D'Aliso (left) was appointed commissioner of the Westchester County Department of Public Safety on January 14, 1996, by Andrew O'Rourke, county executive. D'Aliso joined the Mount Vernon Police Department as a police officer in March 1968. In 1970, he transferred to the Ardsley Police Department, where he advanced through the ranks and was promoted to chief in 1988.

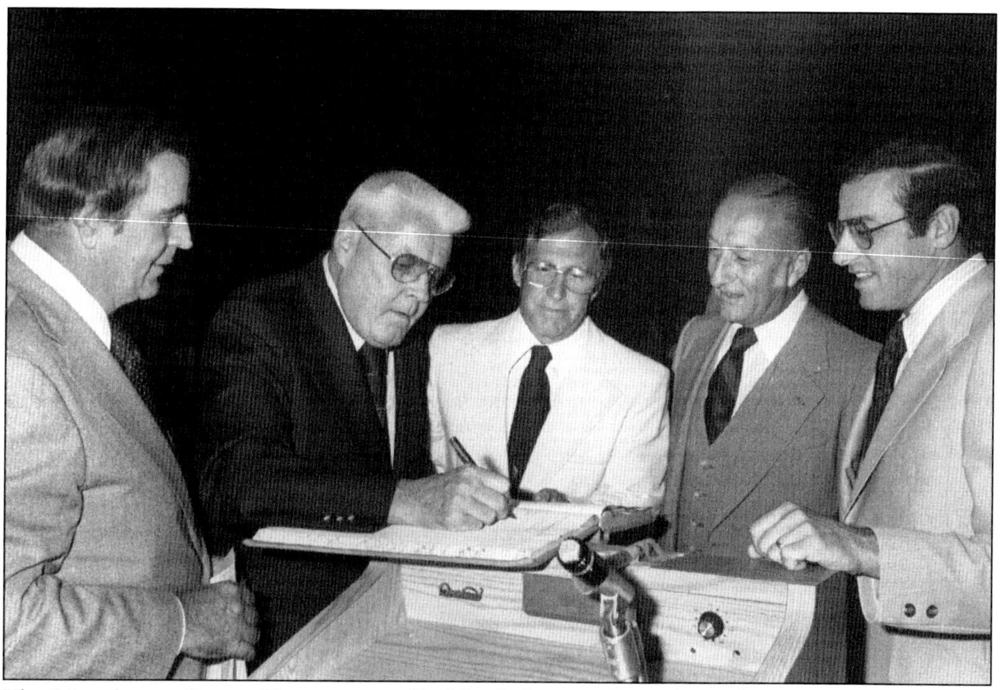

The Westchester County Department of Public Safety was formed on July 1, 1979, by the merger of the sheriff's department with the parkway police. On the left, Sheriff Thomas Delaney and Under Sheriff John O'Brien represent the sheriff's department. On the right, Alfred DelBello, county executive, and Chief Carlo Fulgenzi represent the parkway police at the ceremony in the Westchester County Courthouse in White Plains.

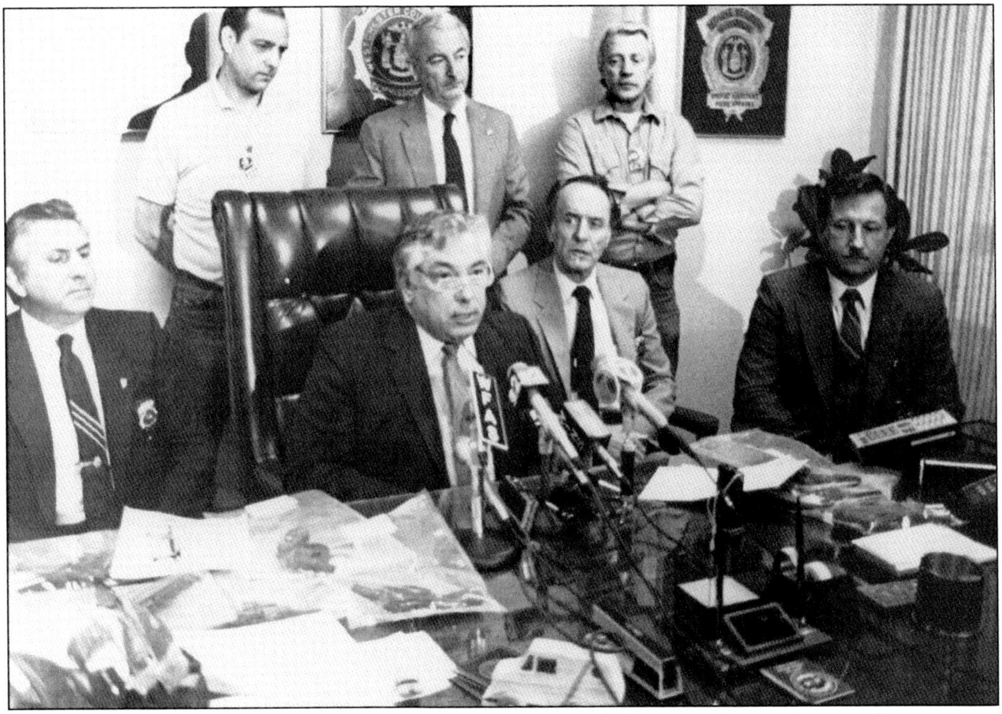

Anthony Mosca (front center) served as commissioner of the Westchester County Department of Public Safety from 1984 to 1993.

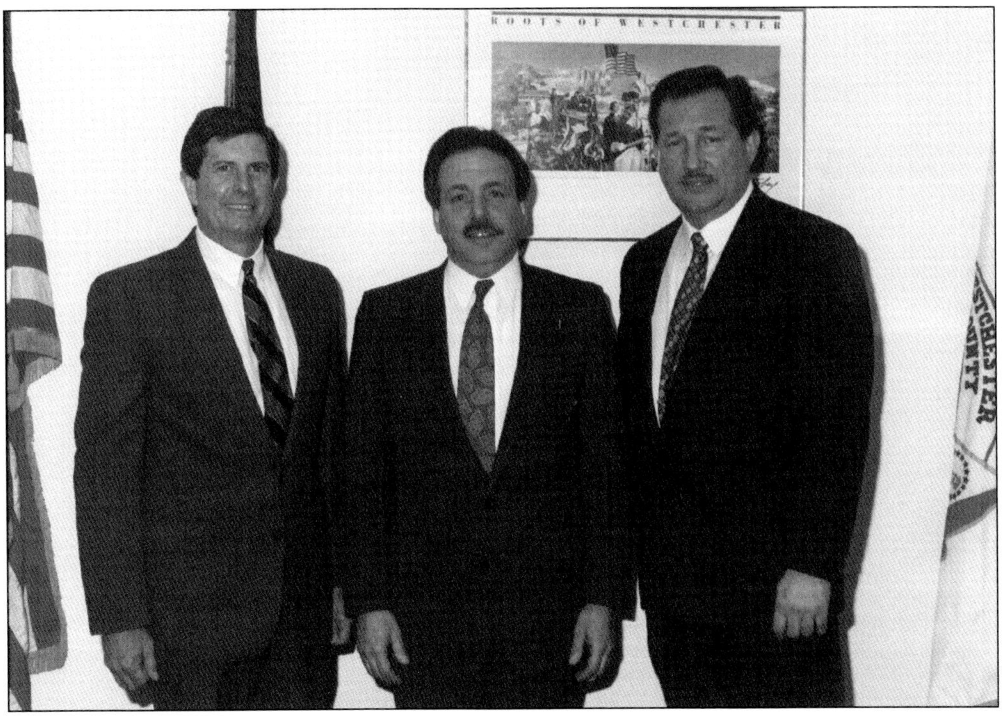

Ernest Colaneri was commissioner of the department from 1993 to 1996. He is seen here flanked by Thomas Vinton (left), deputy commissioner, and Roger Rokicki, chief inspector.

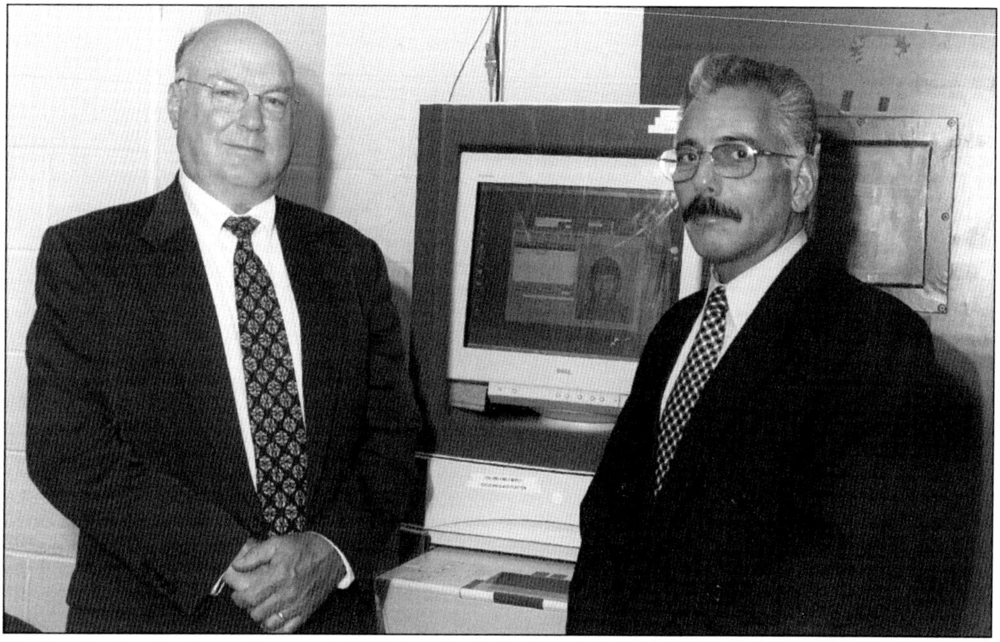

Under the leadership of Louis S. D'Aliso (right), the department implemented a county-wide electronic arrest booking system that makes possible the electronic capture, transmission, and storage of information related to a subject's arrest, including fingerprints and photographs. With D'Aliso at the June 26, 2000 dedication ceremony for the system is Clyde DeWeese, New York State Division of Criminal Justice Services deputy commissioner.

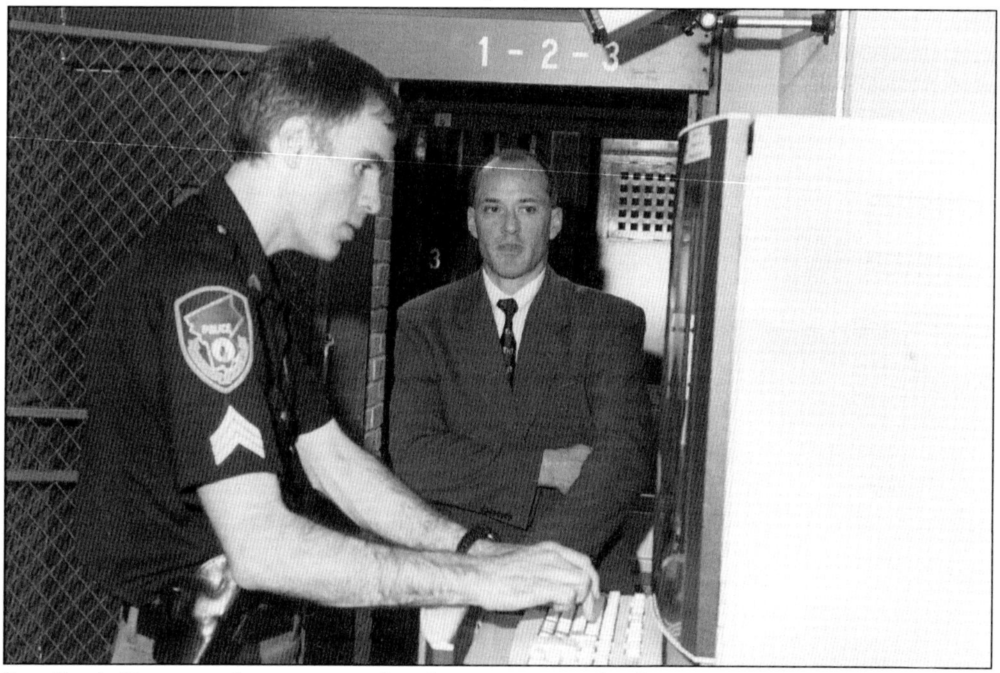

Sgt. Frank Donovan demonstrates the electronic arrest booking system to Thomas Meyer of the New York State Division of Criminal Justice Services on June 26, 2000, at public safety headquarters in Hawthorne.

At ceremonies held on April 10, 1999, to mark the start of Department of Public Safety police patrols in the town of Cortlandt, are, from left to right, Louis S. D'Aliso, commissioner; unidentified; Andrew Spano, county executive; and Linda Puglisi, Cortlandt Manor town supervisor.

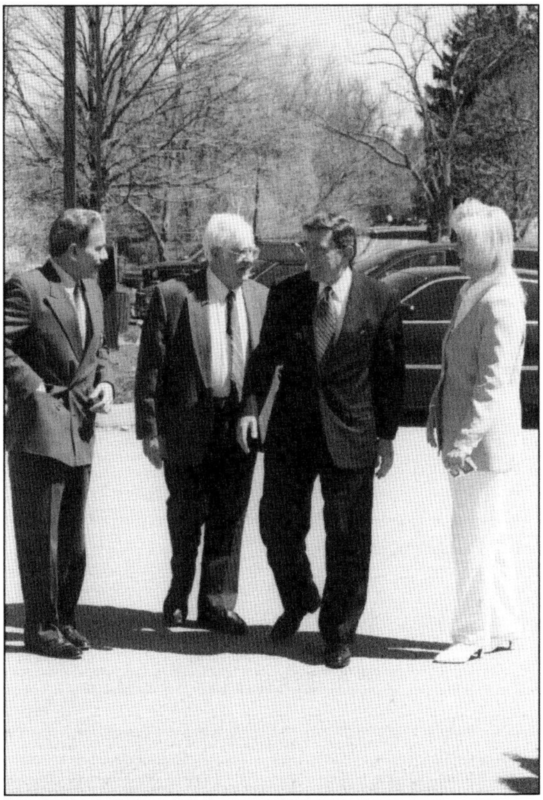

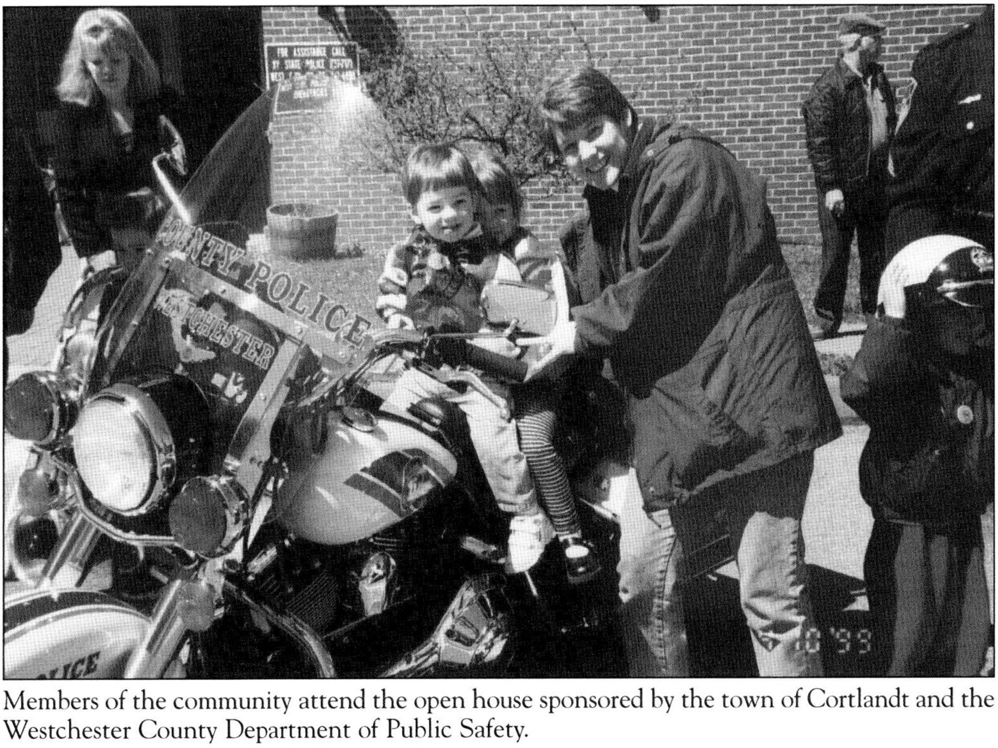

Members of the community attend the open house sponsored by the town of Cortlandt and the Westchester County Department of Public Safety.

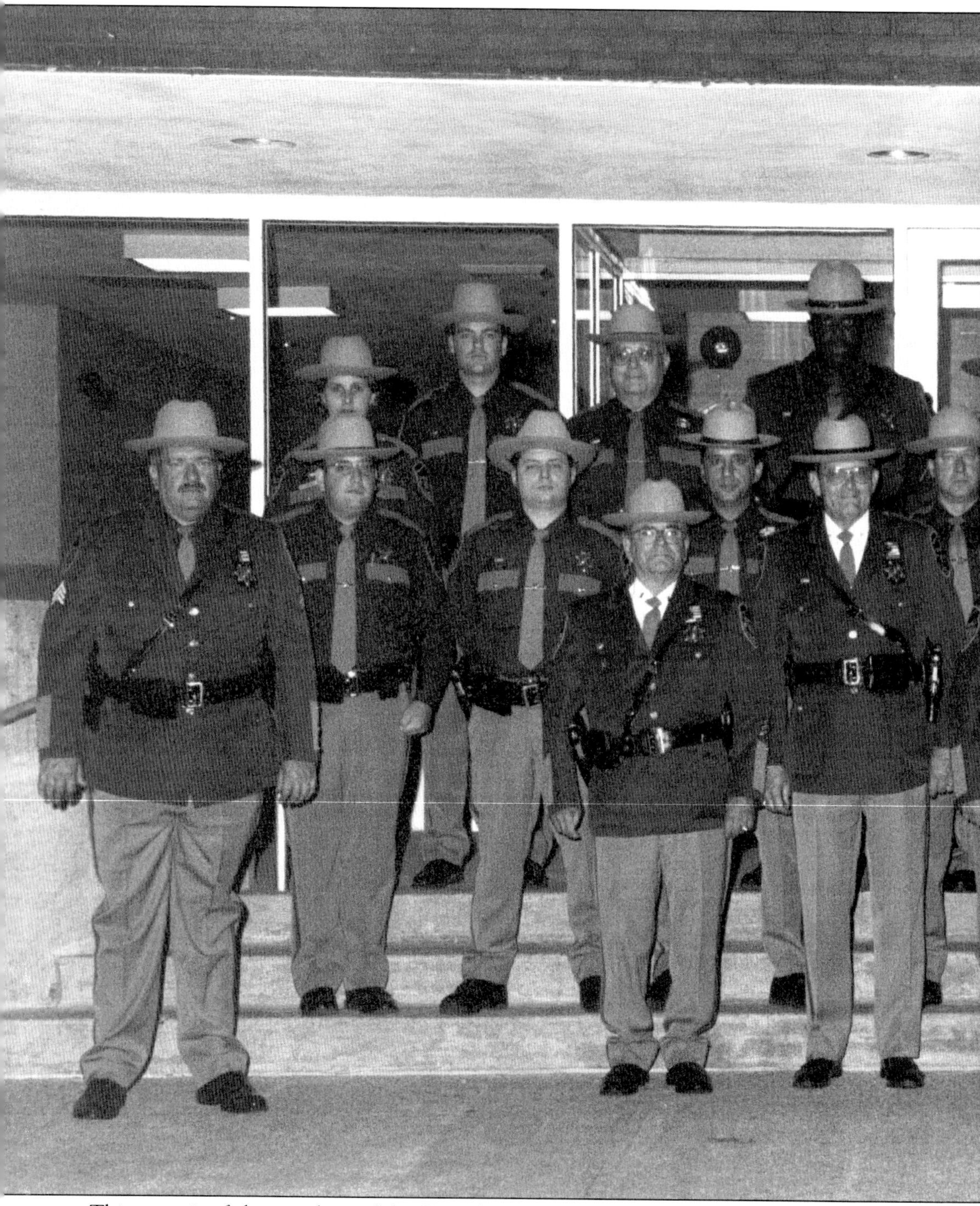

This portrait of the members of the Westchester County Public Safety Emergency Force was taken in June 2001. The members of this organization have a long history of volunteer service within Westchester County. The personnel seen in the photograph are, from left to right, as follows: (front row) Sgt. John Elliot, Lt. Frank Palmer, Chief John Dillon, Capt. Robert Tirella, Lt. August Carideo, and Sgt. William Lougheed; (back row) Deputy Sheriffs Brett Hochron,

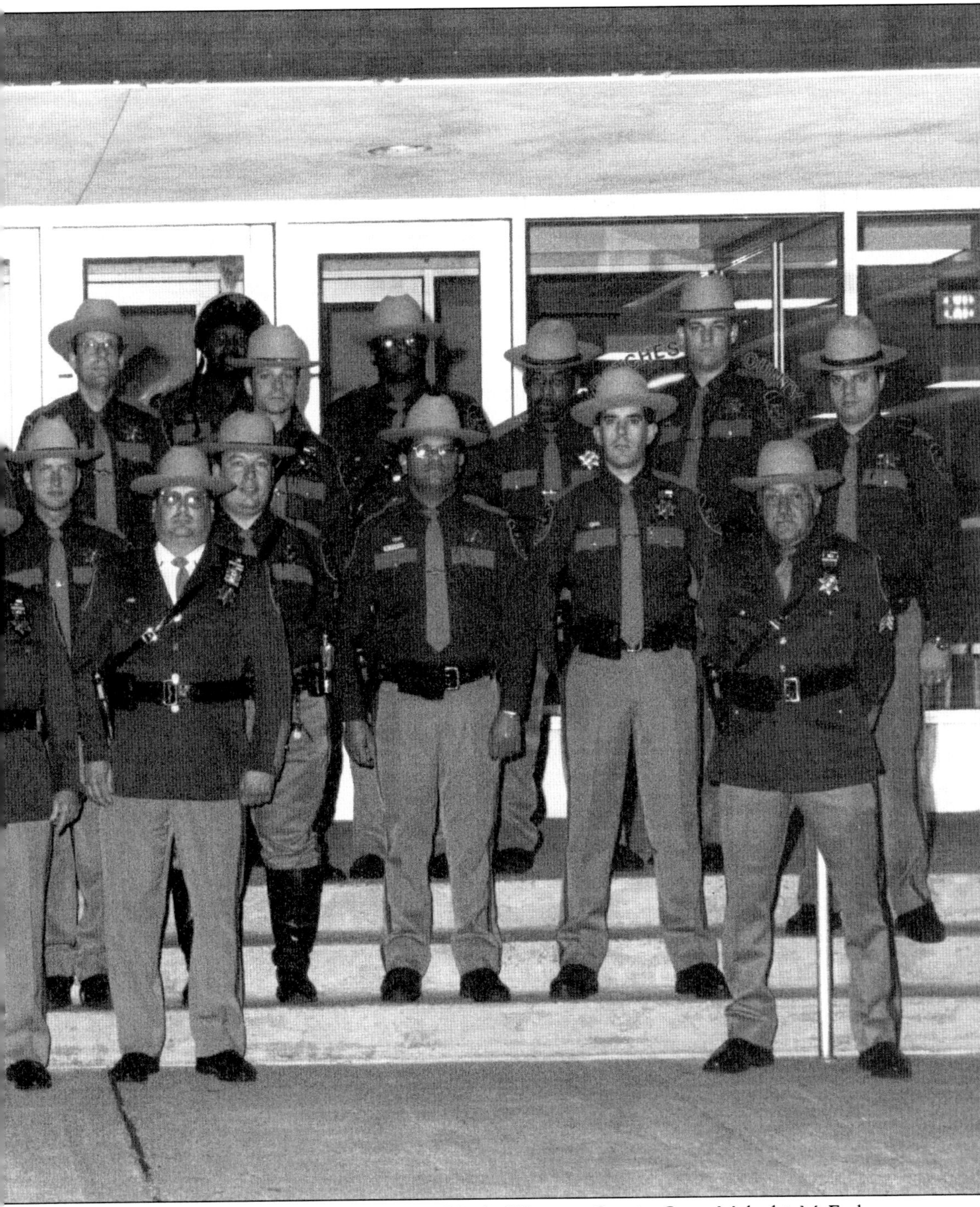

Laura Defeo, Brian Smith, Eugene Sisto, Hugh Winters, Sergio Orts, Malachi McFarlane, Michael Somoza, Sergio Dilello, Dennis Raffa, Andrew Burnstine, James Roberts, Michael Roca, David Metzger, Walter Kirton, Murad Raheem, Henry Coleman, Andrew Shore, Michael Brancamp, and Anthony DiDato.

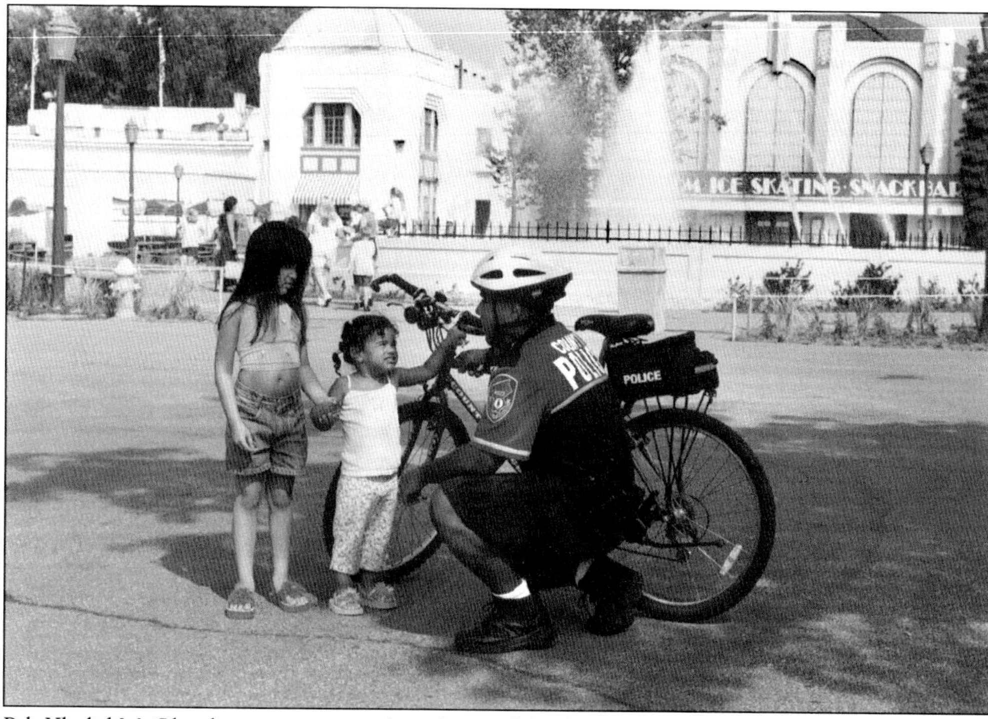

Ptl. Khalid McClendon assists two girls in front of the fountain at Playland Park in June 2001.

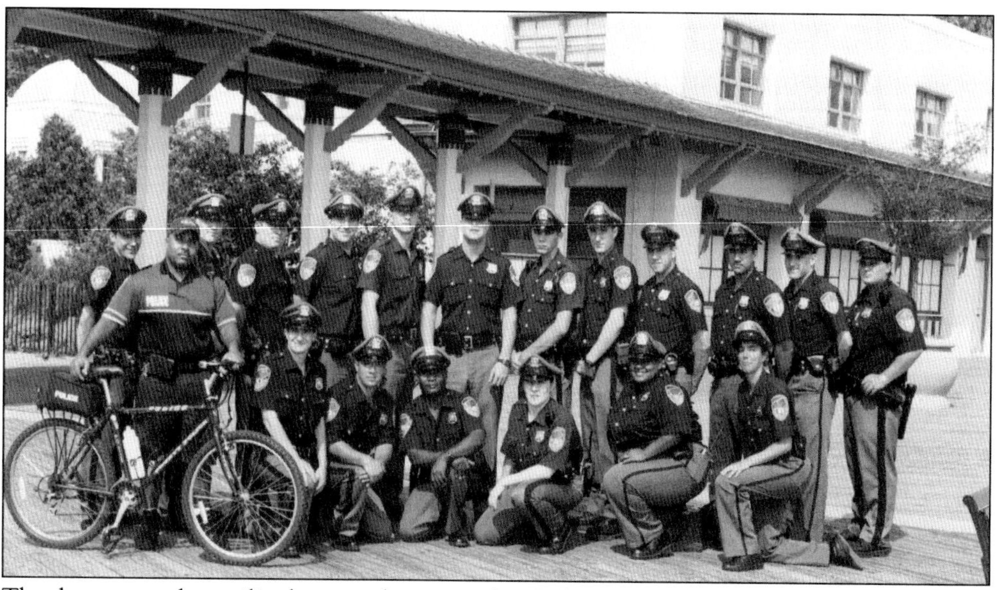

The department has utilized seasonal personnel to help to meet the demands of policing peak summer populations at county parks since 1926. This group of seasonal park rangers were photographed on the boardwalk at Playland Park in 2001. They are, from left to right, as follows: (front row) officers Khalid McClendon, Joseph Fiore, Michael Rivera, Africo Louis, Christine Bruno, Karla McCleod, and Rose Cybulski; (back row) officers Larry Bornholtz, John Roberts, Richard Sheridan, Scott Pfeiffer, Todd Spano, Rick Stanton, Gilbert Lopez, James Harrison, Matthew Kitt, David Delarosa, William Paul, and Michelle DeVito.

Four

In the Line of Duty

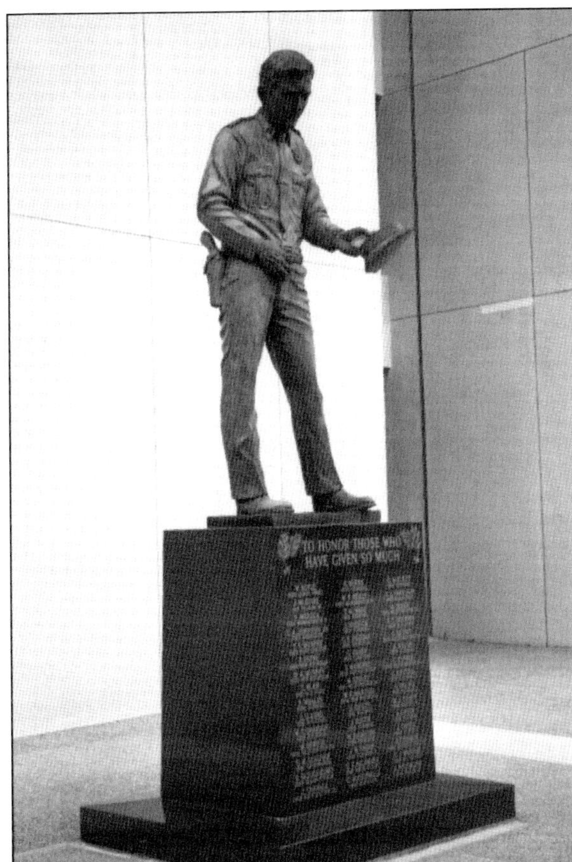

This monument at the Westchester County Courthouse in White Plains is dedicated to all of the police officers who have died in the line of duty in Westchester County. Pres. John F. Kennedy designated May 15, 1963, Police Officers Memorial Day in honor of those peace officers who, through their courageous deeds, have lost their lives or have become disabled in the performance of duty.

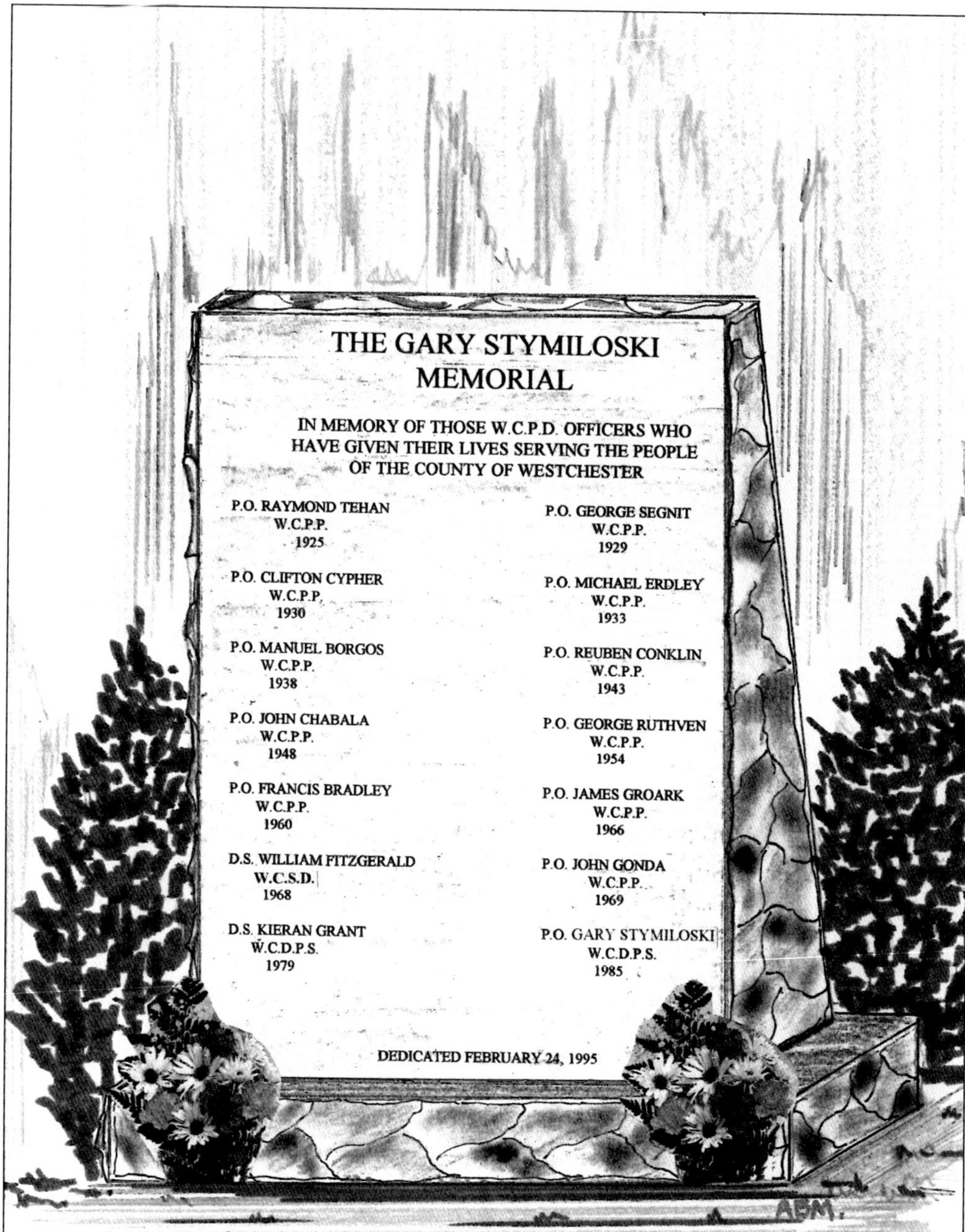

This is the original artwork for the memorial dedicated to all of those members of the Westchester County Department of Public Safety, the Westchester County Sheriff's Department, and the Westchester County Parkway Police Department who have died in the line of duty. This memorial was erected in front of the headquarters building in Hawthorne as a reminder to all of those who pass by of the sacrifices made for the benefit and protection of the people of Westchester County.